# ADVANCE PRAISE FOR
## *NICE WHITE LADIES*

"This nation has never, ever read anything like *Nice White Ladies*, and it shows every single day. Paragraph after paragraph, Jessie Daniels illustrates that it's not enough just to say what no one is saying. We must, as she does, write what is rarely spoken with supreme skill and a desire to substantiate our claims as though our lives depended on it. I'd love to live in a world where every white woman on earth reads this book. It could change everything."

—Kiese Laymon, author of *Heavy: An American Memoir*

"Mixing stories of her own youth and family with current events, Daniels calls in all white women to look at where they were, where they are, and where they are going. Instead of shying away from difficult truths, she invites readers to sit with them—to look across the table or into the next cubicle and see the impact of generations of choices. As uncomfortable as it is necessary."

—Mikki Kendall, *New York Times*–bestselling author of *Hood Feminism*

"Once again, Jessie Daniels has given us a crucial book for understanding race in America. This should be required reading for all who want to dismantle racist systems that limit what could otherwise be possible."

—Safiya Noble, author of *Algorithms of Oppression*

"If the title makes you squirm, this book is for you. Daniels lays bare the inadequacy of gender-only feminism to address the interlocking forms of domination and difference that shape all of our lives and offers an irresistible vision of sociality grounded in solidarity and truth-telling. *Nice White Ladies* is a manifesto for readers who are ready to do the real work of reckoning with our shared racist inheritance."

—Ruha Benjamin, professor of African American Studies, Princeton University

"With compassion, care, and a gentle double-dare, Daniels's book cuts straight through the noise. I now know what I should do to help dismantle systemic racism, and I'm doing it. I'll always be grateful for this book."

—Rev. Dr. Susan Corso, minister and novelist

"A timely call to action for us white women everywhere. Daniels lucidly details the mundane and sadistic ways that white women uphold white supremacy, even when it comes at great personal cost. Her work does not allow 'nice white ladies' to simply wallow in guilt, but encourages us to concretely challenge the ways we reinforce racial hierarchies."

—Alyssa Bowen, PhD, research fellow at True North Research

"This is the book on whiteness we've been waiting for. Jessie Daniels pulls no punches as she unravels centuries of American narratives that cast white women as innocents, victims, and saviors. Drawing a straight line from lynching picnics to Karen-hood, Daniels deconstructs the tiny daily behaviors of 'nice white ladies' that create structural racism across the United States today. This book is a powerful calling-in of her fellow white women, highly recommended for those who want to push past their conditioning."

—Minal Hajratwala, author of *Leaving India*

# NICE
# WHITE
# LADIES

**Also by Jessie Daniels**

*White Lies: Race, Class, Gender and Sexuality
in White Supremacist Discourse*

*Cyber Racism: White Supremacy Online
and the New Attack on Civil Rights*

*Being a Scholar in the Digital Era: Transforming
Scholarly Practice for the Public Good,
coauthored with Polly Thistlethwaite*

*Digital Sociologies, edited with Karen Gregory
and Tressie McMillan Cottom*

*Going Public: A Guide for Social Scientists,
coauthored with Arlene Stein*

# NICE WHITE LADIES

The Truth about White Supremacy, Our Role in It,
and How We Can Help Dismantle It

## JESSIE DANIELS

SEAL PRESS

New York

Seal Press
Hachette Book Group
1290 Avenue of the Americas, New York, NY 10104
www.sealpress.com
@sealpress

Printed in the United States of America

First Edition: October 2021

Published by Seal Press, an imprint of Perseus Books, LLC, a subsidiary of Hachette Book Group, Inc. The Seal Press name and logo is a trademark of the Hachette Book Group.

The Hachette Speakers Bureau provides a wide range of authors for speaking events. To find out more, go to www.hachettespeakersbureau.com or call (866) 376-6591.

The publisher is not responsible for websites (or their content) that are not owned by the publisher.

Print book interior design by Amy Quinn.

Library of Congress Cataloging-in-Publication Data

Names: Daniels, Jessie, 1961- author.
Title: Nice white ladies : the truth about white supremacy, our role in it,
    and how we can help dismantle it / Jessie Daniels.
Description: New York City : Seal Press, 2021. | Includes bibliographical
    references.
Identifiers: LCCN 2021009415 | ISBN 9781541675865 (hardcover) | ISBN
    9781541675858 (epub)
Subjects: LCSH: Women, White--United States--Attitudes. | White supremacy
    movements--United States. | Racism--United States. | United States--Race
    relations. | Social justice--United States.
Classification: LCC HQ1410 .D36 2021 | DDC 305.800973--dc23
LC record available at https://lccn.loc.gov/2021009415

ISBNs: 978-1-5416-7586-5 (hardcover), 978-1-5416-7585-8 (ebook)

LSC-C

Printing 1, 2021

*For Emmett Till*
*and Markis, Hannah, Abigail, Devonte, Jeremiah, and Ciera*
*and*
*For Shirley*

I'd like to be a spoiled rich white girl.

—Venus Xtravaganza

# CONTENTS

# INTRODUCTION

Nice white ladies, and our protection, are fundamental to American culture. And this fact is destroying all of us. You should know that I, myself, am a white woman. I have been helped in my career by many nice white ladies, some of them feminists. I come from a long line of white women ancestors, none of whom would have ever identified as a feminist. When I enter a room, people assume I am a nice white lady. No one can tell just by looking at me that I have spent half my life in a conscious effort to not be a nice white lady. I have learned to disavow the niceness that is a cover for ignoring the pain of others, to distance myself from the safe emptiness of whiteness, and to detox from the poison of ladyhood. Yet, this is what the women in my family hoped for, for me, this narrow dream of nice white ladyhood.

The other thing that you should know about these women I come from, my ancestors in Texas, is that none of them made it past the eighth grade in school. All of them were married by the time they were fifteen years old, and as a point of pride they would have me tell you, not one of those was a shotgun wedding. All of the women I come from were mothers by the time they were sixteen years old.

Not me. I went after as much education as the state of Texas had on offer, divorced a couple of husbands without bearing any children, and found myself in a clutch of radical lesbian feminists. Along the way, I discovered that I was white—my father had told me I was Cherokee. I didn't fully realize I was white until fairly late in life, in my twenties, when I started reading books by people who were actually Indigenous who pointed out how very common it was for white people to claim Cherokee ancestry when there was none. When I would ask my mother, "What are we?" she seemed less interested in ethnic heritage than my father and would dismiss my question with a quick "Scotch-Irish, I think." She did not entertain follow-up questions. "Go play outside" was her most common response to my inquiries, genealogical or otherwise.

In a family photo from 1962, I am the baby held in my great-grandmother's arms. She wears a dress with a floral print, a belt cinched snug under her bosom, wire frame glasses, gray hair swept back in a bun, sensible shoes that lace up the front. What you cannot see in this photo is the tin she carries, a repurposed Vienna Sausages can that she uses to spit out chewing tobacco. My cousins and I called her "Little Granny" because she was quite short and continued to shrink as she aged. It was a rite of passage for each one of us eleven cousins to mark the point at which we grew taller than Little Granny.

Next to her in the photo is my grandmother, "Big Granny," because she is taller than her mother by a couple of inches. She is a stout woman, funny sometimes, and mean. In the photo, she wears moderately high heels and a dress cut the same as Little Granny's but in a geometric print. The dresses are so similar I suspect that they are homemade by one of them, both expert seamstresses. Next to Big Granny in the photo is my mother, the tallest by several inches, slim, and chic in dark sunglasses, shorts, and a shirt with giant polka dots and matching sandals. I do not know the particular details of when the photo was taken or what prompted this self-conscious documentation of four generations of our family, but I think about this photo often. I sometimes use it when I give talks about white women and white feminism, because it so clearly locates me at the end of this line of white women who raised me and it makes me think about how very different my life is from theirs.

Just as I inherited this constellation of identities that I have chosen to interrogate and reject, similarly, I want this book to challenge and subvert both "whiteness" and "ladyhood." This book is not merely an intellectual exercise. Instead, the stakes here are deeply personal for me. I have experienced the destructiveness of whiteness firsthand, in suicide and failed relationships and intergenerational trauma. For me, telling the truth about white supremacy and working to end it are interlaced with my own liberation and yours. I want this book to be a catalyst for dismantling the systemic racism that we, nice white ladies, have upheld. And I want this book to help women raised white to reach beyond the strictures of niceness and the constraints of ladyhood to experience their full humanity and to join the rest of us working toward a better world for everyone.

Although this book is about the distinctive role of white women, from the right to the left on the political spectrum, it is a book meant to be read by everyone. If you are not a white woman, you may have been raised by, worked for, dated, or married someone who was, or perhaps you're simply curious about the many cultural products that feature white women so prominently. Most of the examples in this book are drawn from the American or British context because of the outsized influence of those two nations. But it is meant for readers beyond those borders because those cultures, designed with white women's protection in mind, through very real ways are often destructive to people from the Global South. Further, the intertwined notions of "hot, thin blondes" and who is considered a "good mother" and who gets to keep the children they give birth to are part of the reverence for the supposed specialness of white women, and these ideas circulate globally. I want this book to chip away at these burdensome notions that white women as a category are somehow more beautiful, more deserving of protection, or more nurturing than anyone else. I want this to be an invitation to everyone to resist this pernicious set of ideas.

More than merely refusal of a set of ideas, this book points to another way of being in the world. There are white women who have found new pathways to wholeness and resistance. I write about them with the hope that there will be more of us, and new generations in which these conversations will no longer be necessary.

## WHO IS "WHITE," ANYWAY?

When I misbehaved as a child, like when I rode my tricycle in the house over the bedsheet Big Granny was ironing, she was fond of telling me, "When you're free, white, and twenty-one, you can do whatever you want, but now you're going to do what I say." It was both a way of reprimanding me because I was a child, not yet twenty-one, while at the same time letting me know that someday I would be entitled to all the world had to offer someone who was "free" and "white." But who is "white," anyway?

The truth is, what it means to be white varies depending on time and place and social context. Sociologists and other academics say things like "whiteness is a social construction." Another way of saying that is: Whiteness is a made-up category. Who belongs and who doesn't belong in that category is a list that is constantly changing. Between 2000 and 2010, for example, an estimated 1.2 million Americans of the 35 million who identified in 2000 as of "Hispanic, Latino, or Spanish origin" or "some other race" on the Census changed their race to "white."

The notion of being white is a relatively new one, historically, and one rooted in colonialism. When the British colonized much of the world, they began to see themselves as white and superior to the dark Others they were conquering, and they considered themselves to be making the rest of the world a better place. White women, as long as they were of the right class, served as guardians of the race in their reproductive capacity and provided a guarantee that those in settler communities adhered to British morals. One of the recurring themes in the history of colonial repression is the way the threat of real or imagined violence toward white women symbolized the most dangerous form of insubordination. And protecting the supposed virtue of white women was often the pretext for instituting cruel measures against Indigenous populations. In Papua, New Guinea, for instance, a law called the White Women's Protection Ordinance was passed that made any "native" convicted of rape or attempted rape of a European female eligible for the death penalty.

In the United States, precisely who counts as white is something that has changed over time, and changed rather dramatically. My Little Granny was born in 1886 in either Texas, Mississippi, or Alabama—the records are unclear—at the time when many thousands of southern and eastern Europeans escaped religious persecution and economic hardship by immigrating to the United States. In response to two decades of fearmongering about these immigrants, and how they "brought crime and disease" with them, the US Congress held a series of hearings in the early 1920s. Social science experts of the day testified that immigrants from Middle Eastern nations, India, Japan, and China could never assimilate and, therefore, should be banned from entering the United States. Indeed, one social scientist gave sworn testimony that people from southern Italy were decidedly not white but of a different "race" and therefore incapable of ever assimilating into mainstream American society. The result of these hearings was the Immigration Act of 1924, which put in place restrictive immigration laws for the next several decades. The goal, according to one official, was to "preserve the ideal of American homogeneity." My Little Granny, with her snuff can, homemade dresses, and sensible shoes, ended up "white" because she was born in the southern United States rather than in southern Italy.

But southern Italians, like people from other groups initially categorized as "nonwhite," became white over the next several decades of the twentieth century. A number of scholars have written about this phenomenon of racial transformation. Noel Ignatiev, an American historian best known for his work on race and social class, wrote about how the Irish, at one point considered "ape-like" and "less than human," eventually became white. In her book *How Jews Became White Folks and What That Says About Race in America*, Karen Brodkin documents the way that postwar policies like the GI Bill and those of the Federal Housing Administration effectively translated into de facto "affirmative action" for the male children and grandchildren of immigrants, many of them Jewish, thus promoting the whiteness of southern and eastern Europeans while purposefully excluding African Americans from those crucial mechanisms of economic uplift. Because some immigrant men were able to get good educations and jobs and buy houses through government subsidies, they had the opportunity to access the affordances of whiteness and, specifically, white masculinity.

Brodkin suggests that "becoming white" for Jewish women meant giving up the power they once held in the family in exchange for the lifestyle of bourgeois white women. She argues that to assimilate into the dominant white culture, Jews had to conform to new gender norms and leave behind those they had brought from eastern Europe. In the wake of that shift in gender norms, Jews were left with anxiety and ambivalence, which manifests in, among other things, Jewish American Princess (JAP) jokes and misogyny toward the "Jewish mother." This anxiety is a brief rupture that, according to Brodkin, masks the larger trend of becoming white, of blending into the dominant white culture. In the bid to assimilate into the category "white," part of the deal is accepting the gender norms and relationships of the dominant, white culture.

Writer Natasha Stovall points out the way white identity remains diffuse: "Farm-to-table white or Cracker Barrel white? Rust Belt white or Sunbelt White? Electric car white or pickup truck white? Digital white or analog white? One percent honky or precariat ofay? Italian? Irish? English? Ukrainian? Polish?" For white women, specifically, we could ask: Martha Stewart white or Paula Deen white? Real House-wives of Orange County white or Honey Boo Boo of McIntyre, Georgia, white? Catholic, working-class, Kentucky white or Jew-ish, upper-class, apartment on the Upper East Side and house in the Hamptons white? Ivanka Trump American businesswoman white or Sheryl Sandberg chief operating officer of Facebook white? These distinctions of taste, culture, and wealth divide white women in sig-nificant ways. These different shades of whiteness don't diminish the power of whiteness but rather strengthen whiteness because people reduce these variations into a reassertion of mere individualism.

"I'm not really white, I'm European," is an actual thing that some-one has said to me after a talk I'd given on white womanhood. If not this specific thing, then white women will often say some version of this to me after I make a presentation. It's a deflection meant to put some distance between their sense of self and what I have to say. It's this claim to individuality that is one of the main ways that we try to evade understanding our role in white supremacy. To move forward, we have to begin by acknowledging our whiteness in whatever flavor it comes.

## ISN'T THIS DIVISIVE?

"Talking about white women just divides us" is something that white people, and especially nice white ladies, say to me often. This ignore-it-and-maybe-it-will-go-away approach to race doesn't work and, in fact, plays into another kind of racism known as "colorblindness." White people who were raised in households that valued colorblindness might have been taught that even mentioning race was rude, socially unac-ceptable, and to be avoided at all costs. But there's evidence that this isn't the best approach. We know from child development researchers that even children as young as two years old recognize and respond to racial differences. And researchers have also demonstrated that being able to talk about race and racism actually fosters a decrease in preju-dice among children. So, not talking about the social fact of race and racism amounts to a kind of gaslighting, a denial of what is plainly evident in the social world around us. Some of the most ardent proponents of the idea that talking about race is divisive that I've encountered are white feminists. It seems that when someone tries to bring up the issue of race and racism within feminism, they are accused of being "toxic" and of making people feel "awkward."

In 2011, writer and critic Emily Nussbaum celebrated the feminist blogosphere in *New York* magazine: "Freed from the boundaries of print, writers could blur the lines between formal and casual writing; between a call to arms, a confession, and a stand-up routine—and this new looseness of form in turn emboldened readers to join in, to take risks in the safety of the shared spotlight." But by 2014, Michelle Goldberg, then a contributing editor at *The Nation*, wondered if the online version of feminism was over because of "toxic Twitter wars."

To make her case, Goldberg pointed to the blowback received by producers of the #femfuture report following a convening at Barnard College in New York City. When the meeting and the report were criticized for being exclusionary, the organizers were hurt and some saw the criticism as disproportionate. Goldberg said that the report was "savaged as a cabal by white opportunists" and, later, that there is a "nascent genre of essays by people who feel emotionally savaged" by criticism from other feminists.

Perhaps Goldberg's use of the word *savaged* twice in the same article was a coincidence, or merely bad copyediting, but given that most of the critique of the #femfuture report, coauthored by two white feminists, came from women of color, it is worth considering that the word choice here has deeper meaning. It may be that white feminists feel particularly sensitive to any criticism, especially when it comes to matters of race. This is what researcher Robin DiAngelo has called "white fragility," a kind of hypersensitivity to any critical discussion of whiteness, and it stands in the way of actual solidarity. No amount of positivity, light, and love will help us defeat the patriarchy if white feminists can't tolerate being criticized.

## THE BUILT-IN ADVANTAGE OF BEING A WHITE WOMAN

In the mid-1990s, I was working as a sociology professor when the rise of the popular internet changed the world as I knew it. I left my job in academia to work in the dotcom industry in 2000 and had a great time while the ride lasted. That bubble eventually burst, and I got laid off. My closest friend at that job, the only African American man at the company, also got laid off when the firm's payroll sluffed off about 330 employees over six months in 2001. Following the layoffs, I spent a year piecing together a living from three or four part-time gigs until I landed back in academia at a job with direct deposit and health insurance. My friend, who had previously worked in journalism (which was also shedding jobs), struggled to find employment and hasn't worked in a full-time job since then. The last I heard about him, he was living in a homeless shelter. Although there are differences in education and job sector that shaped our dramatically divergent paths out of the dotcom bust, part of the reason I was able to recover from that job loss was because of the built-in advantage of being a white woman when it comes to getting and staying employed.

Recent employment and income data tell this story through numbers. According to the Economic Policy Institute, in 2017, the median annual earnings for full-time, year-round white women workers was just over $46,513. That is 21 percent more than the annual earnings of Black women, whose average was $36,735. Hispanic women earned even less, just $32,002 per year. And when you look at men's income by race, it tells a further story of advantage for white women. When you consider that most white women who marry (95 percent) marry white men (89 percent), you can see that they have an added advantage because of access to the greater earning power of their partners. Again, according to the Economic Policy Institute, in 2017, white male full-time workers earned an average of $60,388 compared to just $42,076 for Black men and $38,876 for Hispanic men. And, if you take into consideration the disparity in access to the income of those male earners, it compounds the advantage. Black families, for instance, are more reliant on women's incomes than other families since about 80 percent of Black mothers are the sole breadwinners.

There's also a good bit of evidence that we, as white women, are the main beneficiaries of affirmative action policies. The Department of Labor estimates that six million white women workers are in higher occupational classifications today than they would have been without affirmative action policies. This pays off in dividends in the labor force and to (mostly) white men and families.

Although some people of color have been helped by affirmative action, data suggest that women—white women, in particular—have benefited disproportionately from these policies. In many ways, affirmative action has moved white women into a structural position in which they share more in common with white men than they do with Black or Latina women.

Even in the private sector, white women have moved in and up at numbers that far eclipse those of people of color. After IBM established its own affirmative action program, the numbers of women in management positions more than tripled in less than ten years; overwhelmingly, these were white women. Data from subsequent years show that the number of executives of color at IBM also grew, but not nearly at the same rate.

Given these incredible employment gains by white women, it might seem logical that this demographic would be among the biggest supporters of affirmative action. This is not the case. White women often feel aggrieved because of these same policies.

After I finished my PhD at the University of Texas at Austin, I applied for a teaching position at a small college. When I didn't get that job, I was disappointed. The chair of the search committee, a white man, told me, I think in an attempt to console me, "Our hands were tied, we had to give it to her." The "her" he was referring to was the just-as-well-qualified woman of color who got the position. By telling me this, he was implying that affirmative action policies in hiring are unfair to white women and, specifically, that her hire had caused me injury. I can't know his intention in telling me this, but I do know that such stories are an invitation to racial resentment even as they obscure the many ways white women benefit from affirmative action policies, as when we get to count as diversity in an otherwise all-white-male company, organization, or institution.

When Abigail Fisher sued my alma mater, she claimed that UT had discriminated against her in the undergraduate admissions process. Her case went all the way to the Supreme Court. Since the 1970s, the most common plaintiffs in lawsuits against universities for discrimination in the academic admissions process have been white women: Abigail Fisher (*Fisher v. University of Texas*); Barbara Grutter (*Grutter v. Bollinger*); Jennifer Gratz (*Gratz v. Bollinger*); and Cheryl Hopwood (*Hopwood v. Texas*). Despite their incredibly privileged structural position within the United States, these white women still felt aggrieved because they assumed that if they didn't get into their top choice of school, a person of darker complexion and lesser qualifications had taken a spot that rightfully belonged to them. Fisher, like so many white women of her generation, seems to believe that her peers who are Black and Latina have it "easy" when it comes to getting into college, as if they only had to send in their photograph with their application to gain admission.

The popular culture narratives about affirmative action would have us believe that it is a system that offers unfair advantage to Black, Indigenous, or other people of color. Yet, the reality is that it's white women who benefit most, and it is advantage they pass on to their families.

## PASSING ON ADVANTAGE THROUGH WHITE FAMILIES

My family didn't have any wealth to pass on to me. Even though neither of my parents left any sort of inheritance for me, I've witnessed up close the way white people pass on their housing wealth. Around the same time that I first moved to New York City and discovered that I couldn't actually afford to pay my rent on an assistant

professor's salary, a colleague of mine—a white woman like me—
bought an entire brownstone in Brooklyn. She made the same crappy
salary I did, but she was different from me in two salient ways. First,
she'd had the good sense to have middle-class parents who died
properly, with insurance benefits and home equity to pass on to her,
unlike mine who died without any of that. Second, she'd married a
higher-earning white man. She and her husband went on to have a
couple of (white) children and will, I expect, pass on the equity in
their single-family brownstone to them. My former colleague and her
husband are good people and progressive liberals. She was probably
at the Women's March wearing a pink hat she'd knitted herself. And
she and her husband are passing on their financial advantage to their
children, locking in the racial wealth gap for another generation.

Despite all the hand-wringing in the news about economic insecurity among white voters, white women in the United States are doing
pretty well for themselves when you consider their access to white
family wealth. Wealth, in fact, is a more enduring marker of economic advantage than income. Think about the difference this way:
income is what you get weekly or monthly, and wealth is what you
would have if your income stopped. Even average white families have
a huge wealth advantage, but they don't realize it. Census data reveals that the median assets of white families amounted to $132,483
in 2013, compared to just $9,211 for Black families. Yet white Amer-
icans, and especially higher-income-earning whites, vastly overestimate the progress toward economic equality between Blacks and
whites, according to a 2017 article published in the *Proceedings of the
National Academy of Sciences.*

White families are twice as likely to be millionaires as they were
a generation ago. The richest one hundred families control more
wealth than all the Black people in the United States. The list of the
ten richest families in the United States looks like an L.L. Bean catalog: white people are everywhere. The bootstrap lie would have you
believe that these ten families worked harder or were smarter than

everyone else and that's why they have so much wealth. But the current members of the ten richest families list didn't earn that money themselves. All ten are on that list because they inherited wealth from a rich white forebear.

During the early twentieth century, instituting a significant tax on large inherited estates was viewed as a major win for the progressive effort to reduce the gap between rich and poor. A hundred years later, and after a twenty-year campaign by the Right, the estate tax has been rebranded as the "death tax." Anti-tax libertarians like Grover Norquist would have us believe that "eliminating the death tax" will "create jobs," even though there's little evidence to support such claims. Doing away with the estate tax also keeps billions out of the tax base—billions that could be used to help decrease inequality—while increasing the federal debt by between $1.9 trillion and $2.2 trillion over the next decade. Nonetheless, making it easier for the wealthiest white families to pass on their assets is a dearly beloved plank in the GOP's agenda; the latest tax legislation was written to give billions more to these few families.

The estate tax applies to only a tiny fraction of American families, but middle-class white families hoard wealth, too. For them, the wealth is in their houses. A recent Center for American Progress report provides more data on this: For 2016, the median wealth for Black families was $17,600, and for Latinx families it was $20,700. The median wealth for white families was $171,000. Most of this difference can be attributed to home ownership. For the majority of white families, their greatest asset is their home, and they're far more likely than families of color to own a home.

The wage gap also contributes significantly to the wealth gap. White men are still paid more than every other racial and gender group, and white women are the highest paid group of women. Better wages mean more money to invest in home equity. At the same time, Black families have been systematically ripped off in the housing market. Because of the racist practices of the Federal Housing

Administration, banks, and real estate agents—like redlining, racially restrictive covenants, and racial steering by real estate agents—home ownership continues to work in favor of white families.

Even the language "the wealth gap" from the well-meaning Center for American Progress report misses the role that white families play in perpetuating these inequalities. The report describes Blacks as "struggl[ing] to keep pace with their white counterparts," which makes the wealth gap sound like a failure on the part of Black families to "keep pace." The truth is that white families took advantage—and continue to take advantage—of racist housing policies and pass the resulting equity on to their (presumably white) children.

Of course, the American dream that's been sold to us is one of home ownership and of people being able to provide for their families. But taking care of people we love can't be an excuse to actively disadvantage other people's children. White parents who want the best for their kids must find a way to give it to them without pulling up the ladder behind them. To point this out is not to call all white people with kids bad parents; it is to remind them that any action on behalf of one's own family has consequences beyond it.

Consider the issue of school segregation, a classic case of white families—especially white mothers—hoarding resources for their children at the expense of their nonwhite peers. Reporter Nikole Hannah-Jones has documented white parents' efforts to fight the desegregation of public schools, a fight that recalls the violent opposition to integration of the 1960s and the busing riots of the 1970s but that persists today, even in self-proclaimed liberal communities like many in New York City.

The problem of wide gaps in school funding is directly linked to housing segregation, but it doesn't have to be this way. We could fund all schools equally so that all children have access to the same quality education. Instead, we have built—and white families continue to insist upon—a system in which being able to afford a more expensive house means you can send your child to a better school. That's a form of hoarding of opportunity for the children in one community at the expense of all children.

When we form families, we draw a circle around the people we care about. Those within the circle are deserving of our fullest care; those outside, less so. That circle of kinship represents love and acceptance, and too often, white women are instrumental in the decision to stash wealth in white-only families and pass on their advantage for generations to come. Part of what we're passing on, too, are our ideas about what it means to be a woman, and in our society, that's always shaped by the racial category we find ourselves in.

## NICE WHITE LADIES

"Pretty is as pretty does" was a phrase my mother was fond of saying to me. I didn't know the origin of the phrase, I just knew that it meant being cute wasn't going to allow me to get away with anything and I'd better behave myself. As I learned much later in life, this edict was part of the code of ideal white Southern ladyhood. In her book *Being Ugly: Southern Women Writers and Social Rebellion*, Monica Carol Miller writes that tenets like "Pretty is as pretty does" and "You can never be too thin or too rich" and "Don't be a slut" were used throughout the twentieth century to reinforce the status quo of white-supremacist, sexist Southern society in which people recognize, and most importantly, stay in, their proscribed roles.

But surely, outside the South and in the twenty-first century, this notion of white womanhood no longer holds sway? On the contrary, the idea of being a nice white lady is still a powerful force today, and not just in the South.

A key feature of one type of contemporary white womanhood is being nice and nonconfrontational. In 2019, when celebrity lesbian Ellen DeGeneres spent her Sunday afternoon in the luxury box at a football game in Texas with former president George W. Bush, people were incensed that she would have such an easy rapport with someone who many believe is a war criminal. For her part, DeGeneres used the opening of her show to address the controversy, saying, "Just because I don't agree with someone on everything doesn't mean that I'm not going to be friends with them." Ellen concluded, "When I say, 'Be kind to one another,' I don't mean only the people that think the same way that you do. I mean, 'Be kind to everyone, it doesn't matter.'" Many said that her position as a lesbian icon made friendship with George W. Bush antithetical. The fact is that DeGeneres's brand of kindness is really just about avoiding social confrontat and awkwardness by being nice to everyone, even to those who h made the world a worse place. I know, because I recognize this tendency toward niceness in myself.

On a recent afternoon, when I was hanging out at my local library for an afternoon of writing, the announcement came on overhead, "The library is closing, please exit." I packed up my belongings and prepared to leave. Along with several other patrons who were leaving, I stood in line at the bathroom. As we waited, an older white gentleman, perhaps in his eighties, struck up a conversation. I wanted, more than anything, to have a pleasant exchange with him and go on my way. When the Asian woman in the bathroom was, in his opinion, taking too long, he began to say derogatory things about her. He questioned whether she was allowed to be in the building at all and wondered aloud if she could "even speak English"—and I said nothing. My desire to confront this man's obvious racism and boorish behavior was quashed by my compulsion toward niceness. In that moment, I gave in to the desire to be a nice white lady and let it override my better instincts to speak up.

The underbelly of the "niceness" is the harsh commands of the slave mistress and the colonial overseer. Historian Stephanie Jones-Rogers writes in *They Were Her Property* that white women in the United States were enthusiastic in their cruelty as owners of enslaved people on plantations. White women throughout colonialism have wielded power over subjugated people, as Vron Ware writes in her book *Beyond the Pale*. And these historical legacies continue to shape contemporary relationships between women today. On the Upper East Side of Manhattan, for example, it's possible to see these dynamics every day. The neighborhood bounded by 59th Street and 96th Street, Central Park and Lexington Avenue, includes the richest zip codes in the world. And there, nice, rich, white ladies employ Caribbean and US-born Black women to tend their children. Riding the bus along Lexington Avenue, I have heard girls as young as four or five telling their caregivers, "You are not the boss of me. I'll have you fired." This is the voice of the overseer, made new for the twenty-first century.

## NICE WHITE LADIES IN NEED OF TRUTH AND TRANSFORMATION

As white women, we need to tell the truth about ourselves and we need transformation. The results of the 2016 election were made possible by nice white ladies, the majority of whom (53 percent) put their interest in whiteness above everything else, including the collective good. And when some of us went out to protest the results of that election, we looked like we were showing up in superficial ways that performed justice, like those signs at the Women's March that said "If Hillary was President, I'd be at brunch now." Though those events were a wake-up call for some, for others they were just the latest in a long history of white women showing up for themselves, but not for anyone else. We need to grow and move past this; we need to learn to undo the damage we cause as nice white ladies. But how?

This book is meant to offer a reckoning for the damage we've done, as white women, as well as a road map for undoing white womanhood and the destructiveness it causes. In the pages that follow, I explain that "Karens," who call the police on Black people doing ordinary things—from sitting in a Starbucks, to napping in their college dorm, to setting up a barbeque grill in a park, to bird-watching—have gone viral because these white women feel entitled to police others. This "can I speak to your manager" way of going through the world is elemental to the destructiveness of white womanhood. This history stretches from the recent past, with white women prosecutors, and into the deep past, through centuries of colonialism.

White feminists need to find the courage to be critically self-reflexive about how whiteness shapes our capacity to think about gender. For me, it's important to critique white feminism because our effort to smash the patriarchy is hindered by a gender-only feminism. This kind of feminism replays a cycle of harm, especially toward Black and other women of color, and also queer, gender-nonconforming, and transgender women of all races. It is the opposite of sisterhood, the antithesis of feminism. In the chapter on white feminism, I take a hard look at why marching in pink pussy hats and "leaning in" and hashtagging #MeToo may not be the kind of feminism we need if it silently reinforces ideas about the specialness of white womanhood.

For so many of us, when we get an inkling that something might be wrong with the way our lives are organized or what we've come to believe about ourselves, we turn to the array of healing products and services on offer in late capitalism known as "self-care." The trouble with this, as I point out in one chapter, is that the wellness industry connects the "light and love" it's selling to a particular kind of white-hetero-lady identity, one that seems natural and benevolent. Once the discussion in those spaces turns to having your chakras realigned or anchoring your pelvic wall, you're urged to put aside any unpleasant thoughts (about race, or social inequality, or climate change, or why your husband won't do more of the housework) and focus on yourself. It is this turn inward, to the exclusion of all others, that is an essential component of whiteness and why it is a mainstay of the current wellness industry. For some white women, these elixirs offer a respite from their daily lives, and for a tiny few, wellness represents a billion-dollar business. The image of white women as becalmed practitioners of mystical stretching is then repackaged by news outlets that speculate that the "yoga vote" will somehow save us all from fascism. (It didn't; although Donald Trump was voted out in 2020, this was not thanks to white women; 53 percent of white women voted for Trump in 2016 and *55 percent* of white women voted for Trump in 2020.) But this version of light and love doesn't reach much beyond the end of an individual yoga mat and it's not going to make the world better for anyone, except maybe Gwyneth Paltrow and her bank account.

Some white women have responded to social discomfort differently, by trying to escape whiteness altogether. Some have tried a spray-on tan or a different hairstyle, or they have adopted a knock-off version of African American Vernacular English. It can be puzzling to understand why white women like Rachel Doležal or Jessica Krug would adopt a Black identity. Or why women like Andrea Smith, Elizabeth Warren, or BethAnn McLaughlin might claim a Native American identity when no Indigenous people claim them. In one chapter, I look at the desire of white women to consume, and be consumed by, Otherness. This behavior begins to make sense when we understand the cultural and spiritual bankruptcy of whiteness and how agonizing it can be to sit with white identity once you see the destruction it has caused and realize your own complicity in that devastation.

Another chapter explores a more cutthroat version of white womanhood, one that is plain to see when it comes to segregation and hoarding resources in education. In 2018, when a middle school in the predominantly white neighborhood of the Upper West Side in Manhattan announced plans to desegregate the school by including more Black and Latinx students, white parents were furious. One white mother was particularly incensed at what she believed was the threat to her child's education, when she said: "You're talking about an eleven-year-old and . . . telling them that you're going to go to a school that's not going to educate you the same way you've been educated. Life sucks!" This mom on the affluent Upper West Side is just one recent example of the role white women have played in maintaining racial segregation, and it is primarily in, through, and on behalf of white families that this happens. In a chapter to follow, I explain that one of the defined responsibilities of white ladyhood is to create, reproduce, and protect white families. White women are crucial to the endeavor of hoarding resources—like educational opportunities—for their families. If we're to undo the damage caused by white womanhood, we've got to reimagine a new way to form connection that moves us away from the insular "my family first" ethos and toward an expansion of who we choose to care about.

Whiteness operates unconsciously. And, like most unresolved conflicts operating at the subconscious level, it wreaks havoc when not addressed. The CDC reports that rates of chronic pain and mental distress among white people have risen, and for an increasing proportion of white women this ends in death by suicide. Could it be that there is a psychic numbness required to trade one's full humanity for the social standing conferred by whiteness? In a final chapter, I explore the toll that being a nice white lady takes on all of us and the very personal pain it has caused me.

In the end, though, it doesn't have to be this way.

We can learn a different way to be in the world. In the conclusion, I write about some inspirational figures who have been successful at rejecting the role of nice white lady to help dismantle white supremacy. I also describe my own struggle, failures, and transformation in doing this work. This book is a call to think together about the truth of what we've been told we are entitled to as white women, of who we really are, and how we might join with other people who are already engaged in the work of liberation. My hope for this book is that it will *call in* all white women—rather than "call out" or "cancel" anyone. The invitation here is to tell the truth about white supremacy, to uncover our role in it, to think differently about our place in the world, and to begin the work of transformation necessary so that we are no longer contributing to the destruction of ourselves, those around us, and the world we live in. So that we can finally join with everyone else working to get free.

# 1

# "KARENS": WEAPONIZING WHITE WOMANHOOD

"Hi, I have two gentlemen at my café that are refusing to make a purchase or leave. I'm at the Starbucks at 18th and Spruce." That's what the manager of the Philadelphia Starbucks told the dispatcher when she called 911 in April 2018. It was 4:37 p.m., two minutes after Rashon Nelson and Donte Robinson had arrived. Most news reports described her as a "Starbucks employee" or as the store's manager. Few noted that she was a white woman, but it's as significant to the story as the fact that Nelson and Robinson, the people she called the police on, were Black men.

"It's always a Karen. I learned something, if you go to a white people's party, just say you know 'Karen,' they will take care of your ass the whole day. . . . 'Have a pumpkin spice latte!'" Comedian Jay Pharoah included this riff about white women in his 2015 stand-up show called "Can I Be Me?" and claims he's the originator of the "Karen" meme. Memes, these ideas that circulate through the culture through social media, can be hard to trace back to their origin. The website Know

Your Meme suggests that the Karen meme didn't take off until 2019, but that seems a bit late. In fact, it was in 2018 that a succession of recordings went viral of white women calling police on the ordinary activity of Black people, including the white woman at Starbucks who called the police on two Black men sitting in a coffee shop. It was also in 2018 that Alison Ettel called the police in San Francisco on an eight-year-old girl selling water without a city permit, and Ettel became "Permit Patty." That same year, Jennifer Schulte called the police from a public park in Oakland because Black people were setting up a grill, and she became the meme "BBQ Becky." These different nicknames got flattened into one meme: "Karen," as a shorthand for entitled white women calling 911, asking to speak to a manager, or otherwise behaving badly. In the midst of the global pandemic, several Karen memes circulated of white women angrily refusing to wear a mask.

"Memes have power above and beyond just humor," says André Brock, a scholar who studies digital Black cultures. "We often use metaphor, which is often at the heart of memes, and emotion or affect to make shorthand of things which deeply affect us." Part of what people are pointing out with the circulation of these memes is the lethal power of white women. "These memes are actually doing logical and political work of helping us get to legal changes or legislative changes, which is really something to be said," says Apryl Williams, a sociologist who has conducted computational research on these memes. She contends that they are valuable because they "actively call out white supremacy and call for restitution. They really do that work of highlighting and sort of commenting on the racial inequality in a way that mainstream news doesn't capture."

Each time one of these incidents makes the news, I think about the way we are connected, these Karens and me. We are the descendants of white women who instigated, encouraged, and benefited from white supremacy, shoulder-to-shoulder with white men. It's this destructive history that simmers underneath the internet memes. Understanding this, and how integral it is to American society today, can help us understand the world white women have cocreated with white men.

Of course, part of me wants to disavow my connection to these Karens. Sharing the meme on social media is a way I can signal that I understand the harm she causes and that I am not like her. My retweet of a Karen meme says, "I get it," "Don't associate me with her," and "I would never do this." Yet I, like her, want the power to dial 911 and summon protection. But there's a tradeoff in this. My desire for protection and power to summon help from 911 means that I'm activating the launch codes for my body to become a missile that destroys lives and whole communities. One gesture of my nice white lady finger at someone darker, a request to speak to the manager, that call to 911, and my white/queer/femme body becomes an assault weapon. The reality is that none of the women who get spoofed in a Karen meme are ever in any danger, nor did they need the protection of the state when they called 911.

In the Oakland case, Jennifer Schulte witnessed a Black family setting up a barbeque grill in a public park and something in this quotidian act of using shared space set her off. And when the Black people in the park used their phone to record a video of her talking to 911, she cried and ran away. I could speculate about what was going on inside Jennifer Schulte's mind that day: her phantom fear, her seeming pathological need to control others in a public place, her apparent desire to see others suffer. But I'm less interested in her inner world than I am in how we got here as a culture.

What I want to understand is this: How did we, white women, help create a world that gives us this lethal power? Why do we often feel afraid and entitled to protection? And why do we frequently cry and run away when this gets pointed out to us? And is there a way that we can turn, face ourselves, and help to dismantle this system of violence that we're currently nurturing?

## LOCATING NICE WHITE LADIES IN HISTORY

There is a history to white women's lethal power, but it can be hard to locate despite the central role we hold in the culture. We are everywhere, yet we are often unspecified. I have a Google alert set for the term "white women." Almost every morning, the search algorithm crawls the Web for occurrences of these two words together and automagically sends me an email. What I've gleaned from these morning emails is that the word *women* modified by *white* most often shows up in research and news articles about health disparities, as in, "African-American women are 3–4 times more likely to die of pregnancy-related causes than **white women**." Or we appear in reports about voting, as in, "Black female voters are multiple times more likely to vote Democrat than white men or **white women**." There are frequent stories like the one about Jennifer Schulte ("BBQ Becky"), Alison Ettel ("Permit Patty"), Amy Cooper ("Central Park Karen"), and other white women caught on video behaving badly. But there is also a kind of void when it comes to white women, a missing narrative about white women as a collective with a specific history.

Without recognizing this history, the news items about BBQ Becky, Permit Patty, or Central Park Karen devolve into opinion pieces and meta-news items that ask if nicknames in such cases are "too cutesy" or why the internet is shaming white people. In the case of Justine Sacco, the white PR executive who tweeted just before she got on a flight to South Africa: "Going to Africa. Hope I don't get AIDS. Just kidding. I'm white!" and who was fired from her job at IAC by the time she landed, she became the signifier for internet shaming. Her experience became the focus of countless essays, podcasts, and even a book by Jon Ronson, *So You've Been Publicly Shamed.* But what these hot takes miss entirely is the fact that white women collectively wield a deadly power.

I was in my twenties when I realized that I was white and how that was connected to being a white woman. When I started graduate school in 1986, I still harbored the fantasy that my great-grandmother was Cherokee. Fortunately for me, a professor gave me a copy of Vine Deloria's *Custer Died for Your Sins,* and in reading his words, I saw the story my family told about the "inherited" beaded moccasins for what it was: a threadbare but comforting lie about who we were.

Easier to believe that our ancestors had been on the Trail of Tears (as my father had told me) than to come to terms with the much uglier truth that our family had benefited from the theft of Indian land. During my childhood, I believed the lies about our racial heritage, and I'd only come to recognize my own whiteness relatively late in life. At least, because of the slowness of this realization, I hadn't invested a lot of years or emotions into whiteness as an identity. That experience gave me the ability to see whiteness from a different angle, as if from outside it, even though I was inside it all along.

I also didn't learn about the racial terrorism of lynching—and who the intended beneficiaries were—until I was in graduate school. In the public school system that I grew up in, the legislature mandated two years of Texas history and one year of US history—to reinforce the state's sense of its own importance with schoolchildren—but there was nothing in the curriculum about lynching. I had some vague notion that lynching meant hanging, but in fact, it refers to any extralegal murder. Before a widespread court system, vigilante justice was commonplace, and one of the most common reasons for lynching was being a horse thief, which, according to one account, was how one of my ancestors met his end. Before the end of slavery, white people—mostly men—were lynched. But it was after slavery that lynching became a campaign of racial terrorism, and the targets of this form of violence became predominantly Black and Brown people. From approximately 1877 to 1950, thousands died from lynching. In Texas, where I grew up, hundreds of Mexicans and Mexican Americans were lynched. When lynching became racialized, it also became a thoroughly sadistic ritual in which Black men were often tortured, castrated, and dismembered before their bodies were hung for display. In total, some four thousand all across the United States were murdered this way. What lingered in my mind as I read these historical accounts is that these lynchings had so often been carried out in defense of white womanhood. In graduate school, I was a student who wanted to know why, and how, we got here.

Beginning in the 1600s and through to the mid-nineteenth century, white women in the United States were witnesses to, beneficiaries of, and active participants in the practice of enslaving human beings. The women's history I'd been taught as a student at a small state college in East Texas reassured me that white women had a minimal role in slavery and were possibly even "allies" to enslaved people. But historian Stephanie E. Jones-Rogers sets this record straight in her book *They Were Her Property: White Women as Slave Owners in the American South*. In it, she documents women's economic investments in slavery. At a time when white women generally did not own property, they were more likely to inherit enslaved people than land. I was taught in an early women's studies class about women making progress in being able to own property, but in fact this "progress" came through changes to the law that enabled white women to own slaves. This form of inherited wealth gave white women a kind of provisional power: it enabled them to attract wealthier potential husbands and, once married, gave them more power in their marriages. As one reviewer of Jones-Rogers's book noted, "If their husbands proved unsatisfactory slave owners in their eyes, the women might petition for the right to manage their 'property' themselves, which they did, with imaginative sadism." And it is the "imaginative sadism" that comes through in historical accounts of white women as slave masters.

Even the very intimate familial caretaking that we now tend to think of in glossy, soft-focus terms like "maternal instincts" was routinized in brutal and violent ways under slavery. White women expected enslaved women to serve as wet nurses, that is, to breast-feed their infants for them. Although earlier historical accounts insisted this happened rarely, the practice was actually widespread. In Jones-Rogers's book, she tells the story of one woman whose enslaved mother always gave birth at the same time as her mistress so she would be available to nurse the white baby. Being forced to lactate for the convenience of white women, and all that implies—captivity, rape, being used for "breeding"—was but one part of the elaborate cruelty of slavery. This is what I mean by a world that is cocreated: within this system, enslaved women were regularly brutalized by white men for their sadistic pleasure, and for the convenience of white women, which is its own form of sadism.

What white people built and benefited from in the system of slavery lingers today. Scholar Joy DeGruy has documented the Post Traumatic Slave Syndrome (PTSS) of Black Americans who are descendants of enslaved people. She traces how the trauma of that brutal institution gets passed on intergenerationally, like any other family trait. And what is it that the white slave-owning mistress handed down to white women today through this intergenerational process of transmission? The sadism that summons death by dialing 911, the callous disregard for suffering, and the bounty of white wealth. Slavery remains with us in the here and now.

A handful of white women did resist the institution of slavery and advocated for social justice, such as the Grimké sisters, but history tells us that white women who fought against white supremacy were exceedingly rare. More typical of the history of nice white ladies is the United Daughters of the Confederacy.

White women, explains historian Elizabeth McRae, "did all . . . kind[s] of work to sustain the ideology and politics of white supremacy" in the late nineteenth and early twentieth centuries. Although white men may be recognized as official "spokespeople," it is white women who have always done the "daily, mundane work" of ensuring that "the public history of the nation . . . privileged white experiences and white leaders." A key organization in the work of maintaining the ideology of white supremacy after the end of the Civil War was the National Association of the Daughters of the Confederacy. It was founded in 1894 by Caroline Meriwether Goodlett and Anna Davenport Raines to "tell of the glorious fight against the greatest odds a nation ever faced, that their hallowed memory should never die." The organization, which eventually became known as the United Daughters of the Confederacy (UDC), was concerned with

raising money for the construction of statues and other public memo-
rials to the Confederate dead as a way to keep the cause of white supremacy vibrantly alive. As the Civil War faded from memory, white
women took it upon themselves to ensure the Confederacy and its
cause never faded from public consciousness.

According to historian Karen Cox, it is critical to recognize that
the women of the UDC went beyond this goal of memorialization
and became active agents in the politics of vindication, a goal that
focused their attention on the education of the next generation of
Americans in both the North and the South. They pressured textbook committees to spotlight narratives that either minimized the
brutality of slavery, diminished the role slavery played in the founding of the United States, or worked to erase the presence of Black
people from US history altogether. The UDC held essay contests on
the importance of referring to the Civil War as the "War Between
the States" and on why it was an extended "battle for states' rights"
and not a conflict over slavery. And the nice white ladies of the UDC
hosted teacher trainings and speaker series at universities to reinforce
this skewed pedagogy.

In interviews, Bryan Stevenson, the attorney and founder of the
Equal Justice Initiative, has said, "The North won the Civil War,
but the South won the narrative war." He says it's part of why we,
in the United States, have never really come to grips with white supremacy. I agree with Stevenson. And, I would add, if we're going to
tell the truth about white supremacy in this country, we have to lay
a good deal of responsibility at the doorstep of the nice white ladies
in the Daughters of the Confederacy. Today, there are more than fifteen hundred public monuments and statues to the Confederacy that
fought to uphold slavery, and those all exist because white women
raised money for them, oversaw their construction and the stories
they told, and organized the fanfare of an unveiling ceremony for
each one. The UDC is still active, and as of 2015, had over nineteen
thousand members, and on its website claims to be merely a "women's

organization," a turn that was already happening at the beginning of the twentieth century. In 1912, just eighteen years after its founding, the UDC claimed that it was an ally of other women's organizations, especially those within the growing peace movement. As the women of the UDC focused their political energy on vindicating the South, other white women were focused on voting rights.

In 1866, the year after the Civil War ended, white suffragists Susan B. Anthony and Elizabeth Cady Stanton formed the American Equal Rights Association (AERA), an organization dedicated to the goal of suffrage for "all regardless of gender or race," and two years later, started their newspaper called *The Revolution*. But it became clear pretty quickly that their idea of a revolution was one that benefited white women. That same year, 1868, the Fourteenth Amendment granted citizenship to everyone "born or naturalized in the United States," which meant that formerly enslaved people were now citizens. Then debate ensued about the Fifteenth Amendment, and white women saw their rights as pitted against Black men's rights. At a pivotal convention in May 1869, abolitionist Frederick Douglass argued that the AERA should support the amendment, written to protect against discrimination based on race, color, or "previous condition of servitude," while continuing to fight for women's suffrage. Stanton not only disagreed with Douglass but also stood to give an address filled with racist stereotypes: "Think of Patrick and Sambo and Hans and Yung Tung, who do not know the difference between a monarchy and a republic, who cannot read the Declaration of Independence or Webster's spelling book, making laws. . . . [The amendment] creates an antagonism everywhere between educated, refined women and the lower orders of men, especially in the South." Expressing her opposition to the amendment, Susan B. Anthony said, "I would cut off my right arm before I would ever work or demand the ballot for the negro."

In 1894, the same year the UDC was founded, Ida B. Wells, an investigative journalist, suffragist, and civil rights activist, was invited to speak about her anti-lynching campaign in Great Britain by Lady Henry Somerset, head of the British temperance movement. Lady Somerset also invited Frances E. Willard, national president of the Woman's Christian Temperance Union, to share the stage with Wells. Wells knew she had to persuade the white liberals of the day to understand her cause, and she used the occasion to do just that. Willard, who came from an abolitionist family and who was an advocate for women's suffrage, was typical of white liberals at the time who believed in the inherent inferiority of Black people. Wells wanted to expose this. When Lady Somerset asked Wells what she thought of Willard, Wells read an interview Willard had given to the *New York Voice* in which Willard had said, "'Better whiskey and more of it' is the rallying cry of great, dark-faced mobs. The [local tavern] is the Negro's center of power . . . [and] colored race multiplies like the locusts of Egypt. The safety of [white] women, of childhood, of the home, is menaced in a thousand localities." Lady Somerset was so angry about Wells's disclosure of this information that she sent a telegram to abolitionist Frederick Douglass demanding that he publicly reprimand Wells, which he did not do. Lady Somerset and Frances Willard were the nice white ladies whose positions were emblematic of that era, as was their opposition to early Black feminists like Wells.

Regarding the period in the United States from 1848 to 1920, one historian, Louise Newman, refers to the rise of a "white woman movement" that affirmed white women's racial similarity to white men while at the same time asserting their gender difference from those men because they believed white heterosexuality, and all the binary differences it suggests, formed the bedrock of white civilization. When the Nineteenth Amendment passed in 1920, giving white women the right to vote, Black women, Indigenous women, and many Latinx women in the Southwest were still barred from voting because of racist voting restrictions. When those women reached out to the main suffrage organizations of the time, they were ignored, according to historian Lisa Tetrault. "They say basically, 'Help us, we still can't vote,' and those organizations basically say, 'That's a race question, it doesn't concern us,'" Tetrault explains.

Most historical accounts of the campaign for suffrage whitewash the overt racism, or minimize it as an understandable by-product of that historical period, rather than address it head-on as a cornerstone of white women's political organizing. In the 2014 documentary by Ken Burns and Paul Barnes, *Not for Ourselves Alone: The Story of Elizabeth Cady Stanton and Susan B. Anthony*, race is barely mentioned. The 2015 film *Suffragette* reproduces this history and sanitizes it through an all-white-women cast and a script that doesn't give voice to the stories of women of color. Instead, we get this version of history in which white women's racism is reimagined as a noble struggle for justice rather than the intense campaign for white women's voting rights ahead of Black men's and Black women's voting rights. When some white feminists wanted to put a statue of Susan B. Anthony and Cady Stanton in Central Park, Brent Staples, an editorial writer for the *New York Times*, criticized the planned sculpture for presenting a "lily-white version of history." Many people organized to have the statue changed, and when it was installed in the summer of 2020, it had been amended to include Sojourner Truth, the early Black feminist who was often at odds with the nice white ladies of the suffrage movement.

In the 1920s, after white women had won the vote, people began to talk about the modern era and the rise of the "new woman." This referred to the emergence of flapper girls, when fashion favored bobbed hairdos and shorter dresses with more skin revealed, a change that many women experienced as liberating. At the same time, the appearance of the automobile dramatically changed social relationships and made a new kind of dating possible so that courtship could take place away from home and the gaze of chaperones. The 1920s is also the decade in the United States when white women were doing another type of organizing, with the Ku Klux Klan. In 1924, thousands donned all white and marched down Pennsylvania Avenue in the nation's capital in support of a white nation. At the time, there were millions of white women in the Klan.

This is also the time period of the Great Migration of African Americans out of the southern states, pulled northward to the Upper Midwest and to California and the Pacific Northwest by the promise of a brighter future for their children. The way this story is commonly told today is by reporting that African Americans were seeking economic opportunity in the North, and though that's partially true, this mass relocation of people takes on another dimension when you see it in the context of the terrorist campaign of lynching across the South in which white women played a role.

In 1917, as part of what later became known as the East St. Louis Massacre, a group of white women beat a group of Black women with "fists, stones, and sticks" as the latter begged "for mercy" while the white women "laughed." The events in East St. Louis launched an intense, widespread campaign of racial terror throughout the United States from 1917 to 1923, a movement often fueled by white-owned newspapers reporting fabricated instances of Black men assaulting white women. During the Red Summer of 1919, at least ninety-seven lynchings were recorded, thousands of Black people were killed, and thousands of Black-owned homes and businesses were burned to the ground in three dozen cities across the United States. One of the first people killed in violence in Washington, DC, in 1919 was a twenty-two-year-old Black World War I veteran named Randall Neal. In May 1921, the Greenwood section of Tulsa, Oklahoma, a prosperous Black urban area, was bombed and completely destroyed after a young Black man named Dick Rowland happened to get in the same elevator as a white woman. The elevator ride was retold among the white community as an "assault," and then white people grabbed their torches. In the first week of January 1923, Black people were massacred and the town of Rosewood, Florida, was destroyed after a twenty-two-year-old white woman said a Black man had assaulted her.

The Great Migration, then, becomes clearer when we recognize that time and again Black people were forced to run for their lives, often chased by white mobs sometimes composed of white women with "fists, sticks, and stones," and more often made up of white men who would publish, believe, and defend the false narrative of white women's innocence.

One of the worst economic depressions in the United States stretched from the 1930s through 1945, when entering World War II served as a catalyst to jump-start the economy. During this time, people of color were hit harder with economic troubles than white Americans. And yet, when you look at the representations of the Great Depression, it is a photo of a white woman that has become the iconic image that represents that era.

The popular culture of the 1930s is one that reifies this kind of angelic innocence fantasy of white women and white girls. Two examples illustrate this: Snow White and Shirley Temple. These artifacts live on beyond the time for which they were created and resonate in other eras even to today. In large part, the popular culture of the 1930s promoted tropes of purity, innocence, and wholesomeness as defining features of white femaleness. People bought into these fantasies in droves, and the legacies of these roles persist dangerously today. At the same time, an economic depression and an ongoing campaign of racial terrorism against African Americans were occurring, yet white maidenhood became the story that we were telling ourselves about who we were in the United States.

The period following World War II gave rise to the suburbs and dramatic changes in the way many Americans lived. This was also a time of racist deed restrictions. In suburbs like Levittown on Long Island, houses were sold only to white families. These societal shifts also produced another persistent trope of white womanhood: the newly reimagined ideal of the housewife, whose role in this period ballooned—as illustrated, as one example, by the increasing complexity of recipes and cookbooks, which seem almost designed to fill the time of women who were no longer working outside the home.

The intended audience for these kinds of schemes was always the white suburban housewife, never Black women. When Black women were shown in advertisements and in popular culture, they often were depicted as domestics. Black women were relegated to working as maids and nannies for white women, or they worked in a very limited set of clerical jobs.

In the United States, the civil rights movement in many ways began in 1955 in response to the murder of Emmett Till. The sepia-toned history we often hear about the civil rights movement is that it was a nonviolent movement, and certainly nonviolence was a principle held by the movement's leaders. But it was also an incredibly violent movement, and violent on the part of the state and on the part of white people who resisted integration. White women were part of that violence.

"In my opinion, the guilt begins with Mrs. Bryant." With those words Mrs. Mamie Till-Mobley lay the blame for her fourteen-year-old son's lynching in Mississippi on Carolyn Bryant, the white woman who testified in 1955 that Emmett Till made an advance on her.

Till's lynching was a spark that helped ignite the civil rights movement. And until recently, historians widely agreed on this point: Emmett Till did what Bryant accused him of and, in doing so, violated social mores of the Jim Crow South, unjust as those mores were and appalling as his punishment remains. In other words, they believed Bryant. As historian John David Smith told PBS in 2003, "Till crossed the line of white propriety; he committed what whites considered a betrayal of racial lines. Till insulted Bryant's wife and insulted the very bases of white racial control and hegemony." Or so Carolyn Bryant claimed.

Now in her eighties, Bryant has changed the story she told under oath. In 1955, she said Till whistled at her, grabbed her by the waist, and "verbally threatened her." But in a 2007 interview, she told Duke

University researcher Timothy Tyson "that part's not true." In Tyson's 2017 book, *The Blood of Emmett Till*, Bryant is quoted as saying that "nothing that boy did could ever justify what happened to him."

Late in 2018, the Department of Justice reopened the case of Till's murder, although it's not clear whether this action was related to the revelations about Bryant's false statements in court. DOJ officials said that they had "new information" but did not specify what it was. Some speculate that Bryant—who now goes by Carolyn Donham—could face charges. If she does face legal consequences, it will diverge from the norm in instances like this. A white woman customarily goes unchallenged when she turns her social power into a bomb thrown at Black and Brown people. Bryant is the foremother of contemporary white women who call the police on Black people sitting in a Starbucks, barbecuing in a park, or napping in a dorm. These white women know that their accusations have power, that they are readily believed, and that they face few consequences for words that can and do end lives.

Throughout these same decades of American history, only a handful of white women seemed to resist the white power structure. Viola Liuzzo, an Italian American white woman, a wife and mother of five, left Chicago to join the civil rights movement in the South. She was driving some workers who were registering voters in Mississippi when she was shot and killed by the Klan in 1965. In *Deep in Our Hearts*, a book from 2000, the authors profile nine white women who were part of the freedom movement for civil rights. It's difficult to find a much longer list of white women who were doing this kind of work. There weren't thousands, hundreds, or even scores of white women risking their lives for the movement, while so many African Americans were risking theirs. The big picture of white women in US history and in colonialism is this: millions of white women have been heavily invested in violence, domination, and the suffering of racialized Others, while only a handful have tried to resist the invitation to join white men in this terrorism and oppression.

The late 1960s and early 1970s saw the emergence of the women's movement. This second wave of feminism brought together women across racial categories and mobilized action around issues that today we would call "care work," that is, the idea of paying for domestic labor, for state-supported childcare, and for welfare rights. For a brief moment, this multiracial coalition of women challenged capitalism and the patriarchal family and white supremacy. But the dominant cultural narrative about feminism was one shaped to appeal to white women. In a way, the women's movement was a response by privileged, well-educated, white housewives dissatisfied with living in suburban homes and doing housework that the post–World War II advertisements told them made up the American dream.

There is a longer and more detailed narrative of nice white ladies that a skilled historian can create, but what I intend with this brief account is to bring white women into the line of sight. When I gaze backward through history, it is the women in my own family I see looking back at me. I have searched the historical records for our family, and though I've not found any records that we owned slaves, I know my family well enough to know that this was not because of a moral objection but rather a lack of economic resources. But ownership is perhaps the wrong metric. According to one historian, Adam Goodheart, "Many non-slaveholding whites in the South rented slaves from wealthier slaveholders. So it was very common for a white Southerner to be a 'slave master' but not technically a 'slave owner.'" This, I recognize. We are renters, not owners, yet we believe ourselves to be masters. In Jones-Rogers's account of slave-owning white women and their "imaginative sadism," I see my mother's mother, Big Granny. When my mother was born in 1934, she was named after Shirley Temple. Then, in her version of motherhood, Big Granny routinely beat her daughter Shirley until she bled. A middle child of three, Shirley was singled out for a particular kind of cruelty that Big Granny did not inflict on her other two children. That, to me, is an imaginative sadism that must have been learned and passed down through generations.

When I look at the photos of lynchings and see the crowds of smiling white faces turned toward the camera, proud of what they've done, I see the faces of my own family. To be clear, I haven't found evidence in a family album that my ancestors attended a lynching (although there are rumors they did), but when I look at family photos taken in locations where I know that lynchings occurred, I don't see any difference between the people in those crowds and the people in my family. I see no distinction, no moral objection raised by any one of my ancestors to the horrors of lynching.

My father served in World War II as a paratrooper, and when he came back to the United States the skids were greased for him through the GI Bill, which made it possible for him to enroll at the University of Houston (although he never graduated), become an engineer, and buy a house, first in Houston and then in Corpus Christi. When the court decision in *Cisneros v. Corpus Christi Independent School District* was issued and my name was among those that would be bused to comply with the desegregation order, my father said "no daughter of mine" would ride a school bus, and we moved back to Houston to an all-white suburb, where I not coincidentally went to an all-white public high school. The white-flight education I got at Spring High School was an elite one: I took Latin from a man who had written the textbook we used; I studied Beowulf with another teacher who had a PhD and who read it to us in Middle English; in one of my extracurricular activities, I worked in theater on lights and sound with state-of-the-art equipment that would be the envy of a professional theater company. Even so, the education I got in the Texas public school system was not one where I ever learned about the enslavement of Black Americans or the lynching of Black, Italian, and Mexican Americans or the internment of Japanese Americans. We did learn about Caddo, Apache, Comanche, Wichita, Coahuiltecan, Neches, and Tonkawa peoples, who were indigenous to Texas, but what we were taught about them was that they lived in the past, had been wiped out by settler colonialism, and that was for the best. Genocide was just meant to happen. My elite high school experience led me to believe that I could go on and eventually pursue a PhD. When I did, higher education as an institution was set up for me, as a white person, to succeed. And, as a white woman, I got to count as "diversity" in comparison to my white male counterparts.

In my case, as is the case for many white women, being raised with a vague sense of safety and priority over Others (which I could not name until much later on) also meant that I was not able to see how my protection specifically created a hazard for people of color.

In 1964, Kitty Genovese, a white woman from Queens, was stabbed to death outside an apartment building by Winston Moseley, a married African American man with a history of mental illness. When reports told a story (later refuted) that none of her thirty-seven neighbors called police when they heard her being attacked, her death became the subject of social psychological research on the "bystander effect." The Genovese case became one of the driving forces for the 911 emergency call system. In a 2015 documentary film, *The Witness*, about the murder, her brother Bill Genovese describes the 911 system as "one positive outcome" from his sister's case.

So, when the manager at Starbucks or Jennifer Schulte or Alison Ettel picks up her phone and dials 911, not only is she replaying a centuries-old trope about the inherent danger of Black people, or simply activating a key mechanism for keeping public spaces white, she is also using a technology that was designed for the protection of white women, one that presumes our innocence and veracity, even as it relies on the constant surveillance and threat of incarceration of Black and Brown people.

## THE NICE WHITE LADIES OF THE FAR RIGHT

From 1995 through 2008, I spent time looking at Stormfront, at the time the main global portal for "white pride." The watchdog agency Southern Poverty Law Center has documented over one hundred murders that have been committed by people with some connection to Stormfront and its violent, racist ideology of white supremacy. I spent time there because I was researching how the ideas used to uphold lynching in an earlier era were being translated into the digital era. Stormfront used an off-the-shelf software product for its bulletin board–style forum, so it looked like any other online forum. I would log on and look through the bulletin board posts about "White Genocide," racist jokes, and the supposed evils of interracial dating. One of the discussion boards was called "Ladies Only," and there the women of Stormfront gathered. They were openly and explicitly dedicated to discussing the cause of white supremacy, yet they were also espousing liberal feminist views. They were in favor of the right to equal pay for equal work, the right to have an abortion, and even in favor of gay rights (as long as they're still white supremacists). The women in the Ladies Only discussion saw themselves as both white supremacists and feminists, and I took them at their word.

Although someone else might have tried to argue with these ladies, what occurred to me is that their easy embrace of feminism says something troubling about (white) liberal feminism. Without an explicit challenge to racism, this kind of feminism becomes a useful device for furthering white-supremacist goals. This is another way that white womanhood gets weaponized, as a way to justify racist violence to protect the "ladies," and all that white ladyhood supposedly represents.

"I hated myself my whole life because I was white, like ever since I was eleven years old, and the guilt just kept piling on," Emily told a reporter in 2016. She was at a gathering of white nationalists who were celebrating Trump's election as a victory for their movement. When asked how she found the alt-right, Emily, twenty-six, recalled with resentment being made to read *To Kill a Mockingbird* in elementary school and being told that white people were responsible for slavery. She says she found comfort in the ideas of the alt-right, which she encountered through the notorious online forum 4chan. "After joining this movement, I found that it—the guilt—I don't have it anymore," she said.

Whereas Emily may have stumbled upon ideas of white nationalism by hanging out in the Fight Club culture of 4chan, she could
just as easily have encountered these ideas through the microcelebrity
culture of YouTube.

Lana Lokteff believes that feminism, liberalism, and multicul-
turalism are destroying "white civilization." A thin, blonde, blue-
eyed American-born woman, Lokteff looks like the "Aryan warrior
woman" featured in line drawings from the white-supremacist
printed newsletters I explored in my book *White Lies*. I looked at
hundreds of these pre-internet-era propaganda tools, created solely
by white men. While I had expected to find a long list of groups they
hated, instead, the newsletters were filled with discussions and drawings of what the idealized "white man" and "white woman" were in
their imagination. In those publications, there were two kinds of
white women depicted: the Aryan warrior woman, and the faithful,
fecund wife, dutifully reproducing the white race. Lokteff, who is
married to Swedish national Henrik Palmgren, seems to embody elements of both these white-nationalist feminine ideals.

Lokteff and Palmgren are behind *Red Ice*, a radio-on-the-internet
show along the lines of Alex Jones's *Infowars*, without the shouty vi-
tamin hawking. Lokteff curates videos for her white-woman-themed
Radio 3Fourteen, a channel within *Red Ice*, which features titles
such as "Pro White Is Pro-Woman. Feminism Is Anti-White" and
"Women and the Alt-Right: The Awakened White Female." Their
combined audience reaches about 145,000 subscribers.

Of course, there is a long history of talk radio as a vehicle for
spreading racist propaganda, stretching back to Father Coughlin's
anti-immigrant screeds in the United States and Hitler's in Europe.
(Lokteff is a fan of Hitler; she recently claimed that it was women
in Germany who were responsible for putting him in power.) And
there's precedent for women doing the PR for Klan groups and the
Third Reich.

Lokteff, in her remix of these older forms, uses Radio 3Fourteen
to amplify the voices of women across national boundaries that share

the ideology of white nationalism. Sometimes she does this by interviewing other video bloggers, such as "Swan of Tuonela," a Finnish nationalist who aligns her cause with that of the US-based alt-right. In another episode, Lokteff talks with Belgian politician Anke Van dermeersch, who is an elected official in the Belgian senate and president of the organization "Women Against Islamization."

Lokteff's YouTube channel illustrates what I've found in my research about how the rise of the internet helped fuel the spread of white supremacy. In my second book, *Cyber Racism*, I traced the organizations that had produced the newsletters I'd studied in the pre-internet era and found that white supremacists were often early adopters of internet technologies because they saw the potential for spreading their racist propaganda. Part of what the digital era did for white supremacy was make it more readily accessible, globally networked, and easier to participate in. In other words, the Web made white supremacy easy to find and quickly connected people around the globe who shared that interest, opening the formerly all-male process of formulating white-supremacist ideology to white women, just as it's done for Lana Lokteff.

For women like Lokteff, the alt-right is a place where white women can embrace both whiteness and a particular version of femininity in a space unchecked by those who might try to challenge either. The women "embody a glaring contradiction," according to Seyward Darby, journalist and editor in chief of the *Atavist Magazine*, who profiled Lokteff in her book *Sisters in Hate*. Darby claims that the women she interviewed must perform extraordinary "intellectual contortions" in order to "justify participating in a movement so hostile to their freedom." In 2017, *Red Ice* announced it was partnering with Richard Spencer to create AltRight.com, with the immediate goal of creating the consciousness necessary to make a "white ethnostate" possible. The new platform is meant to be "like Breitbart, but further to the right," according to one source.

The most affluent of the white women on the far right is Rebekah Mercer, who has an advanced degree from Stanford University and is the middle daughter of hedge fund billionaire Robert Mercer. She worked as a trader before she had four children, which she reportedly now home schools in her penthouse (she combined six apartments) in Trump Tower. She has become the spokesperson for the Mercer monetary and political agenda, which is to "save America from becoming like socialist Europe," as she has put it to several people. She's trying to disrupt the more traditional conservative movement and invests in projects like Breitbart News, to which she reportedly donated $10 million. Her family also donated an estimated $25 million to sway the outcome of the 2016 presidential election. With 19.2 million unique visitors in October 2016, Breitbart's audience towers over the measly online presence of Red Ice (or even Stormfront, which has about 325,000 registered users). Stephen Bannon, once the driving force behind Breitbart, boasted in August 2016 that it is the "platform of the alt-right." It is also the favorite news source of Donald Trump. According to Joshua Green in *Devil's Bargain*, Trump read Breitbart articles flagged by Bannon, which were then printed out on paper (his preferred way to read) and delivered to him in manila folders by his staff. That is, until Bannon was ousted and various successive White House chiefs of staff tried unsuccessfully to keep the president away from Breitbart.

In addition to the Breitbart website, Rebekah Mercer has also funded other Steve-Bannon-led propaganda enterprises. She chairs the board of the Government Accountability Institute (GAI), founded by Bannon and Peter Schweizer. Reports based on tax records show that the Mercer Family Foundation has invested millions in GAI, which published Peter Schweizer's book *Clinton Cash*, a regular source of excerpts for articles for Breitbart as well as ammo for Trump's attacks against Hillary Clinton.

It's her role as the key funder of Breitbart and Bannon's allied ventures that have earned Rebekah Mercer the moniker "First Lady of the alt-right," according to investigative journalist Jane Mayer. It is a richly deserved appellation. As the underwriter of Breitbart, one of the most successful propaganda arms of the alt-right and a deep well of content for Trump's vitriol, Mercer has effectively used her inherited wealth to elevate white nationalism. With her inherited fortune, Rebekah Mercer has done more for the cause of white supremacy than the women of Stormfront or Lana or Emily could ever imagine. Like the women of the Daughters of the Confederacy, Mercer is using her resources to further white-supremacist propaganda that exploits the existing media ecosystem. And, like the women I discovered in early internet discussion boards, Mercer is deploying a kind of feminism to expand propaganda-making from an all-boys club to include white women.

## THE CRUSHING POWER OF THE STATE: BROUGHT TO YOU BY WHITE WOMEN

"If anyone wants to quibble about whether or not we should call those people animals, perhaps the quibble should be whether we call them something worse," Kirstjen Nielsen, then secretary of the Department of Homeland Security (DHS), said. The US border policy was crafted by white men, but a white woman enthusiastically enforced it and a chorus of white women have acted to justify it. The white women in these roles provide a softer edge to the blunt force of state power, like a velvet glove on an iron fist. In 2017, Nielsen was installed as the leading enforcer of the "zero tolerance" immigration policy of separating children from their families at the border. Media framing of this issue has tried to cast it as a women's issue, presumably because women care more about children and families and keeping them together. All four former first ladies released a statement opposing it. Yet, such framing does not help us make sense of the fact that it was blonde, blue-eyed, skirt-and-heels-wearing Nielsen who did the job of putting children into cages with gusto.

Tempting though it is to assume that Nielsen must, on some level, oppose this cruel policy, there's no reason to believe Nielsen would have empathy by virtue of being a woman. In fact, it's these kinds of assumptions about white women's innocence and outsized empathy that have made them some of white supremacy's most effective agents. To be sure, men like Trump and his former aides, Chief of Staff John Kelly, Attorney General Jeff Sessions, and White House adviser Stephen Miller, are the architects of this policy—but it has been left to Nielsen to implement their inhumane plan and to defend it to the public.

White women like Nielsen have always been part of making white supremacy seem more palatable and less like the brutal ideology it in fact is. Women like Laura Ingraham and Ann Coulter are putting up the ideological lace curtains around the frame of the most abhorrent policies. For the white women of the Trump administration, this is a global project. Following Ivanka Trump's 2018 trip to celebrate the disastrous move of the US Embassy to Jerusalem, Nielsen visited Israel so she could get inspiration for her border wall.

Nielsen took on the job as DHS secretary with a résumé that is generously described as thin. "In a normal Administration, there isn't a chance in hell she would get nominated for anything above an undersecretary job," one national security official told a reporter for *The New Yorker*.

But she had served Trump loyally and had done her part to defend his systematic whitewashing of America. In January, she canceled the legal temporary protected status of two hundred thousand Salvadorans who had been in the United States since 2001. Then, she issued a series of aggressive statements criticizing bipartisan immigration bills that appeared to be gaining support in the Senate. One of the statements from DHS said a bipartisan immigration bill "would effectively make the United States a Sanctuary Nation where ignoring the rule of law is encouraged." She seemed able to use more extreme language than even a few male Republicans felt comfortable with—even Senator Lindsey Graham said that her statements were "poisonous."

Nielsen has defended the policy of separating families, and at the same time she has also denied the policy exists or was created by the Trump White House. In any other administration, such mind-numbing contradictions would be baffling. But in the Trump era, her work was part of a larger propaganda strategy, and Nielsen threw her shoulder into it.

She'd also been quick to mimic Trump's strategy of attacking facts—and the press that reports them. Asked about the images of children abused and warehoused in cages, she called the coverage "hearsay stories" and denied there was any child abuse taking place in detention centers. "Claiming these children and their parents are mistreated is simply not true," she said. In a speech to the National Sheriff's Association the same day, she said, "These minors are well taken care of. Don't believe the press."

The minors are not well taken care of. This brutal form of institutionalized racism has traumatized children at the border. The American College of Physicians issued a statement strongly objecting to family separation, noting the kind of psychological and emotional distress it inflicts on the very young. "Childhood trauma and adverse childhood experiences create negative health impacts that will last an individual's entire lifespan. Separating a child from his or her parents triggers a level of stress consistent with trauma." The damage that the Trump administration inflicted on these children lasts a lifetime.

Nielsen insisted on calling these children "criminal aliens," a dehumanizing phrase she used repeatedly in a speech to the National Sheriff's Association. The double-barreled rhetoric of "criminal" and "alien" is meant to dehumanize the people attempting to cross the border, when they are already fleeing horrific, genocidal conditions. Nielsen was resolute about enforcing the policy, which she mistakenly referred to as "the law." "Illegal actions have and must have consequences," she has said. "No more free passes, no more get-out-of-jail-free cards." But seeking asylum at the border is not illegal, no matter how many times Nielsen—or Trump—say it is.

Meanwhile, Ivanka Trump posted photos of herself on Instagram with her own children as her father's administration kept ripping children away from their parents. As White House adviser, she remained silent about her father's vicious immigration policy. Her hypergroomed appearance made it easy to pose as a palatable mouthpiece to run interference for her father's hateful policies. In January 2017, as she posted photos on Instagram of her glamorous lifestyle with her husband, her father's administration rolled out its first attempt at a Muslim ban. The timing of one of her posts created outrage in some quarters, but her "elegant," soft-focus Insta-life has sailed on, unimpeded by criticism. The exterior Ivanka presents to the world, and the things she gets away with as a result, are wrapped up in being a nice white lady.

## AMY COOPER AND GEORGE FLOYD

In late May 2020, there were two headlines that spoke to the urgency of the destructive power of "Karens" and what's at stake. In one headline story, Amy Cooper escalates a confrontation with an African American man in New York's Central Park. The man, Christian Cooper (no relation), tells the woman to put her dog on a leash, in compliance with clearly marked rules. When she refuses, he starts recording a video of her on his phone. In response, Amy says, "I will call the police and say an African American man is threatening my life." She calls the police, throws her voice up half an octave, and begins to perform "fear" for the dispatcher. The video of her throwing her voice on that 911 call is the starkest display I have ever seen of someone intentionally weaponizing her white womanhood against a Black man.

The other headline story this day is of the killing of George Floyd, an African American man in Minneapolis, Minnesota, again recorded on a cell phone and distributed through social media. In the recording, made by seventeen-year-old Darnella Frazier, Floyd is chest down on the street, his head turned to one side, while a white Minneapolis cop smirks and presses his knee into Floyd's neck, taunting him, for nine minutes and twenty-nine seconds. Floyd says, "I can't breathe," several times, but those pleas are ignored. As the man with his knee on his neck looks at the cell phone camera defiantly, Floyd becomes motionless and the police move his still-handcuffed body. George Floyd died on that street with that man's knee on his neck while we all, at home because of the pandemic, watched the video in our living rooms. Before this encounter with police, Floyd had been a beloved friend, a son, a brother, and a boyfriend. He worked as a bouncer at a club in Minneapolis, and he was originally from Houston's Third Ward, where my mother would have locked her car doors because she believed a lie about Black men like George Floyd.

The deadly power of the police that ended George Floyd's life in Minneapolis is exactly what Amy Cooper was summoning when she called 911 in Central Park. It's the same power that Carolyn Bryant used when she pointed at Emmett Till. It is the power that our society has decided we, nice white ladies, are entitled to. One gesture of my white lady finger at someone darker, a request to speak to the manager, a call to 911, and my body becomes an assault weapon.

# 2

# THE TROUBLE WITH
# WHITE FEMINISM

Feminism has saved my life, broken my heart, and left me with questions I don't know how to answer. What I've come to understand is that there is not just one feminism but multiple versions.

When I was growing up, my father was more of a feminist, in his Texas-styled way, than my mother was. A bumper sticker popular when I lived in Texas read: "God made men and women equal. Smith & Wesson makes damn sure they stay that way." My father subscribed to this brand of feminism. It's part of what prompted him to give me a gun when I turned seventeen and was getting ready to leave home. He took me to a shooting range and taught me how to use the gun. He encouraged me, in the strongest possible terms, that if I ever had to fire on someone, "Make sure you kill the son of a bitch." And he assured me that the law in Texas was on my side if I were to shoot someone who was threatening me, even if they were outside my home. "Drag him over the doorstep before you call the law," he counseled. Finally, he told me, "If you can't kill someone, then you have no business owning a gun."

Smith & Wesson feminism, like other forms of white feminism, appears simple enough at first. It is rooted in a set of reassuring, if facile, ideas about who "men" and "women" are. In this binary view of the world, all women are on the same, disadvantaged side of the bright, wide line dividing men from women. This is what I refer to as a "gender-only" feminism, and it is at the root of white feminism.

When some people describe white feminism, they treat it as a monolith, as if there were only one kind. After observing this phenomenon for the past two decades, it seems to me that there are multiple versions, hence the plural: white feminisms. There is the V-Day feminism, pink pussy hat resistance, the Hollywood version of the #MeToo movement. There is white carceral feminism and white corporate feminism. Sometimes, women of color are active in one of these forms of white feminism, but they are often tokenized within a predominantly white milieu. Or, as in the case of the #MeToo movement, a Black founder and creator had their ideas co-opted and taken over by a young, thin, white celebrity.

"Are you better off than your grandmother?" was a question that many people were asking in 2013 when the fiftieth anniversary of the publication of Betty Friedan's *Feminine Mystique* came around. My answer to that question was a resounding *yes!* My life now as someone who earned a PhD and who now makes a living as a writer and a professor is one that previous generations of women in my family— my mother, grandmother, and great-grandmother—could scarcely have imagined. And this is largely because of feminism.

Even as I celebrate the changes that second-wave feminism made possible in my life, I recognize that Betty Friedan's version of feminism was a narrow one. Her "problem that has no name," the central concept in her book, was really a description of a problem that white, upper-middle-class, well-educated, cisgender, heterosexual women experienced. These were women who, like Friedan herself, had college educations and felt trapped by the lack of opportunities and wanted "something more" than marrying, staying at home, and raising children. Yet, Friedan was no friend to queer women like me, and her vision of feminism was not meant for the millions of women—working-class women and women of color—who already worked outside the home. Friedan's feminism was one that liberated some women (mostly white, upper-middle-class) and contributed to the oppression of other women (mostly queer, poor, women of color).

Shirley, my mother, believed she had no use for feminism. She was one of those women who Friedan described with some disdain that "longed to be a housewife." When she married my father (her second husband), she achieved that goal, gave up her job as an executive assistant, and never worked in the paid labor force again. She spent most of her time keeping the house that we lived in hospital clean. But she imagined something different for me. When I would ask her to teach me something having to do with housework—how to do laundry, for example—she would shoo away my request with a dismissive, "You don't need to know how to do that." And, for the most part, she resolutely refused to teach me such things. When I would press her on why not, she would answer, "You can hire someone to do that." In Shirley's dreams of my upper-middle-class, white (heterosexually) married future, she imagined that I would employ a woman of color to do housework for me.

The feminism I first encountered in the mid-1980s saved me from Shirley's plans in that it helped me imagine a different future for myself, one in which I could choose my own destiny without a man.

These were also the early days of writing about "intersectionality," and one of my professors assigned a 1985 Hazel Carby article on lynching, which introduced me to the writing of Ida B. Wells-Barnett, the journalist, researcher, and activist. Wells-Barnett published *The Red Record* in 1895 with her analysis and eyewitness account of the patterns surrounding lynching. What Carby and Wells-Barnett, writing almost a century apart, taught me was that

there were two myths, two lies, really, at the center of the justification for lynching: Black men were rapists and inherently violent;
and white women were especially susceptible to such attacks and
were, by their very nature, innocent. Black women were, at this
same time, viewed as unrapeable because of the lie of their sexual
availability and their lack of protection under the law. Growing up
in Texas, I found the racist myth about Black men was like ambient
noise, always on in the background. It was why Mother locked the
doors on her Chrysler when we drove through the Third Ward in
Houston. It was why Daddy didn't want me to sit on a bus in compliance with a school desegregation order in Corpus Christi. But
did I ever learn about the other side of that myth, that white women
were inherently innocent? Never once.

## PINK PUSSY HATS GO TO WASHINGTON
## AND #METOO COMES TO HOLLYWOOD

On January 21, 2017, the Women's March drew approximately
470,000 people to Washington, DC, in a protest that was in some
ways a collective outpouring of grief and anger that Hillary Rodham
Clinton lost the election to someone who not only grabbed women
by the "pussy" but bragged about it.

Thousands of women showed up there in knitted "pussy power"
hats, crafted from hot pink yarn. The hats were part of a campaign
launched by Krista Suh and Jayna Zweiman, friends from Los Angeles, in November 2016. Suh and Zweiman wanted to come up with
a way for women to visibly demonstrate their opposition to Trump's
election. Suh said she wanted to turn her despair over Hillary Clinton's loss into a positive contribution. To brace for the colder tem-
peratures in DC, she made herself a hat that was warm and visible.
After she knitted her own, she realized, "we could all wear them,
make a unified statement."

Suh and Zweiman created a pattern that could be shared online
and it quickly caught on and became the Pussyhat Project, with its

own website. In the first few weeks, the pattern was downloaded tens of thousands of times. Based on the downloads, Suh estimated there were sixty thousand hats knitted, but images from the march suggest it was many thousands more. Of the almost half a million marchers in DC alone, a good 80 percent were wearing the hats, knitted by themselves or a friend or purchased on Etsy. According to the Pussyhat Project website, Suh and Zweiman wanted to reclaim knitting and the color pink, derided for their cultural association with the feminine, and make both into symbols of strength. As the introduction to the project explains, "Pink is considered a very female color representing caring, compassion, and love—all qualities that have been derided as weak but are actually STRONG. Wearing pink together is a powerful statement that we are unapologetically feminine and we unapologetically stand for women's rights."

One participant in the march, Andi Zeisler, author of *We Were Feminists Once* and founder of BitchMedia, worried that the hats were "too cutesy" for the political reality of the post-2016 election. "We need to go *full* witch. We need to really scare some folks." That said, Zeisler was cautiously optimistic that for the thousands of women who were exposed to political activism for the first time at the march, the knitted hats might be a way in to more sustained political engagement. "If people take this as an entry point and then take it to the next level, then, yes, that t-shirt or that necklace or that feminist deodorant, even, is good," she said. Considering turnout alone on that day, the march was a big success, and another one was planned for the following January. But some questioned whether the march made any tangible political impact, and the pussy hats began to rankle.

Taylyn Washington-Harmon is a writer and editor based in New York who said she chose not to participate in the 2018 march "mostly because of the idea of performative activism and the lasting action that rarely follows." She was also bothered by the pink pussy hats as a symbol of feminist solidarity. "The vagina, especially a pink vagina, should not and cannot serve as a universal symbol of womanhood across racial and gender lines. To put it simply: Not all women have vaginas . . . and not all vaginas are pink." For her, the coup de grâce came when she was scrolling through her Instagram feed and saw that someone had placed a pink pussy hat on the Harriet Tubman statue in Harlem. "In good faith, I imagine the person felt it was a sweet gesture," Washington-Harmon wrote, "but as a Black woman and feminist, nothing could be further from the truth." Eve Ewing, sociologist and poet, summed up her reaction to the placement of the hat this way: "Harriet Tubman was a disabled Black woman, an enslaved person who risked her life to free other enslaved people. Keep your cutesy symbol of cisnormative, white normative, made-a-supposedly-subversive-joke-about-sexual-assault accessories off her head."

The political fact lurking just below the pink hats is that a majority of white women—53 percent—voted for the pussy-grabber. The cheery resistance narrative about women in pink hats is, once again, a gender-only feminism that assumes "women are women everywhere and they all have [pink] vaginas." But the gender-only feminism on display at the marches in January elevates white, heterosexual, cisgender women's experiences.

In a widely circulated photo taken by Kevin Banatte, activist Angela Peoples nonchalantly nurses a lollipop and holds a hand-lettered sign that reads, "Don't forget white women voted for Trump." She is in the foreground of the shot, and behind her stand three white women wearing knitted pink hats and taking selfies as they stand perched atop a Jersey barrier. The photo of Peoples, who is African American, and the three white women quickly went viral, in part because it works as a visual callout. The juxtaposition is a critique of these specific white women and, by extension, of all white women.

Implicit in this critique is a challenge to white women: Where were you when Mike Brown was killed in Ferguson, Missouri, just three years before? Or where were they in 2015 when Mya Hall, Alexia Christian, and Meagan Hockaday—all Black women—were shot

and killed by police? The image of the three white women taking selfies in their pink pussy hats also punctures the shallowness and per-
formativity of their activism. It implies that they are most concerned
with how they will appear in Instagram shots of their participation in
the march, and they will likely vanish from activism when the day is
over. In 2020, in the wake of twenty-seven-year-old Breonna Taylor's
murder by police in Louisville, Kentucky, Charnessa Ridley, president of the North Carolina group Women United, asked: "Where are
the pink pussy hats when Black women are dying?"

Part of what rankled so many about the Women's March was its
cozy relationship with the police. In the wave of videos and images
from the march, many show women high-fiving cops, women taking
photos with cops, and cops wearing pussy hats. As scholar Lauren
Michele Jackson observed about the march: "The irony that a march
against the state was applauded *by the state* was not only ignored,
but promoted as the crown feature of the Women's March. Unlike
all those *other* demonstrations, participants argued, this was protest
done the right way. The American way: with permits, class, and civility." It was as if the Black Lives Matter protests were erased rather
than amplified that day. Jackson went on about the message that rang
out that day, of "white women chastising the men—all men—so certain misogyny lost them their turn again, too distraught to consider
how much whiteness had won."

The Women's March, like so many social protests in the digital
era, was largely organized online and then quickly dissipated. There is
an inherent fragility to protests organized exclusively through social
media, without a simultaneous and parallel effort in long-standing
face-to-face settings, as sociologist Zeynep Tufekci points out in her
2017 book *Twitter and Tear Gas*. According to Tufekci, part of the
reason the Arab Spring uprising didn't last over the long term is because it was mostly coordinated through social media connections.
In contrast, a movement like the Montgomery Bus Boycott could
last over a year—381 days—with daily car-pooling and walking long

distances to avoid the buses. This movement was sustained because the organizing relied on existing relationships and networks in Black churches. Organizing a protest through social media is like a flash fire: it ignites quickly, then burns out just as fast. To some, this is what happened with the Women's March—it caught fire then faded without having much of an impact. To other observers, the Women's March made possible another feminist uprising: the Hollywood version of #MeToo.

Tarana Burke started the #MeToo movement in 2006 to support survivors of sexual violence. As a Black woman, Burke's effort is connected to a larger movement led by Black women to end sexual violence. It includes contemporary efforts, such as Aishah Shahidah Simmons's *NO! The Rape Documentary* and related activism. And it goes back through decades to include Rosa Parks and Recy Taylor. Historian Danielle McGuire in her 2011 book *At the Dark End of the Street: Black Women, Rape, and Resistance* documents that the roots of activism for many Black women were in the fight against sexual violence, often perpetrated by white men. For Taylor and Parks, as for Burke and Simmons, rape is always interwoven with the politics of race. Not so for celebrity Alyssa Milano.

In October 2017, Alyssa Milano tweeted: "If all the women who have been sexually harassed or assaulted wrote 'Me too' as a status, we might give people a sense of the magnitude of the problem." It's not clear where she got the idea, but she attributes it to a "friend's suggestion." With this tweet, Milano used her platform to launch a gender-only critique of sexual harassment and assault in Hollywood and beyond. She did not mention the way race or white supremacy shapes sexual assault.

For many white women, Milano's tweet resonated. As Black actor and sexual violence activist Gabrielle Union said on *Good Morning America*, "I think the floodgates have opened for white women." Alison Phipps, in *Me, Not You*, observed the whiteness of the movement this way: "The #MeToo hashtag had global reach. But except for

Burke, most key figures in the movement were Western, white, and privileged. The whiteness of #MeToo reflects two related issues: the global ascendancy of mainstream Western feminism (which sees itself as universal and neutral), and the dominance of white bourgeois women within it." As white feminist outrage spread and #MeToo played out in the mainstream media, race was rarely mentioned, and the contributions of Black women, like Burke, were co-opted, or erased.

At the same time, white women in Hollywood sometimes defended men accused of sexual harassment or assault. Lena Dunham, for example, defended writer Murray Miller, who worked on her show *Girls,* when actor Aurora Perrineau accused him of having raped her. Dunham later apologized and confessed to lying about her knowledge of what happened to Perrineau. In the height of the media coverage surrounding #MeToo, it could often appear, as Alison Phipps points out, to be a conversation between white people: the privileged white women speaking out and the privileged white men defending themselves against allegations. In this way, #MeToo became a movement about white women's protection from powerful white men, like Harvey Weinstein.

Allegations, rumors, and even jokey innuendos at the Academy Awards ceremonies had long suggested Harvey Weinstein was a serial rapist. Once the head of Miramax studios, which produced such box office hits as *Pulp Fiction, The Crying Game,* and *Shakespeare in Love,* Weinstein could make careers or destroy them by deciding which actors got work. In October 2017, actors Rose McGowan and Ashley Judd were among the women who came forward to describe how Weinstein had assaulted them, or attempted to do so. When they resisted or objected, Weinstein made sure they quit getting calls for acting jobs. The media news cycles then spent a good deal of time and attention speculating on which white celebrities would be next to speak out. The flurry of allegations began to tumble out for the rest of 2017, and in early 2018 Weinstein's world began to fall apart.

In February 2020, a jury found Weinstein guilty of rape in the third degree and a criminal sexual act in the first degree, and not guilty on three counts, including two more serious charges of predatory sexual assault. He was sentenced to twenty-three years in prison. According to a report in the *New York Times*, at his sentencing, Weinstein, sitting in a wheelchair, said he was remorseful but also "totally confused" about what had happened to him. He compared his experience to that of Hollywood figures blacklisted during the scare over communism in the 1950s.

Cyrus Vance, the Manhattan district attorney who prosecuted the case, heralded the victory for his office in a statement, referring to the survivors: "They refused to be silent, and they were heard. Their words took down a predator and put him behind bars, and gave hope to survivors of sexual violence all across the world."

Feminist icon Gloria Steinem echoed this in her statement following the conviction: "This court victory is due to the courage of brave and diverse girls and women who have dared to tell the truth. I thank each and every one of them!" Steinem was one of the few feminists to mention race in her response to Weinstein's conviction: "Given the fact that this wave of feminism started in a time when the law treated (white) virgins as the only probable victims of rape—and that, if a married woman was raped, it was her husband who had been wronged—we've come a long way in a lifetime." Steinem's parentheses around the word *white* is a sort of clumsy way of acknowledging the racist history of laws covering sexual assault.

Through hundreds of years of US history, it was not possible for Black women to bring a charge of rape because the law did not recognize them as possible victims. In the early 1980s, scholar Hazel Carby elucidated the ways that dominant feminist conceptualizations of rape cast Black women's status as "unrapeable" as a foil for bourgeois white woman who were viewed as sexually endangered. It's a similar point that Harriet Jacobs made a century earlier in her *Incidents in the Life of a Slave Girl*, when she wrote that if white women possess the "true womanhood" characteristics of virtue and domesticity, it is because laws create and protect both of these. Reconsidered in this historical context, the Weinstein verdict, and much of the #MeToo coverage in the mainstream press, was a victory for the protection of white women.

In many ways, the failures of white feminism in the march of pink pussy hats and the takeover and narrowing of #MeToo are just two of the most recent examples of enduring problems in our thinking about feminism. Since the late twentieth century, feminism as led by white women can be grouped into three categories: vagina feminism, carceral feminism, and corporate feminism. It's these iterations of feminism that continually break my heart for the way they ignore the radical insights of Black, Indigenous, and Latina feminism and keep us all trapped in the service of white women's vision of the world.

## VAGINA FEMINISM

"Women are women everywhere and they all have a vagina," Eve Ensler has said of her play *The Vagina Monologues (TVM)*. When a reporter asked her if it is difficult to get women to talk about this, Ensler replied, "It's not getting them started on the subject that's the problem, but getting them to stop. Years and years of secrets and lies and tears and joys just pour out. The story of a woman's vagina is the story of her life."

The play was first produced in 1996 and since then has been performed annually at colleges, universities, and community groups on February 14, Valentine's Day. The money from these performances goes to Ensler's V-Day organization and is used to fund programs and campaigns to raise awareness about violence against women. Women from all over the world have been moved by the show and use it as a way to push for transgressive discussions about women's bodies and the violence against them. In some countries, the women who stage the play do so at great personal risk. Understandably, Ensler is beloved by fans of the play who regard her as a feminist heroine.

Ensler interviewed women about their experiences with sexual discovery and sexual assault, and then reshaped their accounts into *The Vagina Monologues*, a series of dramatized individual stories. The staging of the play includes little set decoration beyond stools and microphones for the actors, who read from scripts directly to the audience. The actors read with accents, and the monologues depict experiences of women from around the world, such as "My Village Was My Vagina," the testimonial of a Bosnian woman's experience of sexual assault in the Balkan wars of the 1990s. Another monologue, "Under the Burqa," opens with these lines: "Last year Eve Ensler had the opportunity to go to Afghanistan. There she witnessed firsthand what the outcome of misogyny would be if it were allowed to manifest itself totally. Under the Taliban, women are essentially living the lives of walking corpses. This monologue is for the brave, tender, fierce women of Afghanistan. That we may all rise up and save them."

The monologues are meant to suggest a "global vaginahood" and to gesture at transnational feminism. However, the very way that the play uses difference—this seemingly arbitrary collection of voices, and stories, and accents to represent "the global"—works to reinforce the normative voice of American whiteness that holds the play together. By using the vagina-self trope, Ensler reduces the differences between women. What this leaves instead of a global sisterhood is "a missionary feminism, where the (white, affluent, Western) feminist is positioned to aid, if not save, others by witnessing their pain," as one scholar puts it.

In the monologues, direct representations of rape happen to women of color and women outside the United States. In contrast, the voices of white women with American accents have their vaginas and selves intact. White women in the imagination of the playwright, and by extension the assumed white female audience who are all at a safe distance from the most dire forms of patriarchal violence, act out the worst elements of white-dominated international feminism. Scholar Tani Barlow describes this kind of feminism as a whole "ideological package—a well-financed, resurgent, neoliberal, United States–focused effort to establish common ground" for gender politics throughout the world. This version of white feminism emphasizes saving women from the dark, Muslim Other in ways that often align with US military goals.

The emphasis on *vagina* as the catch-all term for women's genitalia is an inaccuracy that has puzzled and infuriated women's health advocates for decades. Since the 1970s, many advocates have had the difficult task of speaking honestly about women's bodies in a culture that regards them with disgust and revulsion. This provocation is part of the impulse of *TVM*, which opens with the line, "I bet you're worried," playing on the cultural anxiety about the very word *vagina*. It is strange, though, that the play then perpetuates misunderstandings about female anatomy by collapsing labia, clitoris, vulva, cervix into the term *vagina*. But it is a misnomer that works well for the brilliant, and totalizing, brand enclosure around V-Day: Vaginas, Violence against Women, Valentine's Day.

In the United States, Native American women are twice as likely to experience violence as any other racial category of women. In Canada, Indigenous women are experiencing a decades-long scourge of violence. According to a 2016 report, between 1980 and 2012, Indigenous women and girls represented 16 percent of all female homicides in Canada, although they only make up 4 percent of the female population in Canada. They are also far more likely than other women to go missing. This alarming pattern of violence was the catalyst for an annual day of remembrance and mourning known as the "Memorial March for Missing and Murdered Indigenous Women" held in Canada on February 14. For more than twenty years, Indigenous women in Canada have led events on this date to commemorate those killed and to celebrate the strength and power of Indigenous women's leadership. In 2013, the V-Day organization and Ensler's more recent endeavor, One Billion Rising (OBR), her global antiviolence campaign encouraging women to report rape and sexual assault to law enforcement, made a move to launch their events in Canada. They claimed to want to "spotlight" the issue of violence against women. However, they did not reach out to the Indigenous women who were already doing that activism and had long-established events on February 14 in Canada. As a result, many Indigenous women began to speak out against Ensler. One of the foremost critics has been Native American feminist, educator, and writer Lauren Chief Elk. Following a phone conversation with Ensler, Chief Elk wrote an open letter to her and posted it online. The letter is long, but two passages of it are especially relevant here:

> This all started because on Twitter, I addressed some issues that I had with V-Day, your organization, and the way it treated Indigenous women in Canada. I said that you are racist and dismissive of Indigenous people. You wrote to me that you were upset that I would suggest this, and not even 24 hours later you were on *The Joy Behar Show* referring to your chemotherapy treatment as a "Shamanistic exercise."
>
> You asked me what would it mean to be a good ally. It would have meant stepping back, giving up the V-Day platform, and attending the marches and vigils. It would have meant putting aside the One Billion Rising privilege and participating in what the Indigenous women felt was important.

The "Shamanistic exercise" is a reference to *In the Body of the World: A Memoir of Cancer and Connection*, Ensler's 2014 account of her diagnosis with cancer and subsequent travel to the Democratic Republic of Congo in search of alternative healing. In the book and conversations about it on television talk shows, Ensler equates her uterine cancer to the injuries of Congolese women who have been raped and suffered fistula, referring to the healing from these injuries as a spiritual experience, "Congo Stigmata." Around the time of its publication, many writers, including Mikki Kendall and Mariame Kaba, wrote incisive critiques of the white savior complex and the cultural appropriation embedded in Ensler's work, but those were drowned out by the PR machine behind V-Day and the white gender-only feminists who are the most ardent fans of Ensler.

The relevant issue isn't simply about who Eve Ensler is as a person; it's the cultural product of *The Vagina Monologues* and the work it does in the culture. *TVM* is an engine for reproducing a particular version of gender-only feminism and locking in the perspective of the normative, white female voice at the center of it. Because the play has been so widely adopted as a regularly calendared event at community centers, colleges, and universities, it has become an integral part of many thousands of women's first experience of feminism. The play has shaped how a generation of women think about gender, sexuality, and difference. Even though the play gets updated each year, 1996 was a long time ago, and its roots in essentialist ideas about gender are being disavowed by more recent generations of college students.

"At its core, the show offers an extremely narrow perspective on what it means to be a woman," read an email that circulated among members of Mount Holyoke's theater group in 2015 when they decided to end the decade-long tradition of putting the play on at Valentine's Day. These students argue that it does not do enough to include transgender people and people of color. The email went on to say, "Gender is a wide and varied experience, one that cannot simply be reduced to biological or anatomical distinctions, and many of us who have participated in the show have grown increasingly uncomfortable presenting material that is inherently reductionist and exclusive."

In response, Ensler was steadfast in her defense of the play, saying, "I would like to believe that the play is outdated and irrelevant but sadly it isn't. I travel the planet . . . [and in the United States and many countries] 51 percent of the population have vaginas and aren't able to have agency over those vaginas. We know that one out of every three women will be raped or beaten in her lifetime—so we know we have a long way to go before vaginas are liberated."

Responding to the Mount Holyoke students' critiques about the representation of women of color, Ensler notes that "thousands and thousands of women of color [have] performed *The Vagina Monologues* for the last twenty years," adding that the off-Broadway production featured a woman of color in each cast for four years straight. But the issue that neither the Mount Holyoke students nor Ensler address is the white, missionary feminist viewpoint at the center of the play. Within the boundaries of the play, women of color in the cast can only perform their vaginahood in relation to and in service to that voice.

The gender-only and vagina-focused feminism that animates *TVM* becomes more apparent in light of the growing awareness of trans peoples' rights. In 2005, Ensler added a new piece to the play entitled "They Beat the Girl Out of My Boy," written entirely from the perspective of a trans person. In the context of an emerging trans rights movement, Ensler sounds a little defensive about vaginas.

"I think it's important to know that I never intended to write a play about what it means to be a woman, that was not what *The Vagina Monologues* ever intended to be," Ensler said. "It was a play about what it means to have a vagina. It never said, for example, the definition of a woman is someone who has a vagina. . . . I think that's a really important distinction." Ensler's defense of "vagina" as central to her feminism is ultimately an exclusionary and essentialist way of thinking about feminism.

In July 2020, Eve Ensler announced that she was changing her name to simply "V." In her announcement, coinciding with the publication of a new book, she said, "After finishing *The Apology*, I was able to release my father," who had sexually assaulted her as a child. And thus, she was ridding her name of his influence. I'm all for women changing their names to distance themselves from abusive fathers or grandfathers, but it's worth mentioning what a great branding choice this is. With her name change to V, she moves further along the path to the complete brand enclosure around V-Day, now quite literally a celebration of her. Part of what is heartbreaking to me about V, V-Day, and vagina feminism, is how many other young women it inspires to repeat the error. If one were to imagine a political action that grew out of a generation raised on *The Vagina Monologues*, one might conjure a vast sea of pink pussy hats marching on Washington, DC, or something like what began in Toronto in 2011.

## #SLUTWALKS

When Toronto Police Constable Michael Sanguinetti gave a talk on health and safety to a group of students, he told them that "women should avoid dressing like sluts" so as not to get raped. Perhaps not surprisingly, Sanguinetti's remarks outraged many. Some of these angry young women organized the first "SlutWalk" protest in early 2011 demanding an end to what they called "slut shaming." The hashtag #SlutWalk quickly moved across national boundaries and led to a premature declaration that this was a "transnational feminist movement," with historical antecedents in "Take Back the Night" marches.

SlutWalks were primarily organized by white women who said they "are tired of being oppressed by slut-shaming; of being judged by our sexuality and feeling unsafe as a result." One of the main goals was to reclaim the word *slut* through street protests that were primarily organized online rather than through preexisting grassroots organizations. Through most of 2011, mainstream media reported on the protests in a rather trivializing way, focusing on the "scantily clad" women. Little of the initial coverage, including on feminist blogs popular at the time, such as Jezebel and Feministing, mentioned the fact that the SlutWalk marches seemed to be a cultural phenomenon created for white women of the Global North.

This began to change when women of color writers, such as Aura Bogado, called out the marches. In May 2011, Bogado wrote a blog post entitled "SlutWalk: A Stroll Through White Supremacy" in which she questioned the origins of the movement:

I understand the need to denounce this type of speech (Sanguinetti's remarks), particularly when uttered by a law enforcement officer. But what struck me was the fact that a group of students gathered with law enforcement to begin with. As people of color, our communities are plagued with police brutality, and inviting them into our spaces in order to somehow feel safer rarely crosses our minds. I've attended several workshops and panels on sexual violence and would never imagine seeing law enforcement in attendance. Groups like INCITE! have done a tremendous amount of work to address the way that systemic violence is directed against women in communities of color through "police violence, war, and colonialism," as well as to address the type of interpersonal violence between individuals within a community, such as sexual assault and domestic violence. SlutWalk "want[s] Toronto Police Services to take serious steps to regain [their] trust;" our communities, meanwhile, never trusted the police to begin with.

Bogado was among the first to call out the privileged position inherent in a political movement whose goal is focused on "regaining" a trustworthy relationship with police while immigrant women, Black and Brown women, poor women, and transgender women, whether born in the United States or not, are presumed to be sex workers, are targeted as "sex offenders," and are routinely abused by police with impunity, and their deaths ignored. For months, Bogado remained a lone voice. She revived her moribund blog to self-publish the "Walk Through White Supremacy" because none of the outlets she approached—*The Guardian, Huffington Post*—would publish it. This, Bogado writes, is characteristic of the "ways in which white women have constructed a conversation that women of color can't seem to participate in."

In September 2011, the organization Black Women's Blueprint issued "An Open Letter from Black Women to the SlutWalk." The open letter included this passage, juxtaposing the contemporary Slut-Walk movement with the history of Black women's movements in the United States:

Black women have worked tirelessly since the 19th century colored women's clubs to rid society of the sexist/racist vernacular of slut, jezebel, hottentot, mammy, mule, sapphire; to build our sense of selves and re-define what women who look like us represent. Although we vehemently support a woman's right to wear whatever she wants anytime, anywhere; within the context of a "SlutWalk" we don't have the privilege to walk through the streets of New York City, Detroit, D.C., Atlanta, Chicago, Miami, L.A. etc., either half-naked or fully clothed self-identifying as "sluts" and think that this will make women safer in our communities an hour later, a month later, or a year later. Moreover, we are careful not to set a precedent for our young girls by giving them the message that we can self-identify as "sluts" when we're still working to annihilate the word "ho", which deriving from the word "hooker" or "whore", as in "Jezebel whore", was meant to dehumanize. Lastly, we do not want to encourage our young men, our Black fathers, sons and brothers to reinforce Black women's identities as "sluts" by normalizing the term on t-shirts, buttons, flyers, and pamphlets.

The open letter also explicitly challenged the political goal of "re-claiming" offensive terms, saying, "We are perplexed by the use of the term 'slut' and by any implication that this word, much like the word 'Ho' or the 'N' word should be re-appropriated."

There were dissenting views, to be sure. For example, both Sala-mishah Tillet, writing at *The Nation,* and Janell Hobson, writing at the *Ms. Magazine* blog, wrote responses to the open letter from Black women, expressing concern about what they saw as the "politics of respectability" in the letter. The open letter and these responses were widely circulated through social media networks and, presumably, among SlutWalk organizers, but given what happened next, it doesn't seem like the message was received.

Three weeks after the open letter was published, there was a Slut-WalkNYC march in Union Square. A young white woman held up a hand-lettered sign with a quote from Yoko Ono, "Woman is the N-* of the World." The intentionally provocative line was meant to evoke women's subjugation through an analogy rooted in gender-only feminism and tried to make the point via the use of a racial slur. It was controversial when Ono first said it in 1969, and as writer, activist, and filmmaker Aishah Shahidah Simmons reminds us about that time, "Several Black feminists, including Pearl Cleage, challenged Yoko Ono's racist (to Black women) statement. 'If Woman is the "N-*" of the World,' what does that make Black Women, the 'N-*, N-*' of the World?" Simmons, who describes herself as a supporter of the goals of SlutWalk, further challenged the organizers, writing: "How can so many White feminists be absolutely clear about the responsibility of ALL MEN TO END heterosexual violence perpetrated against women; and yet turn a blind eye to THEIR RESPONSIBILITY TO END racism? Is Sisterhood Global? This picture says NO! very loudly and very clearly." The organizers of SlutWalkNYC apologized, but other white feminists continued to defend the use of the term, saying things like "but rappers . . ."

By mid-October of that year, organizer J. (Jake) Kathleen Marcus described the "implosion of SlutWalk" on her blog and apologized for the movement's failure and her own complicity in the racism of it. Marcus basically taps out of the movement, saying to fellow activists, "I hope our paths cross again," but it won't be at a SlutWalk march. In 2016, D-list celebrity Amber Rose created the SlutWalk Festival in Los Angeles to raise awareness of the issue of slut shaming. Rose canceled the 2019 event to protect her "energy and peace" from the "toxic" people who had gotten involved in the event. No SlutWalks were scheduled for 2020 even before the pandemic scuttled most public events.

## TERFS

"We need to give a voice to those most oppressed in order to make everybody better," twenty-nine-year-old Monica Weeks said in her speech to National Organization for Women (NOW) members. NOW was founded in 1966 in Washington, DC, by those attending the Third National Conference of the Commission on the Status of Women. Betty Friedan, among NOW's founders, served as its first president. In 2017, Weeks ran for vice president of the political organization born in the feminist movement's second wave. In making her speech, she continued her definition of "everybody," saying, "That's women of color, that's disabled people, that's LGBTQ people." Then she was interrupted by shouting from the audience of mostly older white women at the Brevard County NOW chapter in Melbourne, Florida.

"White women, too!" one woman yelled out.

"And then, yeah, don't forget the white women," Weeks improvised.

"Just the women with the pussies!" another woman in the crowd called out.

"All women!" someone else shouted.

Weeks was eventually able to finish her speech, but she didn't win election to become VP of NOW. In 2020, she told the story about the hecklers and her experiences of racism at NOW to a reporter, including being called a "hot-headed Latina." Weeks said, "I thought when I was coming into the feminist movement I was joining this big sisterhood." But the reality of what she encountered at NOW "was the biggest disappointment in my life." Emily Shugerman reported in the *Daily Beast* a devastating account of the everyday, systemic, and quite abusive racism that women of color experienced at the hands of white women in the organization. In one allegation, Toni Van Pelt, the white president of NOW, threw papers and chased Gilda Yazzie, the Native American vice president of the organization, around the office, screaming, "You won't be here in three years!" Yazzie (who resigned) filed a lawsuit, which is pending, that calls for Van Pelt to resign and for NOW to end systemic racism. For her part, Van Pelt denied these allegations. Koleika Seigle, chair of the California chapter of NOW, says, "The call to end systemic racism is laughable. We haven't committed to ending racism within NOW." Unexplained in this eviscerating account of racism at NOW is the way white women's racism connects with their transphobia.

The hecklers in the audience for Weeks's speech, with their shouts of "white women too" and "just the women with pussies," are joined together in a gender-only feminism that is obsessed with drawing boundaries and maintaining control. These women are part of a recent backlash to trans rights within feminism known as TERFs: Trans-Exclusionary Radical Feminists. TERFs only want to acknowledge "womyn-born-womyn," that is, those designated female at birth, raised as girls, and who identify as women (or womyn, to eliminate *men* from the spelling of the word).

The TERF rhetoric is much louder in the UK than in the United States at the moment, and British feminist scholar Alison Phipps offers a sharp analysis of the phenomenon in her 2020 book *Me, Not You: The Trouble with Mainstream Feminism*. Phipps calls this "reactionary feminism" and says that it is rooted in a capitalist-colonial mentality intent on "owning and setting boundaries" for what does, and does not, count as feminism. The obsession with trans women is "peak political whiteness," Phipps writes. Feminists like the ones shouting down Monica Weeks "magnify mainstream feminist narcissism, not only centering themselves but also acting as gatekeepers who withhold the designation 'woman' from others." This especially applies to trans women, who TERFs define as "biological men" while they proclaim themselves "adult human females."

When Phipps writes about "political whiteness," she is referring to the kind of alertness to threat that characterizes white women's need to keep out dark Others. When used by reactionary, gender-only feminists, trans people become "them," and thus gender identity gets mapped on top of racial and geographic difference. For example, English reactionary feminist Julie Bindel frequently uses the term "trans Taliban" to describe critics who challenge her or fellow TERFs. In such a worldview, "they"—trans people—have all the power and must be stopped. Obscured from view for white TERFs (and they are almost exclusively white) are the murders of trans people for simply existing.

In a report released by Transgender Europe, over 330 trans and nonbinary people were killed across the globe in 2019 alone. Of those, 130 were killed in Brazil, 63 in Mexico, while 30 died in the United States, and 10 were killed across the UK and Europe. In the United States, trans women of color were the most likely minority to be murdered as part of a hate crime. This is to say, of all the protected groups listed in hate crimes legislation, Black, Indigenous, and people of color (BIPOC), LBGTQIA, religious minorities, people with disabilities, and so forth, the minority most likely to be murdered in a hate crime were trans women of color. According to the Human Rights Council, all the trans people killed in 2019 were trans women of color.

Vagina feminism is appealing because it is a shorthand for a world of meaning. To say, "women are everywhere and they all have vaginas" or to don pink pussy hats is to invoke a set of beliefs about biology, about gender, about race, and about difference. Taken to its logical conclusion, vagina feminism reinforces gender as an inherent, unchangeable identity. And it reinforces a set of binaries—of "women" and "men," and of white and Other, of those who are innocent victims and those who are perpetrators, of those in need of rescue and those who can and should be saviors.

## CARCERAL FEMINISM

When my father gave me that gun when I turned seventeen, to his way of thinking he was giving me a weapon that would protect me from sexual assault and other dangers. I believed his justification for the gun until I turned twenty-one and was living alone and a man stalked me and tried to break into my home. I knew that if I shot him, the law would have protected me, a white woman, even though the man stalking me was white. But I couldn't pull the trigger, couldn't shoot him, because I didn't want to deal with the collateral damage.

I didn't want to know who he was, or what little town he'd grown up in, or his parents' names, or even why he'd decided to come after me. I just wanted him to go away and leave me alone. And I knew that if I shot him, I would learn all about him and never be able to unknow him. I knew that if I shot and killed that man, he would always be with me, he would never go away.

It was then, I think, that I outgrew my father's Smith & Wesson feminism. It was at the moment when I decided that I didn't want my safety to depend on someone else's death. Unfortunately, white feminism only offers empowerment and protection through the agreed-upon marginalization and endangerment of people of color.

In 2019, President Trump pardoned boxer Jack Johnson. It's a good bet that most people were not aware that the Mann Act Johnson was convicted of violating was still on the books. The Mann Act, also known as the White-Slave Traffic Act of 1910, was passed in the midst of a moral panic about protecting white women's sexuality from Black (and other nonwhite) men. As white women gained more autonomy in the early twentieth century, for shopping and other activities unaccompanied by men, advocates raised an alarm. Popular books like *Fighting the Traffic in Young Girls: Or, War on the White Slave Trade* warned white parents about the dangers of living or working in cities, taking public transportation alone, visiting ice cream parlors or restaurants, and congregating in dance halls. There was widespread concern about the sexual enslavement of white women and some even suggested it was far worse than the enslavement of African Americans. The public tended to imagine the perpetrators of white slavery as men who were Jewish, African American, or Chinese immigrants, who would lure, deceive, drug, or otherwise coerce white women into the sex trade. Rescuing white women from such men became a popular cause.

The same year the Mann Act was passed, Jack Johnson defeated the heavyweight boxing champion James J. Jeffries, who was white. So angry were white people about the outcome of this boxing match, they took to the streets and rioted. Johnson's victory also drew increased scrutiny from law enforcement. Johnson was known for dating white women, including a woman named Lucille Cameron, and this fit with the kinds of suspicions that had helped to pass the Mann Act. In 1912, Lucille Cameron's mother accused Johnson of kidnapping her daughter and transporting her across state lines, a violation of the Mann Act. Although Johnson and Cameron were in a consensual relationship (and would later marry), law enforcement nevertheless pressed their case against Johnson. He was convicted and sentenced to a year in prison. But Johnson fled the United States and fought in boxing matches abroad for seven years until he returned in 1920 and served his sentence at the penitentiary in Leavenworth, Kansas.

The Mann Act and the concerns about the "white slavery" issue transformed law enforcement in the United States and gave rise to the modern FBI. As Jessica R. Pliley describes in her 2014 book *Policing Sexuality: The Mann Act and the Making of the FBI*, the bureau expanded from sixty-one officers to more than three hundred agents in the space of three years because of the respectable white men it recruited and deputized to become "local white slave officers." The cultural obsession with policing sexuality continues today in the rhetoric around trafficking. Although contemporary advocates have dropped the term "white slavery" and replaced it with "modern slavery," or simply "trafficked," the subtext is often the same as it was in 1910. The current campaigns and popular culture narratives still rely on the trope of a "dark Other" kidnapping, drugging, or trapping an unwilling and unsuspecting victim. The story is the same: traffickers are men of color who should be punished, and white women and girls are always innocent victims to be rescued by law enforcement. What this narrative reinforces is the danger associated with Black men and other men of color, and the supposed innocence, lack of agency, and need for rescue for white women, even as it completely erases the experiences of Black women and other women of color.

The missionary impulse to save white women and girls who are trafficked is one that binds together feminist activists with white evangelical Christians. Despite rather profound disagreements around the politics of sex and gender, these two groups have joined forces to advocate for harsher penalties against traffickers and their customers within the United States. And they have exerted pressure on elected officials to use the power of the US government to punish nations deemed to be taking insufficient steps to stem the flow of trafficked women. In a broader sense, white evangelicals have been at the forefront pushing for harsher criminal justice policies since the postwar era, with the National Association of Evangelicals favoring the death penalty and FBI director J. Edgar Hoover penning regular columns about "lawlessness" in the pages of *Christianity Today* in the mid-twentieth century. Scholar Elizabeth Bernstein argues this is not simply a case of politics making "strange bedfellows"; rather, it is an alliance that reveals a shared commitment to "carceral paradigms of justice." That is, both white feminists and white evangelicals are thoroughly invested in prison as the solution to gender inequality while ignoring systemic racial inequality. To understand carceral feminism, and the way it has permeated the culture, there is no better case study than Linda Fairstein.

Until 2019, Linda Fairstein was regarded as a feminist heroine. Fairstein was a prosecutor in Manhattan's Sexual Victims Unit and was said to be the model Dick Wolf used for his *Law & Order* TV series. After she retired from the prosecutor's office, she turned to writing mystery novels. Her crime novels feature the fictional Manhattan prosecutor Alexandra Cooper, who "tried to do justice for [victims] in a court of law." The novels feature titles such as *The Kills, Killer Heat, Killer Look,* and *Blood Oath.* Her 2017 novel *Deadfall* includes this passage: "I knew that doormen in the most expensive properties lining Central Park were often as powerless to stop [murder] from entering the dwellings they guarded as the less fortunate who encountered it in random exchanges with strangers on the street." As one critic describes this passage, "Fairstein's writing portrays crime as a dark, seedy invader that even the 'doormen in the most expensive properties' cannot keep from harming their pristine, vulnerable inhabitants. It reads like a nightmare inspired by the 1988 Willie Horton attack ad." Fairstein has done quite well for herself peddling these novels about white women as prosecutors and feminist heroines, and reportedly has a net worth estimated between $12 million and $17 million. Fairstein was an honored speaker at galas for feminist causes, and she sat on several boards of directors, including Safe Horizon, a nonprofit for survivors of sexual abuse. That all changed in the summer of 2019.

In late May 2019, Ava DuVernay released *When They See Us*, a dramatic TV series about the Central Park jogger case in which a white woman was raped. In the series about the group once known as "the Central Park Five," DuVernay portrays a fictionalized Fairstein as a hard-charging prosecutor who is intent on getting the career win of locking up the five teens, ages fourteen to sixteen, despite very flimsy evidence. DuVernay's retelling of this story removes the frame of the New York tabloids at the time that portrayed a "gang" that was "wilding" and savagely attacked a jogger in the park. Instead, she offers a depiction of a group of teens who were shoved into the system by a prosecutor positioning herself as being tough on crime. Now known as "The Exonerated Five," after someone else confessed to the crime and their convictions were vacated, the men sued and received a settlement from New York City. But Fairstein is not contrite about her role in their wrongful conviction. In fact, she's defiant. She wrote a letter to the editor of the *New York Law Journal*, "In Defense of the Central Park 5 Prosecution," and an op-ed for the *Wall Street Journal*, "Netflix's False Story of the Central Park Five," and she sued Netflix for defamation (the case was thrown out).

In the weeks after the series aired, the hashtag #CancelLindaFairstein began trending on social media. Amid the backlash, Fairstein resigned from the board of Safe Horizon and stepped down as a trustee at Vassar College. Her award for Woman of the Year from 1993 was revoked by *Glamour* magazine. Then Fairstein was dropped by her book publisher. Fairstein's defenders were quick to say she'd been the victim of a "mob mentality." And Fairstein herself took to social media to say that the backlash is akin to being "lynched." The belated reckoning for her points to a deeper problem with white, carceral feminism.

*Carceral feminism* is one of those clunky academic terms that's starting to make its way into regular conversations. The idea behind it is that the capital *S* State, as in the government's systems of laws and criminal penalties, is the best way to protect women from sexual assault, domestic violence, and trafficking. It's rooted in a mostly white feminist notion that the State is the best hope for addressing harm to women. However, there's plenty of analysis to confirm that the system we refer to as "criminal justice" protects only certain kinds of people (white, middle class, heterosexual, cisgender) while it harms everyone else, especially communities of color. This harm to people of color seems to be architected by women like Fairstein who have hitched their feminist career wagon to the system of criminal punishment. There is perhaps no greater indication of the pervasiveness of carceral feminism than our collective embrace of *Law & Order* culture, which has us cheering for lock-ups instead of liberation.

People of all political persuasions turn to the *Law & Order* franchise, and particularly to *SVU*, for the balm of genre television. *SVU* was recently renewed for a twenty-first season, making it the longest-running show in television history. The show has been touted by some as "dismantling gender stereotypes," because it portrays women as "strong-willed and hardworking alongside their male (DA) counterparts." But it can only fulfill this feminist edict by symbolically destroying communities of color through the repeated story of incarceration as the solution to all social problems.

What the *Law & Order* franchise does so well is use the patina of gender equality to reinforce the racial order. By creating recurring white women characters who are agents of the State, whether as cops or prosecutors or both, the series reinforces a set of ideas about who needs punishment (people of color) and who needs protection (white people). By returning to that narrative with the veneer of gender equality, white women playing detectives or ADAs on *Law & Order* become the embodiment of carceral feminism.

In a case of art imitating life, Fairstein both made carceral feminism tangible as a real-life prosecutor and used it to enrich herself through her roman à clef crime novels. For white women like Fairstein, their experience of the system of incarceration is probably going to be from administering it or from completely outside it. The expected rate of incarceration for white women is 1 in every 111. Among Black people, 1 in 3 men and 1 in 18 women will go to prison at some point during their lifetimes; among Latinx people, 1 in 6 men and 1 in 45 women will go to prison at some point; among white men, 1 in 17 will go to prison. In other words, white women are far less likely to be incarcerated themselves or to have loved ones who are locked up. So, while white women are largely exempt from the harms of the carceral state, they are prominently featured in sympathetic entertainment—like SVU and Fairstein's mystery novels—as benevolent agents of it.

Carceral feminism begins with the premise that the State can help women achieve feminist goals like gender equality or, at least, justice for crimes committed against women. When carceral feminism is dressed up in a nice suit and served to us in an hour-long television drama with a predictable beginning, middle, and end, it can feel reassuring. And, if you have the luxury of not having any experience with incarceration, these dramas can convince you that justice operates effortlessly. But the reality of carceral feminism's collateral damage is this: Black and Brown boys in cages in our vast gulag of prisons in the United States and along the border, young Black women shot and killed by police with no-knock warrants, and Black men suffocated under the knee of a cop. The results of our criminal justice system are not feminist victories. Carceral feminism helps ensure the smooth operation of the machinery of white supremacy, which is a war machine.

## WHITE FEMINISM AS WAR MACHINE

In the CBS television drama *Madam Secretary*, blonde, angular Téa Leoni plays a US secretary of state who, in between managing geopolitics, balances the demands of being a wife and mother. Through the show, we learn that even though her job requires that she order drone strikes that kill Brown people on the other side of the world, she explains how conflicted and upset she is about this. She wears attractive pantsuits, engages in playful banter with her kind and handsome husband, and loves her kids. Despite the drones, she can't be that bad. Téa Leoni's character is, of course, a proxy for Hillary Rodham Clinton, who was the secretary of state. Both the fictional character and the actual politician are part of a state apparatus that engages in necropolitics.

Necropolitics is literally the power to decide who will live and who will die. The term comes from theorist Achille Mbembe, a philosopher and political theorist from Cameroon who uses the idea of the "war machine" to characterize contemporary militias, both the kind sponsored by the state and those created in opposition to it. All contemporary political sovereignty is necropolitical, Mbembe argues; sometimes this is accomplished actively, through drone strikes or military invasion. Other times, it is done through a deadly level of neglect: people left to drown in New Orleans or die without protection from COVID-19 or locked in cages along the border. This power to decide who lives or dies is a war machine. Alison Phipps makes the connection between Mbembe's necropolitics and feminism when she writes that "white feminism is a kind of war machine."

White feminism functions like a war machine in that it wants to accomplish feminist goals in and through the State. It's part of why we can so easily see Téa Leoni/Hillary Clinton as a feminist heroine, because we have embraced a version of feminism that fits neatly with state power rather than challenges it. Phipps points out that this is distinct from other political movements, which mobilize *against* the state, such as Antifa and Black Lives Matter. For such movements, inclusion by the State is seen clearly for what it is, a concession of the movement's goals. For white feminism, and particularly white carceral feminism, harnessing the State in the service of (supposedly) feminist goals is a taken-for-granted, rarely questioned assumption.

Yet, when white women seek equality with white men in wielding state power, they are signing up to be part of a war machine that works hand in glove with racial capitalism. This produces the genocide of Indigenous peoples, the enslavement of Africans, and drone strikes on Brown people around the globe.

As of 2019, white women were the CEOs of four of the five biggest US defense contractors—Northrop Grumman, Lockheed Martin, General Dynamics, and Boeing. Do these CEOs think of themselves as feminist? Perhaps, perhaps not. But Phipps asks the more relevant questions here: "Whose bodies are forfeited when white women mobilize punitive state and institutional power to achieve [that power]? Who are the real casualties of the white feminist war machine?"

Shows like *Madam Secretary* make us feel better about the actual white women holding high-level positions in this neocolonial war machine. They do so by reassuring us that these women are feminist heroines in nice pantsuits, and they encourage us to ignore the collateral damage in lives lost.

## WHITE CORPORATE FEMINISM

"I've got a head for business and a bod for sin," Tess McGill purrs in *Working Girl*, the 1988 film that sums up the ethos of white corporate feminism. Spunky, sexy, and driven to succeed, McGill's ingenuity wins her a chance to move out of the secretarial pool and onto a career path at her corporate job. Her physical transformation from Staten Island gauche to Wall Street chic is part of how she wins the job and her man, Jack Trainer (played by Harrison Ford). The new clothes, hair, and makeup are an integral part of her success and their own reward.

Pop culture narratives like this one about the charming Tess McGill make individual career triumphs into vaguely feminist victories. We are expected to cheer on the less-than-sisterly acts of Tess McGill, who leaves behind her best friend (Joan Cusack) and undermines her boss (Sigourney Weaver) in her aspirational career climb in this whites-only fantasy of New York. The narrative also happens to align with corporate interests in denuding feminism of its political edge. What was once a political movement for equity in pay and advancement, for parental leave and free childcare, has now been individualized to the point where any setback must be the result of a personal failing rather than a result of systemic oppression.

Any story of a woman's career success seems to take on the patina of feminism in a way that distracts from the need for a movement for systemic change. Soft-focus fables like Tess McGill's are part of how white corporate feminism has insinuated itself into the culture. Don't get me wrong, I loved *Working Girl* when it came out and could watch it again. But what I see now is a film that tells a particular story about corporate culture, about whiteness, and about feminism. When I root for Tess McGill's victory, I am applauding her access to an exclusive club in which luxury goods are both evidence of her power and the means to accrue even more power, which is only available to her as a white woman. A generation later, white corporate feminism still sells.

As public relations executive Audrey Gelman tells the story, she was tired of spending the odd few minutes between meetings in Manhattan looking for a bathroom to freshen up in or a hotel lobby where she could check her email and charge her phone. Then it occurred to her that this need for a "feminine pit stop" must be widespread in the city, so she decided to launch Refresh, a sort of coworking and hangout space geared exclusively for women. In 2016,

Gelman partnered with Lauren Kassan, a former director of business development at a fitness start-up, and together they rebranded the enterprise as The Wing, and expanded the vision into an aspirational "place for women on their way" and a "women's utopia."

Gelman and Kassan launched The Wing from a penthouse at 45 E. 20th Street in Manhattan. The site was selected in part for its proximity to the historic district known as "Ladies Mile," which, at the end of the nineteenth century and beginning of the twentieth century, catered to well-to-do white women of the "carriage trade." Several reports say that Gelman and Kassan enlisted the historian Alexis Coe to research early American women's clubs and traced a line between those clubs and The Wing. Those reports neglect to say whether Coe explained the racial segregation of those clubs, restricted as they were to white women, and the parallel growth in African American women's clubs at the time. Despite winning endorsements from high-profile women of color like the rapper Remy Ma and the congresswoman Alexandria Ocasio-Cortez, The Wing has seemingly reproduced the tradition of white lady's clubs, this time with a carefully curated Instagram presence.

Within a short time after The Wing's launch, it grew to include multiple locations across New York City and in other urban centers: Boston, Chicago, West Hollywood, Georgetown, San Francisco, and London. New clubs were set to open in Toronto and Paris. Membership at The Wing costs $3,000 a year and, at one point, there was a waiting list of around nine thousand women. The vibe inside was, as one writer described it, "a fusion of sisterly inclusion and exclusive luxury." Once inside, members could buy merchandise such as key chains, tote bags, socks, and stickers with slogans like TAKING UP SPACE, PAY ME, or WOMEN SUPPORTING WOMEN SUPPORTING WOMEN.

Gelman became the public face of The Wing and an avatar for the kind of feminism that works for corporate branding. In 2017, she appeared in a video ad for Chanel fine jewelry. Intercut with close-ups of her earrings, Gelman says, "Be inspired," then flexes both her Chanel-suit-clad arms and says, "Be empowered." Another cut to the rings on her fingers, and she says, "I think you should always listen to your gut. If your gut is telling you to go in a direction, I think you should follow it." This is the sort of hazy declaration of white corporate feminism: "Go with your gut, especially if it's telling you to buy something, and thus, you will be empowered." But there is a more radical feminism lurking just under the surface at The Wing.

In 2019, Gelman was featured in a spot for Air France in which she reflected on the pleasures of business class as a kind of self-care. And, sure, why not. The seats are roomier and the food is better. But Gelman's pitch for that indulgence becomes corporate feminism when she notes that the business-class seats tend to be dominated by guys, and she says, "Hey, I'm a CEO and I belong here, too." It becomes white through Gelman's image—thin, long brown hair, impeccably groomed—she is the real-life inspiration for the character "Marnie" on *Girls*, the HBO series created by her lifelong best friend, Lena Dunham. But getting a seat with the guys in business class isn't what inspired Gelman to start the company; it was a vision without men.

"There was something about that night. I felt like there was this lightning that I wanted to bottle," Gelman says of an all-women's karaoke party that she threw for herself on her twenty-eighth birthday. What made it feel so special: "It was the absence of men." An earlier generation of feminists felt the same exhilaration in space that was safe from men, like the radical lesbians who began the Michigan Womyn's Music Festival—popularly known as MichFest—in 1976. Where MichFest featured camping and acoustic guitars, The Wing is trying to sell a brand of gender-only feminism as a luxury good. It's not clear whether Gelman and Kassan were aware of these earlier efforts, but the Michigan festival's policy of admitting only "womyn-born womyn" (cisgender women) led to a crescendo of condemnation from a variety of human rights and LGBTQ organizations. The festival held its final event in August 2015. The Wing faced a challenge that echoed that earlier one.

In 2019, a fifty-three-year-old man filed a $12 million gender discrimination lawsuit over being denied access to The Wing, and the New York City Commission on Human Rights began an investigation into the company's gender policy. The Wing then simply reversed its policy and began allowing men, never mind the "women's utopia" marketing. In an extensive report for the *New York Times Magazine* in March 2020, Amanda Hess interviewed twenty-six current and former employees at The Wing and found the branding of "empowerment" fell short for staff working to provide that experience for members. Working at The Wing was no utopia but rather more like other service industry jobs with low wages, long hours, fickle bosses, and a demanding and predominantly white female clientele.

In 2019, a Black member wrote on the company's Instagram account that she had found The Wing to be a "majority-white capitalist co-working space." She had been harassed by a white woman "over a parking space." While Wing employees had been pointing out racist incidents for years, it was this post to The Wing's Instagram that received press attention. Following that, there was a series of meetings at the company, but little changed. This member's experience tells the truth about The Wing: it is built as a fortress to protect a majority-white capitalist coworking space. When criticisms of the company would surface, Gelman would get defensive and suggest such critiques may be sexist. "A guy wouldn't be criticized for starting a co-working space with a paid membership," Gelman said—"why can't a feminist be a capitalist, and why can't a capitalist be a feminist?"

Gelman, like all of us, is seemingly trapped by capitalism and patriarchy. As Jia Tolentino writes in *Trick Mirror*, "Women are genuinely trapped at the intersection of capitalism and patriarchy," yet "the trap looks beautiful. It's well-lit. It welcomes you in." Being a member, or CEO, at The Wing isn't feminist in the sense that one is participating in a political movement; it's niche marketing with vaguely feminist keychains for sale. The kind of "gender-only" feminism that The Wing is selling also relied on whiteness for its marketing and its customer base. In June 2020, with a business model decimated by the coronavirus pandemic, mass layoffs, and employees speaking up about a disconnect between the company's branding and the realities at the firm, Audrey Gelman stepped down as CEO and sold off the company. Gelman was not the only white woman in leadership to face a reckoning.

That summer saw a spate of white feminist business and nonprofit leaders held to account for their failure to live up to their professed ideals of equality. Christene Barberich, editor in chief and cofounder of *Refinery29*, a publication focused on women, decided to step down after Black women and other women of color said they faced discrimination at the company. Yael Aflalo, CEO and founder of Reformation, a sustainable women's clothing retailer, resigned amid allegations of a racist company culture. Nancy Lublin, CEO and cofounder of Crisis Text Line, a nonprofit providing mental health counseling, was fired because of allegations of rampant discrimination and "inappropriate conduct." According to multiple reports, Lublin engaged in daily microaggressions, referring to staff of color as "difficult." She also promoted white staff with less experience and paid them more than their Black, Indigenous, and people of color (BIPOC) counterparts. Jen Gotch, chief creative officer and cofounder of Ban.do, a women's lifestyle brand, took an extended leave of absence after allegations arose of a racist and "overall toxic culture." A former employee wrote about experiencing "overt and covert racism" and witnessing "a colleague who is a (person of color) being described as someone who looked like 'he didn't speak English,' . . . stating that they 'don't hire black people, as they would feel out of place.'" As important and necessary as these moves are, it is premature to call these instances of a reckoning on a grand scale. Plenty of white women still hold power in companies that do immeasurable harm to the people that work there and to the wider world. Sheryl Sandberg, COO of Facebook, comes immediately to mind.

Sheryl Sandberg, the second in charge at social media giant Facebook, in 2013 published *Lean In: Women, Work, and the Will to Lead*, which sold over two million copies. Her popular TED Talk introduced her to about the same number of viewers. In both the book and the twenty-minute talk, Sandberg shares her upbeat, nonconfrontational, aspirational message about women's equality.

One of her goals is to transform the perception of "every little girl who gets called bossy" into young people with "leadership potential." I am with her on this. My second-grade report card from my teacher at Meadowbrook Elementary School described me as "a good student, but she wants to run the class." No one who knows me is ever surprised at this story—they just raise an eyebrow and offer an understanding nod. So, I am here for the little girls who got called bossy.

What is holding girls back? According to Sandberg, it's not just being called bossy but is the aversion to the label and internalizing a kind of temerity in the workforce. Sandberg's central message is that women are limiting themselves and that we must just get out of our own way, and "lean in"—by which she means assert ourselves in male-dominated offices and boardrooms. Then the entire "power structure of the world" will be changed and this will "expand opportunities for all."

For Sandberg, the root cause of inequality rests at the individual level of women's choices and, to a lesser extent, society's beliefs about women. Within Sandberg's view, there seems to be nothing wrong with the way society is set up; women just need to shake off the limitations they accepted when they were trying to avoid being called bossy, sharpen their elbows, and claim their space at the corporate table. Her version of gender-only feminism is also known as "liberal feminism." Within the framework of liberal feminism, the goal is for women to attain the same levels of representation, compensation, and power in the public sphere as men. In order for change to happen, liberal feminists rely primarily on women's ability to achieve equality through their own individual actions and choices. The actual work involved becomes the "motivational work" women must do individually to fit into the male-dominated corporate structure.

Along with the book, Sandberg launched a public awareness campaign in partnership with the Girl Scouts called "Ban Bossy." One of the cornerstones for the campaign is that "girls are twice as likely as boys to worry that leadership roles will make them 'bossy.'" This factoid is drawn from a small subsample within a larger 2008 report by the Girl Scout Research Institute, *Change It Up!* Of those in the subsample of 360 children, 29 percent of the girls but only 13 percent of the boys said they weren't interested in being leaders, and when asked about the reasons for this disinterest, "I do not want to seem bossy" was mentioned. On the basis of this data, it does seem that girls could use more self-confidence when it comes to being called "bossy," or perhaps just more indifference to other people's opinions.

But there's more to this than an easy gender-only story. In the larger survey pool, girls and boys were more similar than different in their views of leadership. Girls were just as likely as boys to say that they wanted to be leaders and to agree with the statement: "I think of myself as a leader." In terms of race, the study had an interesting racial difference. African American and Latina girls aspired to leadership *more than* the white girls in the study. African American and Latina girls also reported *greater and more positive* leadership experiences than did their white counterparts. Taken together, the broader findings of the study suggest that it is white girls, specifically, who might be most in need of the "Ban Bossy" message.

The images for the promotional campaign feature Sheryl Sandberg flanked by Condoleezza Rice (former US secretary of state) and Anna Maria Chávez (CEO of the Girl Scouts of the USA). The fact that Sandberg enlisted prominent women of color to sign on to her campaign doesn't change the reality that liberal feminism aligns with white supremacy. These successful women of color lend a powerful credibility to Sandberg's brand of liberal feminism, but they cannot change the central flaw in the underlying proposition. Feminist cultural critic bell hooks writes:

> To women of color young and old, along with anti-racist white women, it is more than obvious that without a call to challenge and change racism as an integral part of class mobility [Sandberg] is really investing in top level success for highly educated women from privileged classes. . . . Let it be stated again and again that race, and more importantly white supremacy, is a taboo subject in the world according to Sandberg.

What bell hooks names is precisely the problem with gender-only feminism: it cannot deal with race. For so many of us, the "Ban Bossy" message resonates because there is something that stings in that label for those of us who grew up as girl children in a culture that wants to make us docile, quiet, and subservient to men. Yet many of us also know, at least at some level, that the solution Sandberg is offering us with her invitation to *Lean In* is more than inadequate; it is damaging.

The version of feminism that Sandberg is marketing actively creates harm against women of color by reinforcing the idea that success in the corporate world is entirely the result of an individual woman's ability to stand up for herself and make demands. It's not that individual effort doesn't matter, it does; it's just that it pays off for white women in ways that it doesn't for Black women and other women of color. And the *Lean In* message does nothing to address the persistent structural barriers that women of color face in the workplace. More than that, it means that when women of color face these obstacles and are fired or stuck in the dead end of diversity positions or otherwise not crushing it in the C-suite, they alone get blamed for their putative lack of success. The harm from white feminism spiderwebs out beyond corporate office parks and into people's everyday lives.

Mikki Kendall reminds us of this harm in her 2020 book *Hood Feminism*. Kendall writes, "Whether it is Abigail Fisher suing to undermine affirmative action or Sheryl Sandberg leaning into Facebook's pandering to alt-right conspiracy theories, the reality is that white, mainstream feminism has to confront the idea that power to do harm rests in women too." Meanwhile, issues like food insecurity, affordable housing, and ending poverty get left out of discussions about feminism.

## CONCLUSION

Feminism, which my mother didn't live long enough to embrace, saved me because it offered me a way to imagine the world with queer women at the center of it. That freed me from the kind of life she lived, always truncating her desires to fit within the expectations of her husband. Because of feminism, I didn't have to put my desires for a full, rich life on hold for a man. Because of radical lesbian feminism, I knew I could value other women enough to build my world around them. And at the same time, because of Black, Indigenous, Latina, Asian, and other women of color's intersectional writing, I knew that feminism without an understanding of critical race theory easily maps onto white supremacy.

In July 2015, I was invited to give a talk to a group of high school girls about white feminism. These girls were part of a program known as the "Feminist Seminar," or "FemSem," organized by Alondra Nelson, then at Columbia University, and Merle McGee, from the YWCA of New York. The girls I spoke to were young teens, thirteen or fourteen, from New York City, and from an array of backgrounds. They listened intently while I explained the ideas I've discussed in this chapter, about how feminism has saved my life, how white women have been complicit in creating white-supremacist culture, how flawed some of the usual versions of white feminism can be. Then, one of the young women in this group raised her hand and asked, "Do *you* identify as a white feminist?" I didn't know how to answer her question that day, and I still don't. I am white-raised, and I can't slip off my racial identity that easily. I'm a feminist the minute that a straight, white man tells me to sit down and shut up, or really anything else. But do I identify as a "white feminist"?

Later that same summer, Flavia Dzodan and I sat in a coffee shop in the Binnenstad district of Amsterdam. Dzodan, a writer, feminist, and Latina immigrant, and I talked about the trouble with white feminism and the way that it seemed to be gathering strength behind Hillary Clinton's candidacy for president. She told me that a saying of hers that I'd seen on Twitter had been printed on T-shirts and tote bags without her permission, or attribution, and, of course, without paying her. It was then I realized that Flavia's phrase, "My feminism will be intersectional or it will be bullshit," is how I wanted to go back and answer the young woman in the FemSem. The feminism that has saved my life is joined with the feminism that leads to the liberation of other women, like Flavia, like Alondra and Merle, like the young women in the seminar, and it has always been intersectional.

# 3

# THE SHALLOW
# PROMISE OF THE
# WELLNESS INDUSTRY

In 2019, a new device, Mirror, entered a crowded field of at-home workout options, competing with high-end home exercise products like Peloton, Echelon, or MYX fitness bikes. The *New York Times* called it "The Most Narcissistic Equipment Ever." Mirror is, as one might expect, a reflecting surface with a fitness instructor inside. "I legit use it as my full-length mirror," one user from Brooklyn said. "You would never in a thousand years know it was a piece of workout equipment." For it to become workout equipment, a user stands before the mirror and sees themselves, along with a scaled-down image of the instructor. The Mirror retails for $1,495 and, like its competitors, requires a $39 per month subscription fee for classes. It is a big hit with celebrities such as Jennifer Aniston, Ellen DeGeneres, Gwyneth Paltrow, and Lady Gaga, who have all purchased one. The device is perfect for the era of the selfie, when people are, like the Narcissus of Greek mythology, taken by the beauty of their own reflection. The Mirror is part of the $4.5 trillion global wellness market (in 2018 figures from the International Monetary Fund). This is a market driven by the buying power of affluent white women.

This all became personal for me when my partner began to dive into the world of wellness and self-care. I was glad, at first. She'd always suffered from severe anxiety, so frankly I was relieved when she began to meditate. Then, she got a diagnosis of endometriosis, which had often left her doubled over in pain. Endometriosis, a disorder that affects the uterus, is a tough diagnosis for someone who, like her, is masculine-of-center. Imagine not identifying with, or having much interest in using, your biologically female parts, only to have them turn against you. It's a cruel twist.

For most of our relationship, then marriage, I'd tried to get her to take better care of herself; I urged her to eat vegetables, and after her diagnosis I was glad to see her take them up with gusto. I had no interest in some of the healing practices she began to explore to address her pain, such as dry brushing, breathwork, Buddhism, and doing burpees with her personal trainer. And she had no interest in my version of self-care: working with a psychotherapist on why I hated to see my image so much. After eighteen years together, there were only three photos of us together, and that was my fault because I avoided cameras whenever possible, and it was almost always possible. We didn't own one, but I came to think of the Mirror workout device as the perfect metaphor for the dividing line between us: I could not look at my image and she only ever wanted to see herself reflected back. Both our responses, I suspected, had something to do with whiteness.

We were not the only ones investing in self-care at that time. Following the 2016 election, there was a significant uptick in a constellation of wellness-related activities by Americans. Collectively, we in the United States spent more time on yoga (34 percent increase), meditation (up 16 percent), and therapy (up 17 percent) in 2017 than in the previous year. These data, as is so often the case, are not broken down by gender and race, so it's impossible to know if white women were leading this trend or trailing it.

The banner held aloft over so much self-care is Audre Lorde's famous quote, rooted in her experience as a Black, radical, lesbian warrior-poet. You've probably seen it on Instagram, accompanied by the hashtag #radicalselfcare. "Caring for myself is not self-indulgence," Lorde wrote, "it is self-preservation, and that is an act of political warfare." Feminist writer Sara Ahmed talks about self-care as a form of warfare for women of color surviving under late-stage capitalism. Philosopher and activist Angela Davis said in a 2014 speech that "self-care has to be incorporated" into a "holistic approach to organizing."

In the summer of 2020, *Glamour* magazine featured interviews with six Black women about their self-care routines. The ad copy ran, "Being a Black woman in America has never been easy, but with today's historic civil rights movement hitting a fever pitch, stress is at an all-time high. . . . From skin-care routines to virtual therapy, six Black women share how they're prioritizing self-care while continuing to fight the good fight." The strategies the women named included stretching more, breathing deeply, physical exercise, mental health counseling. One woman shared, "I'm still in this collective grieving state, so my self-care is me being super kind to myself." After the profile and brief interview of each woman, there is a list of products for sale, such as a Goddess Candle, Summer Fridays Lip Balm, and Deep Detox Bath Soak, from which, readers are advised, *Glamour* "may earn an affiliate commission."

This is the shallow promise of the wellness industry as served to Black women. *Glamour*, run by a masthead of mostly very-well-meaning nice white ladies, curates interviews with Black women about their trauma following the lynching of George Floyd and the murder of Breonna Taylor, all amid a pandemic disproportionately killing Black and Brown people, and asks with great concern, *How are you managing?* And to make sure that Glamour/Condé Nast sees a return on its momentary interest in the lives of Black women, there are product endorsements. This approach to self-care makes it the individual's responsibility to heal from racism, and her duties to herself extend to her ability to pay for Deep Detox Bath Soak. I'm not sure this is what Audre Lorde envisioned when she referred to self-care as an "act of political warfare."

Koritha Mitchell, writer, professor, and avid runner, takes a different view of self-care. In a 2018 peer-reviewed article, she acknowledges that "the need for diligence about physical, spiritual, and emotional health is nothing new." Mitchell explains that the real harm done to her and other Black people in everyday life is "whenever there is know-your-place aggression, no matter how subtle, and whenever whiteness is treated as if it is always merit." The know-your-place aggression occurs through interactions sometimes called "microaggressions," where white people push back against the success, or even just the existence, of Black people. To upend this dynamic, Mitchell "flips the script on impostor syndrome," and rather than allow herself to absorb microaggressions, she reframes those same encounters by asking herself, "Would that person even be here if they weren't white?" As she tells it: "I most often find myself answering, 'Nope!' As a result, I am less likely to run myself ragged."

For Mitchell, "noticing white mediocrity is a form of self-care." This may be the first time this strategy has been named in a peer-reviewed journal article, but it is by no means unique to Mitchell. Rather it highlights the creative coping strategies that Black people, particularly middle-class Black people like Mitchell, have been forced to engage in for decades (and longer) as they deal with the harm white people cause. In her article, Mitchell very pointedly locates her self-care as a form of resistance to the oppressive Trump regime. When viewed from this angle, self-care for Black women is indeed an "act of political warfare"—but clearly the politics of self-care is not the same for everyone.

For the most part, self-care today is not part of any political resistance. The kind of self-care on offer from the wellness industry is not an act of political warfare, nor is it engaged in sustaining people as they conduct warfare against capitalism; in fact, it is crucial to ensuring the smooth functioning of capitalism. While I went to psychotherapy and tried to figure out how my self-loathing related to internalized misogyny and whiteness, I also worried that my therapist's advice—such as the recommendation that I needed to take more air-conditioned cabs in the summer—was just making me more comfortable with my place within a capitalist system. I also began to see how wellness culture was changing my relationship.

Self-care became a totalizing experience for my partner and changed her into someone I no longer recognized. For me, the collective turn inward promoted by the wellness industry seemed to be destroying the minds of some of the smartest white women I knew, including my partner.

Self-care is a billion-dollar business. Although that industry often deploys the Audre Lorde quote to help sell the promise of wokeness along with a Deep Detox Bath Soak, it is white women who are the primary audience and the main profiteers. What makes this so destructive is that it feeds a gendered form of white narcissism, which is at the heart of the very culture that's destroying all of us.

## "CLEAN EATING"

In April 2019, nutritionist Arielle Haspel opened a Chinese restaurant in Manhattan's West Village. She called it Lucky Lee's and, in the Instagram marketing for the restaurant, described it as a "clean" alternative to the "oily," "salty" Chinese food that she said makes people "feel bloated and icky the next day." The reality is that to the extent that the food served in Chinese American restaurants is sweet and starchy, it is so because once traditional cuisines have been adapted and tailored to white American tastes, a nuance that seemed lost in the marketing for Lucky Lee's. Articles quickly appeared with headlines like WHITE WOMAN'S NEW 'CLEAN' CHINESE RESTAURANT PROVOKES IMMEDIATE BACKLASH. And the original Instagram post disappeared from Lucky Lee's account soon after a journalist questioned Haspel about the language. Haspel explained that she was creating dishes for people who want to avoid monosodium glutamate (MSG), even though there is no definitive evidence to suggest that MSG causes allergies. She tagged images of her dishes on Instagram with #nogluten #nowheat, #norefinedsugar, hallmarks of a practice known as "clean eating." As New York–based foodie publication *Grub Street* pointed out, there is a long-standing, and racist, stereotype about Chinese restaurants being dirty that Haspel's marketing seemed to replay. Lucky Lee's closed after eight months, but the idea of "clean eating" lives on, and it seems to be a food trend that white women are especially susceptible to.

Clean eating isn't based in science or nutrition, it is about purity and a defense against pollution. With clean eating—or, the idea that it is important to eliminate toxins from one's diet—by cutting out such "pollutants" as dairy or meat or fruit, adherents attempt to optimize their physical health.

Although the clean eating fad may be new, it has roots in the pure food movements that swept the United States and British Empire during the nineteenth and early twentieth centuries. Concerns about food contamination fit seamlessly with calls for racial purity and the regulation of racialized food workers' bodies. Such workers, white reformers said, were unclean and diseased and, therefore, could transmit germs into the food supply, which would in turn infect (white) consumers. Scholar Donica Belisle documents how the movements for purity in food and against "race-mixing" overlapped in anti-Chinese sugar adds in Canada. In a campaign by western Canada's largest sugar company, BC Sugar, from 1891 and 1914, the company sought to convince white Canadians to avoid sugars imported from Hong Kong (BC Sugar's biggest competitor). Doing so would not only support local industry but also safeguard consumers' health because, said the company, Chinese men worked in the Hong Kong sugar industry. As such, these sugars were laden with "filth." This food purity campaign coincided with efforts to remove all possibilities of contact between white women and racialized men. In the Canadian provinces of British Columbia and Saskatchewan, specifically, it became illegal for white women to work for Chinese men.

Today, the murky label "clean eating" is used as a marketing tool directed at those looking to improve their lives. Anthropologist Danya Glabau has been paying close attention to the cultural meanings of wellness influencers like Amanda Chantal Bacon, the white woman who founded the Los Angeles–based company Moon Juice, which has an estimated annual revenue of $12.9 million. A promotional video on the Moon Juice Instagram account advertises something called "moon dust," purported to be a blend of powdered mushrooms, tree bark, and root extract that retails for $38 per 1.5-ounce jar. In the video, clouds of the dust are taken out of a jar and tossed into the frame by a white woman's hand, with text and images that tout the power of this elixir and suggest the many ways it can be added to one's daily nutritional intake. The implication, Glabau explains, is that when what we eat is sold to us as Moon Juice or moon dust, it is meant to be something more than food, "it is magical fairy dust that promises to rev up our cognitive, bodily, sexual, and even spiritual prowess." What's at stake in what Glabau calls the "beautiful food trend," is a kind of perpetual self-improvement through better eating. And it is a form of self-improvement often created by and especially geared toward white women. The harm comes when white women consume purity under the guise of good health and use it to generate a self-righteous superiority over others while insisting on their own racial innocence.

Clean eating, as marketed by people like Bacon, also reinforces a particular social order in which white women—particularly thin, heterosexual, affluent white women—are regarded as "moral authorities on what is right for individual bodies, for children, and by extension, for the health of the nation," writes Glabau. If a white man—even a straight white man—were selling "moon dust," he would run the risk of being called a snake-oil salesman or a charlatan. In a *New York Times Magazine* cover story, "How Amanda Chantal Bacon Perfected the Celebrity Wellness Business," readers learned that Alex Jones, the Austin-based right-wing conspiracy theorist, sells some of the same supplements as Moon Juice on his *InfoWars* website. It is our ideas about white womanhood—our assumptions of innocence, of nurturing, of the expertise implied in "mother's intuition"—that are part of what helps wellness influencers like Amanda Chantal Bacon make millions.

It is those same assumptions of innocence and trusted expertise that enabled Australian food blogger and wellness "expert" Belle Gibson to perpetrate a fraud via Whole Pantry, an app, cookbook, and front for soliciting donations. Gibson built her burgeoning wellness empire on the claim that she cured her brain cancer with healthy eating. It all came to a dramatic end when a journalist uncovered the fact that Gibson had never had cancer, much less cured herself by eating certain foods. Nevertheless, she used the story of her cancer and healing-through-eating to raise over $400,000 in donations for cancer charities, which she then kept for herself. A judge in Gibson's fraud case said that she had a "relentless obsession with herself." It may be this sort of narcissism that is at the center of why so many white women have fallen for the ruse of #eatclean.

All modern cultures have concepts about what is clean and unclean. Anthropologist Mary Douglas argues in her classic 1966 book *Purity and Danger* that elaborate rules around what is pure and impure (e.g., kosher and traif) are a way to reassure people that the world is more certain and under control than it actually is by offering a set of rules to follow that are easy to understand and act on. When the rules are followed, order is maintained, and we are becalmed. Following Douglas's argument, it may be that clean eating reassures us somehow. British food writer Bee Wilson gets at this when she writes, "Clean eating . . . is perhaps best seen as a dysfunctional response to a still more dysfunctional food supply: a dream of purity in a toxic world. To walk into a modern western supermarket is to be assailed by aisle upon aisle of salty, oily snacks and sugary cereals, of 'bread' that has been neither proved nor fermented, of cheap, sweetened drinks and meat from animals kept in inhumane conditions." As farmer and food sovereignty activist Leah Penniman points out in her 2018 book *Farming While Black*, our food system in the United States is built on stolen land and stolen labor and needs a radical redesign.

Farm ownership and management is today among the whitest of professions, but it wasn't always. In 1920, 14 percent of all land-owning US farmers were Black, but today less than 2 percent of farms are controlled by Black people. Penniman notes that this represents a loss of over fourteen million acres of land that is the direct result of discrimination and dispossession that continue to this day. Yet, at the same time, the people who harvest produce are predominantly Brown and exploited, while people of color disproportionately live in "food apartheid" neighborhoods and suffer from diet-related illness. The way white people have approached the issue of our food supply is, according to sociologist Rachel Slocum, to create local-organic food spaces such as regional farmer's markets as well as chains like Whole Foods that cater to predominantly white shoppers, perhaps unintentionally. The comedian Chris Rock riffs on this in a 2017 stand-up routine. "Whole Foods does not say 'No Blacks Allowed,'" he jokes. "But a $7 orange does. That's the new Jim Crow." And it's not only about pricing; it's also about access. In 2020, for instance, the largest farmer's market in the Washington, DC area at DuPont Circle repeatedly denied spaces to Black vendors. Managers at the market acknowledged they "dropped the ball" and promised to try to do better.

For white women, the clamor for wellness and "clean eating" is a hyperindividualized response to our bland, corporate, and denatured food system. Rather than respond to this collectively as a political issue, white women have turned it into an individual issue about what we put into our mouths. And we are reassured at every turn this is the right thing to do. An aphorism that has become the cornerstone of the wellness industry is "the airplane oxygen-mask theory: If you don't put on your mask first, you won't be able to save anyone else." This has become the banner behind which white women march, and it is a form of narcissism that can only center the individual, never the collective.

In early January 2011, the meme "Women Laughing Alone with Salad" went viral. Edith Zimmerman created the original post on the feminist blog The Hairpin, with eighteen images and no text. It took off because people recognized the trope of mostly white women feigning exaggerated, open-mouthed enthusiasm over leafy greens. The original post included fifteen images of white women and three of Black women, but there was little mention of the whiteness as the meme circulated online. In response, Getty Images partnered with Sheryl Sandberg's nonprofit LeanIn.org to create more "realistic" images of women for use in advertising. By 2015, when playwright Sheila Callaghan transformed the meme into a stage production in Washington, DC, it featured three white actresses. Callaghan, interviewed at the time, said, "Nobody likes salad that much—[salad] will never be that kind of satisfying." The meme, the play, and the earnest Getty/LeanIn.org counterprogramming are all meant to work against the sexism implicit in the portrayal of orgiastic responses to lettuce, and that's important. But these responses miss entirely the fact that the women are eating salad *alone*, disconnected from other people eating, or the mostly Brown people growing, harvesting, or preparing food. Human beings are social creatures, and eating is meant to be a communal activity where we gather in each other's presence to break bread slathered with butter, raise a glass of wine, and chew together. These are elemental and abundantly pleasurable rituals which solidify our connections to one another. In the rigidity and narcissism of clean eating, we have all become the deranged Woman Laughing *Alone* with Salad.

The quest to eat only certain foods deemed pure and clean can look a lot like an eating disorder. In her clinical practice, eating disorder specialist Renee McGregor says that for a time, "every single client with an eating disorder who walks into my clinic doors is either following or wants to follow a 'clean' way of eating." In her 2017 book *Orthorexia: When Healthy Eating Goes Bad*, McGregor writes that people can cross into the terrain of disordered eating when they care more about the purity of their food regimen than the pleasure eating gives them.

It happened to Ruby Tandoh, a finalist on the Great British Bake Off series, who found herself slipping into an eating disorder after she discovered wellness culture online. "I became fearful and thin. I had found wellness. I was not well," she wrote in 2016. Tandoh found herself immersed in the world of #eatclean Instagram accounts and clean eating cookbooks that are selling two contradictory messages: our self-worth is not in our appearance, and we should guard against fatness at every turn. If the only "clean food" is that which won't make you fat, then wellness is just the dieting industry with a rebranding campaign. Social scientist Julie Guthman, in her 2011 book *Weighing In: Obesity, Food Justice, and the Limits of Capitalism*, takes issue with the current fashion of promoting food that is local, organic, and "farm fresh" as a remedy for obesity. While locavore food may be tastier and more ecologically sustainable, it reinforces a set of practices that can whitewash food justice and the feminist issues of fat women's bodies. Guthman argues that ours is a political economy of bulimia—one that simultaneously promotes consumption while also insisting upon thinness. There is not a woman or femme raised in the contemporary United States who has not been exposed to the tyranny of thinness disguised as wellness or aspiration or whiteness, sometimes all three.

The damage that comes from this sort of wellness is immense. White women's narcissism causes them to use their privilege and resources to turn inward and focus on their own bodies and delude themselves into thinking their self-care is an act of political warfare. This turn inward also reinforces a smug self-satisfaction and barricades off any connection with, or responsibility to, a wider community or the environment. As white women obsess about clean eating, the people of Flint, Michigan, haven't had clean drinking water since 2014.

## PURE "BARREBIES"

Women who are devotees of the fitness boutique Pure Barre refer to themselves as "Barrebies," a reference to the doll by Mattel that is a simulacrum for white womanhood. According to its website, Pure Barre, the ballet-themed boutique fitness franchise launched in 2001 by Carrie Rezabek Dorr, offers clients "self-focused time to transform the body and mind." While the text goes on to say that Pure Barre is open to "people" at "all levels of fitness," it is a wellness franchise that caters to and cultivates a particular kind of woman who aspires to have a ballet body. For the 550,000 dedicated customers, mostly women, mostly white, the ballet body is an aspiration that is within reach. The ballet body is one that is achieved through discipline and conforms to a particular aesthetic standard. As writer Joanna Nova explains, "Pure Barre cultivates sameness, a one-size fits all model of long, lean lady-strength. [Their] promotional photos feature women my age, somewhere between twenty- and thirty-something. They're all white, all tank-topped, all with the same trim body-type: toned but not overtly muscular." What is on offer at fitness boutiques is a certain kind of community among those who can afford to pay the $40 per class fee several times each week in order to achieve that "long, lean [white] lady-strength." But as journalist Harriet Brown points out in her 2015 book *Body of Truth*, the kind of community created by the "insider speak" of fitness boutiques suggests that anyone who is not part of the community is "other" and "impure."

"When we talk about the ballerina," says Theresa Ruth Howard, a former dancer and curator of Memoirs of Blacks in Ballet, a digital platform that preserves the stories of Blacks in ballet, "we're talking

about the ideal, our stereotype of the desirable woman, and that is reserved for white women." Cultural critic Chloe Angyal interviewed
Howard for her 2021 book *Turning Pointe*. For Angyal, who writes
thoughtfully about bodies and race and ballet, the dance itself is reproducing a version of white womanhood that adheres to a Western European aesthetic. Within this aesthetic, white women's bodies are all the
same: thin, controlled, toned, but not too muscular. In other words,
the same kinds of bodies that Pure Barre is in the business of creating
and selling as wellness. Other fitness boutique franchises sell a slightly
more muscular version of women's bodies, more warrior than ballerina,
but still adhering to a white, Western European aesthetic.

The business model at Pure Barre is one that assists women with
optimizing their pursuit of the ideal body that is not merely thin
but also suggests high art. As writer Jia Tolentino puts it in *Trick
Mirror*, "ballerinas meet the beauty standard not just in the name
of appearance or performance but also in the name of high athleti-
cism and art." Tolentino exposes the bargain that barre classes offer:
"People pay $40 a class for [an] investment that always brings back
returns" for women who can get their bodies to conform to that
ideal. "It can feel like license and agency to approach an ideal, to
find yourself—in a good picture, on your wedding day, in a flash of
identical movement—exemplifying a prototype." As someone who
resists the camera at every turn, I don't know the pleasure of which
Tolentino writes, but I believe her when she says that this is one of
the rewards for succeeding under capitalism and patriarchy if you
are willing to work under those terms. I wonder if it's my resistance
to white supremacy that has made me hate my own image, or if it
is merely my failure to properly optimize my body according to the
constraints of capitalism and patriarchy? I'm not sure, and I'm not
sure how to know for sure.

Idealized notions of what constitutes a healthy body circulate globally through the trillion-dollar wellness industry in ways that seem

contradictory. Consider for a moment two products, Unilever's Fair & Lovely, a skin-lightening cream, sold as a way to "detox" skin, and Tropical Blend Tanning Oil, marketed to "capture the savage tan." The first product is part of the international skin-lightening industry that generated $23 billion in business in 2020. The second product is part of the $1.47 billion self-tanning industry, not including the $4.6 billion in revenue from the tanning bed business. To be clear, it is the skin-lightening products that garner more revenue, by at least a multiple of four. In India alone, more than $432 million worth of skin-whitening products are consumed annually. In South Asia, much of this revenue goes to Unilever's best-selling Fair & Lovely product. The marketing for the face cream features a dark-skinned girl unable to get a job or get married until she lightens her skin with the product. Many feminist scholars have written about the way the skin-lightening industry reproduces white, European, and American ideals of beauty. But what about skin tanning, and specifically, what does it mean, then, to be a white American woman with a tan?

In her research into US consumer culture of the 1920s and 1930s, visual arts scholar Patricia Daigle found that it was this historical moment when the suntanned white body emerged as a symbol of "health." Nineteenth-century medicine recommended "heliotherapy," that is, sitting in sunlight, as a cure for everything from tuberculosis to lupus to rheumatism. This was also the time that camping and other outdoor activities began to emerge as popular activities for white people with leisure time and disposable income. Thus, having suntanned skin for white Americans became a physical marker of differentiation from "the unhealthy, amoral, and pallid bodies lurking in the darker regions of the city," as another writer put it. Daigle, in her assessment of visual culture from the interwar era, such as Alfred Stieglitz's photographs of a very suntanned Georgia O'Keeffe he dubbed "playing Indian," argues that this was a way that white people could appropriate Native American cultural references through changes in skin tone. The irony, of course, is that even these slight transgressions in racial boundaries by altering skin tone to signal health are heavily laden with the eugenicist ideas that dominated the political discourse at that time.

In the current era, skin tanning perpetuates something called "cosmopolitan whiteness." White cosmopolitans are perceived as being sophisticated enough to transcend their own culture and incorporate cultural "difference" into their lives with openness, curiosity, and tolerance, according to scholar Ghassan Hage. In an ingenious empirical study of cosmopolitan whiteness, sociologist Ayu L. Saraswati analyzed the advertisements in two versions of *Cosmo* magazine over the same time period: in the Indonesian version, she looked at skin-lightening ads; in the US version, she looked at skin-tanning ads. Saraswati argues that both of these practices perpetuate and strengthen cosmopolitan whiteness. Skin lightening is less a desire to pass as a part of the "white race" than it is a desire to belong to the unrooted world culture and to gain the freedom to move transnationally, which involves proximity to whiteness. It is a nonessentialist cosmopolitan whiteness that skin lightening seems to offer.

Skin-tanning products are advertised so that white supremacy and white skin color are reinforced but in subtle ways that foster a cosmopolitan whiteness. Unlike whitening ads, none of the tanning ads Saraswati examined used words like *blackening* or *browning*, which have racial connotations in the US context. Instead, they used words like *tan*, *bronze*, or *deepest bronze*. None of the skin-lightening ads suggest the user's ability to take control of how white one's skin can be, but the skin-tanning ads explicitly use the language of "choice and control," key mechanisms of white supremacy. In skin-lightening ads, people are advised to "detox" their skin, but not in skin-tanning ads, where white-skinned users are not insulted with language about their skin being "toxic." Saraswati argues that skin-tanning practices become a way for white female consumers to inhabit "the exotic other," as in the "capture the savage tan" advertisement. Part of what this does is generate a form of longing for the

purity of a colonial past and a fantasy of superior health unquestion-
ably residing in white bodies.

## THE WHITENING OF YOGA

"Yoga is the effort to experience one's divinity personally and then to
hold on to that experience forever," Elizabeth Gilbert writes in her
mega-hit memoir *Eat, Pray, Love* from 2006. Yoga takes up the middle portion of Gilbert's memoir, the "pray" alluded to in the title, and
it includes her quest for spiritual enlightenment through studying
yoga in India. In many ways, Gilbert's memoir (and the 2010 film of
the same name starring Julia Roberts) helped to expand the popular-
ity of yoga among white, middle-class women in the United States.

Yoga has also become the sine qua non of wellness for white
women, holding the promise, as it does, of both thinness and enlightenment. Pure Yoga is the signature fitness boutique owned by the
same Republican billionaire who owns Equinox and SoulCycle, but
there are over six thousand smaller, nonfranchised yoga studios in the
United States. According to a 2016 Yoga Alliance and *Yoga Journal*
study, other locations where practitioners attempted a sun salutation
or a downward dog included at home, in a gym or club, in a community center, or in a park. The same study reported that there are
approximately thirty-seven million Americans practicing yoga, and
they spent upward of $16 billion on classes, clothing, equipment, and
accessories in one year. Of those thirty-seven million practitioners,
72 percent are women. Although the study did not ask a question
on race, one can safely assume that a large majority of the 72 percent
of thirty-seven million yoga practitioners (roughly 26,640,000) are
white women.

"I realized with horror that despite the all-inclusivity preached by
the studio, despite the purported blindness to socioeconomic status, despite the sizeable population of regular Asian students, Black
students were few and far between," Jen Polachek wrote in a piece
for the online magazine *XoJane* in January 2014. Her realization

about the whiteness of her yoga studio came to her when a Black woman attended her yoga class and Polachek found this distracting. "I was completely unable to focus on my practice, instead feeling hyper-aware of . . . my skinny white girl body. Surely this woman was . . . judging me, stereotyping me, resenting me—or so I imagined." Polachek refers to the woman as "heavyset" and remarks on her struggle to do certain poses, wondering, "What could I do to help her?" Polachek imagines that the woman may not have wanted anyone to look at her, so she writes, "I tried to very deliberately avoid looking in her direction each time I was in downward dog, but I could feel her hostility just the same."

Afterward, Polachek seems to have had a meltdown over the encounter. "I got home from that class and promptly broke down crying. Yoga, a beloved safe space that has helped me through many dark moments in over six years of practice, suddenly felt deeply suspect. Knowing fully well that one hour of perhaps self-importantly believing myself to be the deserving target of a racially charged anger is nothing, is largely my own psychological projection, is a drop in the bucket, is the tip of the iceberg in American race relations, I was shaken by it all the same."

Polachek's essay lit up the internet for a few weeks as all kinds of people reached out to let her know that her response was problematic. People were eager to make several counterpoints: first, there are women of size who practice yoga; second, there are Black people who practice yoga; further, there are Black women of size practicing yoga. Jessamyn Stanley, a Seattle-based yoga instructor and a full-figured Black woman with natural hair, has been practicing yoga since 2011 and has an Instagram following of over 350,000 people. "If we lived in a world that did not denigrate Black female bodies—and specifically fat Black bodies—then I doubt that anyone would've ever paid attention to anything that I've put on the internet," Stanley says. But women like Stanley remain exceptions to the overwhelmingly thin, blonde, white women who have come to dominate the practice of yoga in the United States, and like Polachek, think of it as a "beloved safe space."

The marketing for yoga may be all "love and acceptance," but the desire for a "safe space" is really a euphemism for homosociality, notes feminist scholar Rumya Putcha. The recognition that many white women identify "safe spaces" as those with only other white women reveals that their sense of safety depends on exclusionary practices and often structural forms of inequity. In her decades of research on race in US yoga studios, Putcha has documented the way that white women's dominance of these spaces relies on necropolitics masquerading as "self-care." In the hands of whiteness, Putcha writes, self-care has been elevated to an ideology of virtue, and the self in this virtuous formulation exists in opposition to both the other and the collective. What this means is that white women yogis use the vague association with nonviolence to absolve themselves of any responsibility for social justice. The effect is to reproduce and center white feelings, as is clear in the Polachek essay. This can be difficult to reconcile with the pronouncements about light and love and acceptance that adhere to yoga culture in the United States.

The practice of yoga for white women is not only about stretching but also about enlightenment through consuming Otherness. Gilbert's *Eat, Pray, Love* spawned a cottage industry of similar self-help-themed memoirs and films, many of which locate their white women protagonists in India. The draw to India has deepened through an idealization of Gandhian nonviolence, without any acknowledgment of Gandhi's sexism and anti-Blackness, and a fantasized version of yoga, stripped of religious connotations. This "India" is a fantasy of redemption that adopts a Hindu India while ignoring the systematic dispossession of Muslim Indians, and it comes to represent an idealistic antidote to violence, stress, and corruption, as scholar Shefali Chandra points out. In the memoir *Dreaming in Hindi* (2009), Katherine Rich is launched on her journey by someone who says, "India will change you forever." In this imagined India, the country becomes a destination for the late-imperial white woman, a place where she can control her pain and transform her alienation so that she is stronger upon her return to her metropolitan home. And she can take this journey without ever considering how her individual experience connects to the geopolitical reality that makes her vision quest travel possible.

*Eat, Pray, Love*, for example, opens with the unraveling of Gilbert's marriage, and as it comes undone, she wakes from a "troubled night's sleep to find that hijacked airplanes were crashing into the two tallest buildings of my city, as everything invincible that had once stood together now became a smoldering avalanche of ruin." Rarely mentioned in discussions of Gilbert's memoir is that her story emerges from the ruins of 9/11. Little questioned, too, is what it means for a white American woman to be traveling, eating, praying, and loving as a global tourist in a post-9/11 world that is dealing with America's retaliation for those attacks. Gilbert travels to India and consumes yoga much the way she travels to Italy and consumes pasta, with a nod to the culture providing it but with no consideration of how her presence there is complicated by her whiteness or her Americanness. Beginning a yoga practice for white women in the United States is now denuded of its association with Brown people, or Hindu religion, but is instead a form of consumption that suggests self-care and an individual quest for a bland enlightenment that requires the very least pain and sacrifice.

"I started practicing yoga because I thought it might help me figure out why I hated sex," Glennon Doyle writes in her 2016 memoir *Love Warrior*. After she accidentally finds herself in a hot yoga class, she decides to "stay on the mat" until the end of the class. She is trying to recover from the discovery of her husband's infidelity and heal from her lingering trauma from her girlhood bulimia, which was caused by a "culture that taught me that small, thin women are worth the most." Doyle stays on the mat through the ninety-minute class and, upon reflecting on her survival of the ordeal, she recalls a line from *When Things Fall Apart* by Pema Chödrön, an American Tibetan Buddhist: "So even if the hot loneliness is there, and for 1.6 seconds we sit with that restlessness when yesterday we couldn't sit for even one, that's the journey of the warrior." Thus, *warrior* becomes the leitmotif for the book about one white American woman's healing through yoga and the Buddhist teachings of another white American woman, born Deirdre Blomfield-Brown. In Doyle's pursuit of individual enlightenment ("why I didn't like sex") through hot yoga, the Indian and Hindu origins of yoga are easily replaced with Buddhist teachings from another white American woman. Pema Chödrön is an American-born woman and a Tibetan Buddhist nun, in a tradition that emphasizes ritual, mantras, and yogic teachings. Thich Nhat Hanh is a Vietnamese-born man and Zen Buddhist, in a tradition that emphasizes meditation. The nuanced distinctions between Tibetan and Zen Buddhism, not to mention these two teachers, are lost on most Americans who pull inspirational quotes, à la carte, from what may be denser texts. In the United States, the teachings of both Pema Chödrön and Thich Nhat Hanh get blended together into "mindfulness."

## MINDFULNESS

*Time* magazine's February 3, 2014, cover is headlined THE MIND-FUL REVOLUTION: THE SCIENCE OF FINDING FOCUS IN A STRESSED-OUT, MULTITASKING CULTURE. The accompanying photo (by Peter Hapak) features an unidentified young, thin, blonde, white woman with her eyes closed in blissful contemplation. The article by Kate Pickert describes the mindfulness-based stress reduction (MBSR) program, designed by Jon Kabat-Zinn. The practice of mindfulness, a mental state achieved by focusing one's awareness on the present moment, and the MBSR based on it have permeated corporate culture. The same year as the *Time* magazine article, Thick Nhat Hahn visited Google headquarters. He and a group of other monks spent a day on the Google campus, giving a lecture, talking with senior managers, and leading around seven hundred employees through meditation. So many Google staff members wanted to take part that the company had to open up two additional locations to live stream his lecture.

In fact, mindfulness has become "the new capitalist spirituality," writes Ronald Purser, in his 2019 book *McMindfulness*. Purser notes that corporations like Google, McKinsey & Company, Deutsche Bank, and Procter & Gamble began to enthusiastically embrace mindfulness at about the same time the recession of 2008 hit. At that time, perhaps not surprisingly, discontentment among workers grew, and corporations regarded it as a potential threat to the smooth flow of capitalist profits. The economic realities of massive layoffs and the rise in gig economy jobs with long hours, unpredictable schedules, and barely survivable wages all create disaffection and alienation as if by design. The accompanying stress, depression, low motivation, and absenteeism from jobs prompted a corporate interest in mindfulness and "spurred a burgeoning wellness and happiness industry," Purser observes. But the mindfulness popular with corporations is one that is stripped of its cultural and religious origins. In his 2014 book *Mindful America*, Jeff Wilson points out that the roots of today's mindfulness are in Transcendental Meditation. As Wilson notes, MBSR has replaced TM at least in part because of racism. Wilson paints a picture of TM's guru: "The Maharishi was a brown-skinned Indian man with a big beard and long, somewhat unkempt hair worn forward of the shoulders, who typically appeared in yoga robes with Hindu prayer beads." Then he contrasts that to: "Jon Kabat-Zinn, the face of MBSR, a clean-shaven white American doctor with short hair and rimless glasses, who delivers his teachings in business attire."

The belief among CEOs is that mindfulness can help increase profits, and white women CEOs are no less susceptible to this than their male counterparts. Arianna Huffington, who founded *Huffington Post* in 2005 and *Thrive Global* in 2016, which she describes as an "American company that provides behavior change technology and media to support individuals struggling with stress and burn-out," is among the advocates of mindfulness. Huffington sees a di-rect connection between mindfulness and increased profits. She said, "There's nothing touchy-feely about increased profits. This is a tough economy. . . . Stress-reduction and mindfulness don't just make us happier and healthier, they're a proven competitive advantage for any business that wants one." In Thich Nhat Hahn's message to Google executives, he said, "If you consider mindfulness as a means of hav-ing a lot of money, then you have not touched its true purpose." But this decoupling of mindfulness from money seems lost in the drive for corporate profits. In this turn inward, toward the self, mindful-ness as it is often practiced in the United States looks like a retreat from social injustice. As author Ronald Purser points out, "Unless it raises awareness of the social origins of suffering, mindfulness is merely self-management." For white women executives, this new fo-cus on mindfulness and spiritual well-being is baked into contempo-rary neoliberal feminism.

Sociologist Melissa Fisher has conducted ethnographies of in-ternational women's conferences designed for female executives. At these, Fisher observes there is often a "spiritual element" to the pro-gramming. At a 2014 conference in Berlin, for example, the program opened with Doug Manuel and his male drummers from Sewa Beats, a Swiss-based management company that teaches business skills through participatory "traditional" African drumming. Manuel is white and British. Some of the drummers are also white and British; others are Black and West African. Manuel began by instructing each attendee at the women's conference to find a drum, called a Djembe, under their seats. For the following hour, Manuel and his bandmates taught all seven hundred women how to play various rhythms. As Fisher recounts Manuel's explanation: "Drumming provides a way for women to locate their 'authentic feminine selves.' It allows them 'to communicate' with their senses and to 'be present.'" This cor-porate embrace of women's empowerment through spirituality, and drumming, is a kind of training ground for a new global white corporate female elite who are now expected to be "mindful" and calm as they climb the corporate ladder. For the upwardly mobile white woman looking for some self-care, the one-stop shop is Goop.

## GOOP

In the last decade, Gwyneth Paltrow has made a $250 million fortune selling wellness through her lifestyle company, Goop. Goop's wellness section offers up a variety of seemingly dubious products and treatments, from Emotional Detox Bath Soak to supplements and "clean" food, to vaginal eggs and vaginal steams. In an interview in 2017, Jimmy Kimmel asked Paltrow about the practice of "earthing," one of many self-care techniques recommended on Goop.

"So one of the things we like to do on Goop is find what the alternative world says about feeling good in the modern-day world," Paltrow said. "I don't actually know that much about earthing, and it came out of me not knowing anything about earthing but hearing about it. They say that we lost touch with sort of being barefoot in the earth, and there's some sort of electromagnetic thing that we're missing. It's good to take your shoes off in the grass."

Paltrow's answer reveals the cultural appropriation at the heart of her enterprise, as well as what appears to be a clueless mediocrity. There is something gratifying about hearing Paltrow admit that she doesn't know much about what she's hawking on Goop. More than that, her vague call for reconnecting to the land by "being barefoot in the earth" speaks to a kind of entitlement of the white lady settler who is at ease with "finding" what "the alternative world says" and using it for her own, electromagnetic, ends. The problem, though, is not simply the questionable efficacy of the products promulgated by her brand, or her own lack of awareness about her privilege; the problem is the whiteness of the wellness industry more broadly.

The editors at *Self* magazine recently proclaimed that "wellness has a race problem," but it would be more accurate to say that wellness has a whiteness problem. Wellness is pitched to consumers through a constellation of luxuries that white women are more likely to enjoy, such as spare time and disposable income. It's often provided in facilities—spas, gyms, retreats—with aesthetics that are implicitly white, upper middle class, and walled off from any consciousness about their own place in American society's racial landscape. One journalist who attended the In Goop Health Summit in California in 2018 described the scene in which there were "more blondes than one is accustomed to seeing in one place at one time." The problem with wellness isn't that white women are the target market for these products, or that white women like Paltrow make gobs of money off of them.

The problem is that health magazines, wellness gurus, and In Goop Health Summits all work to make a particular kind of white-hetero-lady-identity seem natural and in need of care. Once the discussion turns to having your chakras realigned and anchoring your pelvic wall, what doesn't get mentioned, or likely even noticed, is that there are only white women talking to other white women in those spaces. The combination of making the straight, upper-middle-class, white (heterosexual) woman's identity seem both natural and in need of care while never mentioning it as a specific racial and gender identity or class position is part of what gives whiteness a soothing power for those who have access to it. There does seem to be something in this particular version of white-hetero-lady-hood that requires this kind of personal care to sustain itself. Could it be that there is something in being raised white that damages us and that we look to recover in self-care? Could it be that the work required to maintain our position in a white-dominated society, while remaining subordinate to white men, is quite frankly exhausting? Could it be that nice white ladies' emotional work of managing—"up" to white men in positions of power over them, and "down" to other white women and BIPOC folks—requires such ferocious energy that we in turn need a bevy of self-care aids?

The type of wellness that Paltrow and others like her are selling ignores the things people actually need to be well, such as ending poverty and systemic racism, keeping carcinogens out of our air and food
supply, and providing ready access to free, reliable health care. Instead, these versions of wellness ignore the large, structural problems
that affect everyone's health, while they work hard to reflect back the
special, precious individuality of each and every white woman who
subscribes to their services. And this sort of wellness drives home an
entitlement to all the things from the "alternative worlds" that Goop
and other purveyors of wellness are unearthing for their benefit.

What Goop sells is part of what feminist scholar Rumya Putcha
calls the cult of white woman wellness. And it was to this cult that
I lost my partner when she folded her arms across her chest and told
me she was "making healthy choices for *me*," and ended our relationship to pursue her health. Maybe she was right, and that is what her
health demanded. The truth is that we should have gone our separate
ways years before the moment she put her oxygen mask on her own
face first. And, tragically, all the dry brushing, blueberry smoothies,
and Buddhism didn't protect her from the breast cancer she developed after we split up. The kinds of individual self-care solutions on
offer from Paltrow's Goop or Bacon's Moon Juice are no match for
the carcinogens that invade our everyday lives under American racial
capitalism, and they certainly weren't helping me deal with the damage that whiteness had done to me.

There are Black women who are working to take the whiteness
out of self-care. The Chicago-based Lauren Ash, for example, created
Black Girl in Om, a space that encourages "self-care, self-love, and
self-empowerment for communities of color." What Ash is doing—
situating self-care and self-love within communities of color—is
the key difference between her endeavor and the narcissism inherent in the whiteness of the dominant self-care culture. It is vitally
important to center Black, Indigenous, and other people of color in
wellness practices so that they can heal from the damage of living

in a white-supremacist culture. And to do that is a distinct project from the kind of self-care that we buy into as white women to disengage from the ways we are connected to, and damaged by, white supremacy.

## WHITENESS ON THE COUCH

In a 2019 essay on Longreads, writer and psychoanalyst Natasha Stovall describes her therapy practice this way: "The couch in my therapy office is occupied mostly by white people. Anxious white people and depressed white people. Obsessive white people and compulsive white people. White people who hurt people and white people who hurt themselves. White people who eat too much, drink too much, work too much, shop too much. White people who are bored, envious, guilty, numb. Racist white people and antiracist white people. White people who look across the room and see a white therapist listening. We talk about everything. Except being white." She goes on to ask why it is we don't talk about whiteness in therapy. Stovall reminds us of the old saw about therapy that "the thing you don't talk about is *the thing*." Then she asks the provocative question: "What if whiteness is *the thing*?" By this, Stovall means, what if *whiteness* is the underlying issue and a root cause of all those secondary problems she lists?

Reading this article so resonated with me that when I first encountered it, I recommended it to everyone I talked to, with a "here, read this . . ." I sent it to my therapist. I sent it to friends. I sent it to colleagues. And, when it was my turn to organize the materials for a Harvard discussion group, I paired Stovall's article with Chelsea Handler's Netflix documentary *Hello Privilege. It's Me, Chelsea.* In the well-meaning but cringe-worthy 2019 documentary, Handler sets about to explore the impact of white privilege in America, a journey that leads her to the doorstep of her former boyfriend Tyshaun, whom she dated as a sixteen-year-old. The two of them were busted multiple times with drugs, and each time, he was arrested and she was sent home. She hadn't seen Tyshaun again until she made the film, when she is invited into his home where she talks with him, his mother, and his grandmother all about their drug use. Unexplored in that scene, or in the rest of the film, is Handler's own background. I was eager to talk about what I saw as the connections between these two cultural artifacts: Stovall's willingness to interrogate the whiteness within her own therapy practice and Handler's instinct to examine her own privilege—even though Handler avoids digging into her own psychopathology and dysfunctional family (whom we never see onscreen) by focusing on Tyshaun's family. As we went around the room in the discussion group, I will never forget the white-identified Argentinian woman who objected to the very premise of the article by saying, "I just don't think therapy is the place to talk about whiteness." The conversation about the article stopped at that point.

I was disappointed that day that we couldn't dive into the nuances of Stovall's argument, but I think I understand the resistance. Therapy is a place that many of us go to try to reconnect, re-create, and re-form the strained relationships from our childhood; we expect to be taken care of there, not challenged. For those who think so infrequently about their racial identity that they never realize it shapes everything, including their psyche, the suggestion that it does can seem like an affront. Trying to understand what it means to be a white woman in this culture is impossible without going deep into structures internalized in childhood. It's hard work, and painful, and few of us are ready to do it. And, as Stovall points out, there aren't many psychotherapists equipped to help us do that work even when we are ready.

## CONCLUSION

Most of the way that wellness has been organized, marketed, and sold in the United States feels a lot like a fraud. Its main function is to sell us stuff—Detox Bath Soak, classes, Moon Juice, and all the rest—that may make us feel better in the short term. This is how buying things feels when you live in capitalism and why people sometimes call it "retail therapy." But these purchases don't address the things that actually threaten our health, and they don't assuage the underlying problem for any of us. And we do seem to be suffering from something, if the trillions of dollars we're spending on the wellness industry are any indication. But what if all this clean eating is a dysfunctional response to a dysfunctional system? And what if that dysfunctional system is white supremacy and what it's done to our world? Maybe the truth is that at least part of what white women need is the kind of regimen that helps us confront our involvement in the white-supremacist, capitalist system that we've helped to create.

In her discussion of white mediocrity, Koritha Mitchell talks about how it becomes a social problem that everyone must deal with. The tendency within American culture is to "manufacture innocence and merit" for white people. This lowers the bar for society as a whole. Mitchell writes, "White Americans are consistently taught that it is only right for them to focus solely on their own opportunities and resources. This is more of a social problem than a personal one; it's about American society's low expectations and how those low expectations shape behavior." I wonder if self-care for white women is about managing our disappointment at how little we have settled for, what a meager, mediocre world we've helped to create, and how lonely it is to only ever think about yourself and your individual family. White mediocrity is an often unacknowledged part of being a nice white lady, and I think it must be connected in some way to white guilt and shame.

Writer Ijeoma Oluo observes that white mediocrity is not "something bland and harmless." In her 2020 book *Mediocre*, she describes it as a "cultural complacency with systems that are horrifically oppressive." The cost of benefiting from, and being trained to ignore, these mechanisms of suffering is unprocessed guilt and shame.

Recall Emily, the young woman I mentioned earlier who resented being told that white people were responsible for slavery and said that after finding the white-supremacist movement, "the guilt—I don't have it anymore." For Emily, getting involved in the white-supremacist movement was a kind of escape hatch out of the dead-end feelings she associated with being white. This seems to be one way to respond to circumstances, when you have been raised white by people you love, only to realize that your whiteness is part of a system that destroys peoples' lives. This realization can get so uncomfortable that people look for some kind of release to make it go away. This is what psychologist Janet Helms calls the "reintegration" phase of white identity development, in which a person tries to lower the cognitive dissonance of their whiteness by doubling down on the idea of superiority.

Closely related to white guilt is shame. Self-help favorite Brené Brown has made a career for herself talking about shame, but she hasn't yet written about how we face the shame of whiteness. Basically, there are two types of shame. There is a good kind of shame, which I tend to think of as a healthy emotional reaction to learning about atrocities. If you learn about genocide, slavery, lynching, and police brutality, and you learn that the country you live in is founded on those practices, then feeling shame is an appropriate emotional response. However, if that "good shame" doesn't get metabolized—processed—in some way, then it can become toxic shame. And toxic shame leads to all kinds of weird, awful behavior by nice white ladies, not least of which is white fragility. So, how does one metabolize that kind of shame?

It took a long time, but I eventually realized that it was shame I felt when I couldn't stand to see my own reflection. After years of studying gender and plenty of therapy, I had figured out that part of the aversion I felt to seeing my own image was that I didn't have a thin "ballet body." The tyranny of thinness again. But, if I knew that, if I knew that my worth wasn't tied to my appearance, why did it still sting? More than just my disappointment at being a size 18 rather than a size 2, what was painful for me to realize was that the size and shape of my body were a perennial disappointment to my mother,

Shirley. I can still hear Shirley saying to my Big Granny about me, "We'd so hoped she'd be petite." For me, the thought of going to a Pure Barre class is a nightmare of potential humiliation. Even so, I understand why it might be seductive for someone, gendered femme, for whom having a ballet body is within reach. But it wasn't only the tyranny of thinness that made me hate seeing a picture of myself.

I wanted more, demanded more, from my therapist than this rather ordinary gender analysis of my self-loathing. I suspected it had something to do with my whiteness, and maybe with my relationships. So, I sent my therapist the Stovall article and insisted we work on it together. We are still doing this work, and part of what I've discovered about myself is how I allowed myself to settle for white mediocrity in countless ways. For me, this included not expecting much reciprocity in my relationships; I was fine serving, doing for, looking after, but not asking anything for myself. As far as I thought I had traveled from Shirley's example of abject servitude through housewifery, I realized that I had re-created a perfect queer femme/butch lesbian version of her life and marriage in my relationship. It was when I began to ask for more than that, to think I deserved better than the white mediocrity of being a mirror for someone else, that my relationship began to end.

In grappling with my family history of a sadistic grandmother (maternal) and a Klan and pedophile granddaddy (paternal), I've had to come to terms with the guilt and shame of that. The awareness that my ancestors helped to construct white supremacy and worked to keep it in place so that it could benefit me is a bitter reality, and it is no comfort to try to wall off those facts from my consciousness or dismiss them with platitudes about a different era. My feelings, I imagine, are similar to Emily's, who was disturbed to learn that white people, her ancestors, were responsible for slavery and who found comfort in the arms of unapologetic white supremacists. Probably because I had more resources than Emily, like lots of education and radical lesbians who helped me reimagine kinship,

I chose another way. For me, I've found that metabolizing the shame of whiteness is work to be done on your own (in therapy), in workshops and groups with other white people who get this, and in community with other people who are engaged in dismantling the damage white supremacy has done and continues to do. Usually, this is not the kind of thing on offer from the wellness industry or from those advertising "self-care," but maybe it should be. What if self-care for white women looked like processing guilt and learning to metabolize the shame of white supremacy? What if instead of figuring out how to make Moon Juice at home, we tried to create a more equitable social world and become what author Layla Saad calls a "good ancestor"?

Without connection, care, and community, self-care is packaged and sold to us in ways that wall us off from our individual responsibility for the damage that racist systems cause. Without engagement in real, political efforts to change the status quo, the ideology of self-care amounts to a reinvestment in the narcissistic self and in neoliberal capitalism. Wellness without a radical, collective politics doesn't offer resistance to regimes of power but rather a way to remain in them. The shallow promise of the wellness industry, from Goop to clean eating to Pure Barre to #radicalselfcare influencers, is that it tries to sell us tinctures, potions, and vaginal steams to help us accept the lonely mediocrity of being a nice white lady.

# 4

# LOVE AND THEFT

"That's not my baby!" is, according to family lore, the first thing Shirley said when she saw me after I was born. In the days when women went to sleep to be delivered of a child and then a nurse brought the child to the mother later, Shirley had been expecting to see my father's dark-haired, high-cheek-boned, and faux-Indian good looks reflected in the presentation of a similarly dark-hued child. Shirley's next question, "Where's my little *Indian* baby?" was answered by the nurse handing her the bundle that was me, with my disappointingly pinkish-white skin and strawberry blonde hair.

Every Halloween after that when I had a choice in the matter, I would dress up as some version of "Pocahontas" (Powhatan nation) or "Sacajawea" (Shoshone nation) or the unnamed Cherokee princess I believed myself to be. My mother's assertions about her ancestors being "Scotch-Irish" held no purchase on my imagination, and my fair-skinned and tow-headed complexion could not dissuade me of my right to Indianness. Instead, like so many other white women, I grew up cherishing the somatic evidence of our Indian ancestry in my father's high cheekbones, dark hair, and skin that easily tanned to a medium brown, believing this was sufficient to belong among the Cherokee. Perhaps, too, my Halloween excursions into fantasies of Otherness were a way to become the "Indian baby" my mother had wanted and whose place I had usurped.

When I was ten years old or so, my father, J.T., told me about the Trail of Tears in a way that made me believe that it was us, our family, our ancestors, who were forced off their land in Georgia because of the Indian Removal Act and made to walk to Oklahoma through the long winter of 1838 and 1839. Within the family possessions there was an old cigar box that held a pair of beaded moccasins, with the soles missing, walked out, probably, on the Trail of Tears. When J.T.'s grandfather and grandmother married in 1889, the location listed on the marriage certificate read simply "Indian Territory," and that seemed proof enough of their Indianness, somewhere. Never mind that this was the same grandfather who, a short two weeks after he married, "made the run" to steal 160 acres in the land rush of 1889, plundered from the Choctaw, Creek, Chickasaw, Seminole, and Cherokee nations by the US government. We ignored the federal government handout that made us settler colonialists and didn't talk about Granddad being in the Klan (or liking little girls). In our retelling, we were "Native Americans," noble, righteous, and above all, *entitled* to lay claim to whatever we wanted in this country. It is a sleight of hand that is common in the United States, and maybe everywhere, that people would rather imagine themselves to be among the casualties of settler colonialism than among the beneficiaries of it.

By the time I applied to college, my anti-government-help father encouraged me to check "Native American" on the questionnaire about my racial identity because he was convinced there was easy money available with that checkmark. Like many teenagers, I had begun to question what my parents told me, and I'd begun to suspect that my Indianness might not be real enough for a scholarship, so I checked the box "White/Caucasian" on the forms. A few years later,

I read Vine Deloria Jr.'s book *Custer Died for Your Sins* and it punctured a hole in the gossamer genealogical fabric I'd inherited. Deloria writes about working at the National Congress of American Indians, during which time white people would come through his office almost every day claiming they had a "Cherokee grandmother." It didn't take me long to recognize myself in those pages, to see that my childhood belief in a Cherokee ancestor made me a cliché, to realize those family moccasins were probably from a dime store. That realization anchored me in whiteness in a way I'd never felt before. What is whiter than claiming a fictive Cherokee grandmother? Not much. Embarrassed at my own foolishness, I let go of this false narrative about my family's heritage that was equal parts love and theft.

Minstrelsy was a popular form of entertainment in the northern United States during the 1830s. This practice of white men darkening their faces with makeup, donning costumes, and performing for largely white, male, working-class audiences contained a tension between envy and repulsion, identification with and fear of the Other. In his classic investigation into the cultural meanings of this practice, *Love and Theft*, American cultural historian Eric Lott writes about these opposing feelings at the heart of minstrelsy. According to Lott, the minstrel show continually transgressed the color line through white men's mocking portrayal of Black men. At the same time, it enabled the formation of a self-consciously *white* working class who was the intended audience for these performances. White performers and audiences were also fascinated by and afraid of Black male sexuality, and that, too, was woven into these elaborate homoerotic dances. Although the nuances of minstrelsy may seem archaic to the current-day reader, once aware of it, it seems there are traces of it everywhere in contemporary popular culture. In a 2017 book, *Black Mirror*, Lott extends and expands his argument to include white women such as Grace Halsell and Joni Mitchell.

Grace Halsell published a 1969 book, *Soul Sister*, based on her experiences passing as a Black woman in Mississippi and Harlem.

The book sold over a million copies in paperback and the dust jacket included a blurb from President Lyndon Johnson. Halsell had been inspired by John Howard Griffin, who, a decade earlier, had written *Black Like Me* about his experience as a white man passing as a Black man in the Jim Crow South. Halsell used medication intended to treat vitiligo to help darken her complexion and tied her hair in a headscarf to complete her six-month disguise. Halsell was not trying to upend systemic racism as much as she was on a personal journey, as she wrote "to open my mind, my eyes, my pores, to the dilemma of race in America, and share my experiences." Lott is rather generous to both Griffin's and Halsell's efforts, suggesting that they were part of a "liberal civil rights template that captured the imagination" and made possible a "new politics of sympathy" among whites. Black feminist scholar Alisha Gaines is more skeptical. In her 2017 book *Black for a Day: White Fantasies of Race and Empathy*, she critiques the publishing industry that promoted Halsell's writing at a time when Black women, such as Maya Angelou, Toni Cade Bambara, and Michelle Wallace, were fighting to get their words published. Gaines is also critical of Halsell for trying to "appropriate blackness as a representative mouthpiece for Black women . . . although Black women have been articulating their own intersectionality since Sojourner Truth queried, 'Ar'n't I a Woman?'"

Singer-songwriter Joni Mitchell released an album in 1977 called *Don Juan's Reckless Daughter*, which features a photo of her in blackface. This was not a one-off for Mitchell, who did this "on several occasions." In a 2015 interview, she told a reporter of her identification with Black men, "When I see black men sitting, I have a tendency to go—like, I nod like I'm a brother. I really feel an affinity because I have experienced being a black guy on several occasions." That Mitchell has dealt with very little disapprobation for her embrace of blackface compared to Ted Danson, another celebrity who, in 1993, appeared in blackface and experienced widespread condemnation, is perhaps both a measure of Mitchell's pop icon status and a tell about what white women can get away with. As with any cultural practice, blackface has changed with time. Lott observes that today "neo-blackface performance is also around us, usually (but not always) without the blackface." The neo-blackface that Lott identifies has only expanded with the broadened array of forms of cultural appropriation that are popular today.

Scholar Lauren Michele Jackson contends that cultural appropriation "gets a bad rap." In her 2019 book *White Negroes*, Jackson notes that appropriation is "considered one of America's hallmarks." Rap, for instance, borrows from the styles of other musical genres—soul, disco, funk, gospel—and even borrows from the likes of Billy Joel and Paul Simon. Appropriation, she writes, "is everywhere, and it is inevitable." What we must attend to, Jackson says, is power, because it is always at play in appropriation. White people get away with borrowing fashions, musical styles, and language, using "Black aesthetics without Black people." The pull to take on Blackness or Otherness more broadly is driven at least in part by an economy and a culture where everything, including the accoutrements of racial identity, can be bought and sold. Writing about this in 1992, Black feminist bell hooks observed that "the commodification of Otherness has been so successful because it is offered as a new delight, more intense, more satisfying than normal ways of doing and feeling. Within commodity culture, ethnicity becomes spice, seasoning that can liven up the dull dish that is mainstream white culture." What concerns me here are the specific and peculiar ways that white women go about appropriating culture and what this suggests about how uncomfortable we are existing within the subject position "white woman," especially as we move in realms that require multicultural fluency and that demand authenticity or, at least, a convincing performance of it.

## WHITE WOMEN'S FANTASIES OF OTHERNESS

From skin to hair to booty shapes, white women love playing with Blackness. In August 2020, pop singer Adele put her hair in Bantu knots and sported a Jamaican flag bikini top to wish people a good "would be Notting Hill Carnival" after the usual celebrations were canceled due to the pandemic. In 2009, Lady Gaga appeared on the cover of a fashion magazine with an "extreme tan" on her face that prompted many to say it was blackface. This trend is not new. The Victorian bustle dress that was popular from 1870 onward was, according to several scholars, inspired by the shape of Sarah Baartman's body. Baartman, an enslaved African woman with full breasts, a narrow waist, and large buttocks, was put on naked display against her will throughout Europe from 1810 to 1815. What Western Europeans once paid to gawk at, and said they were repulsed by, they later tried to emulate. The Victorian bustle dress became a sign of high fashion and evidence of proper white ladyhood. A similar version of this kind of love and theft continues with the Kardashians.

Since the 2007 debut of their popular reality-based television show *Keeping Up with the Kardashians*, all five of the Kardashian sisters have built lucrative careers by lifting from predominantly Black designers and influencers and making their aesthetics desirable to new markets. The Kardashians' signature look draws on the Black aesthetics of accentuated lips and prominent curves. Several of the Kardashians have admitted to surgical augmentations of their lips and butts. And they often sport traditionally Black hairstyles like box braids, cornrows, and laid edges. At the 2018 MTV Awards, Kim Kardashian appeared with her hair in Fulani braids. Although Kardashian said she was "totally respectful" of "where the hairstyle came from," many people were angry, including one Twitter user who said, "For the thousandth time, what we're mad at is that when Kim [or any white woman, for that matter] wears styles such as these . . . they get praised all the way around for it. But when black women do it . . . we get told that it's unprofessional, or that we look unkept. Or that we're a distraction. Not to mention the fact that they don't even consider giving credit where credit is due. . . . It's honestly a triple slap in the face." The overall Kardashian brand seems to be profiting from trends or looks that Black women have been wearing for decades.

Less well-known social media influencers on Instagram have been "blackfishing," a term coined by cultural critic Wanna Thompson to describe the phenomenon of white women pretending to be Black through a combination of makeup, hairstyle, and fashion. For example, a young woman named Emma Hallberg fills her Instagram account with images of herself with brown skin, thick ebony curls, and full lips. Based on these images, her followers were shocked to learn that she is actually white. Although Hallberg says she never pretended to be Black, many online said she was blackfishing. Of course, these younger Instagram influencers are inspired by the riches that the Kardashians have pulled in through their appropriation of Black aesthetics. Kim and Khloe Kardashian have a reported net worth of $350 million, and Kylie has been named the world's youngest billionaire by *Forbes*. "How popular the Kardashians are speaks volumes and can't be overlooked," says Ericka Hart, a Black Instagram influencer. "They have been able to capitalize off Black bodies, and people will want to emulate that." Scholar Alisa Gaines told a reporter, "They put themselves out there and have all of these followers thinking they're someone that they're not," Gaines said. "It's so deeply rooted in white privilege because they can take up a space that an actual Black woman could have had." In this way, blackfishing is akin to Grace Halsell's performative account of Black womanhood in *Soul Sister*, which took away publishing op-portunities, and dollars, from actual Black women.

Margaret B. Jones wrote *Love and Consequences* in 2008, a memoir published by Riverhead Books about her experience as a half white, half Native American girl growing up in foster care in South Central Los Angeles. There, surrounded by gang violence and street life, she soon turned to dealing drugs for the Bloods. A review in *Entertainment Weekly* called it a "powerful story of resilience and uncondi-tional love," while a reviewer for the *New York Times* said it was a "humane and deeply affecting memoir." Except none of it was true.

Margaret Seltzer, the actual woman behind the pen name Marga-ret Jones, made it all up, including her persona as a half Native drug dealer in a mostly Black neighborhood in LA. When she, as Jones, appeared in a magazine explaining her past, her sister called the publisher and told them it was all a lie. In fact, she'd grown up in Sherman Oaks, the neighborhood in Los Angeles where the Brady Bunch house is located. She lived with her all-white family and graduated from a private Episcopal day school, her sister revealed. Margaret had never been in foster care and never dealt drugs for gang members. The publisher then immediately recalled all nineteen thousand copies of the book and canceled the scheduled book tour.

When confronted with these allegations, Jones/Seltzer admitted that it was all an elaborate prevarication. "For whatever reason, I was really torn and thought it was my opportunity to put a voice to people who people don't listen to," she told a reporter shortly after her charade came to light. "I was in a position where at one point people said you should speak for us because nobody else is going to let us in to talk. Maybe it's an ego thing. . . . I don't know. I just felt that there was good that I could do and there was no other way that someone would listen to it." It's not clear who the "people" are in her plea, perhaps Black people? Or perhaps all the Black/Latinx people of South Central LA? What Jones misunderstands is that "the position" she was in, as a white woman, is what made the "ego thing" possible. Her convoluted attempt to become Jones in order to write and publish *Love and Consequences* ultimately tells a story about the hubris of white women who believe that to do "good" one must "speak for" people because there was "no other way" they would be heard.

At around the same time, police records in Spokane, Washington, reveal that a woman who identified herself as "African American" or "biracial" began to report a series of racially motivated bias crimes, including threatening letters, intimidating calls, and nooses left on her front porch. The woman had graduated with a master's degree from Howard University and taught a course called "The Black Woman's Struggle" at nearby Eastern Washington University. In 2015, the woman, then known as Rachel Doležal, ran for and won the election to become president of the local chapter of the National Association for the Advancement of Colored People (NAACP). There were rumors about her racial identity, though. "It was discussed among close members to me, and we kept it like that," said James Wilburn. It was Wilburn, who is Black, whom the woman defeated in the local NAACP election. Her new role brought increased scrutiny about her history of claims to the police concerning bias crimes. An anonymous source contacted the local television news station KXLY and shared photos of Doležal's biological family, along with their contact information. On Facebook, however, Doležal had posted a photo of an African American man she described as her father. A reporter from KXLY, Jeff Humphrey, set up an on-camera interview with her, ostensibly to ask her about the police reports of the bias incidents. Then, he changed course to ask about the Facebook photo and her family.

"Ma'am, I was wondering if your dad really is an African American man," Humphrey asked.

"I don't understand the question," Doležal responded. "I did tell you [he] is my dad."

"Are your parents white?" he asked. At that, Doležal blinked twice, removed the microphone, and walked away.

Once video of that interview became public, Doležal's racial identity and family history became a messy national story. In the days that followed, the *Washington Post* reached out to her parents, Lawrence and Ruthanne Doležal in Troy, Montana, for comment. Her mother, Ruthanne Doležal, said the family's ancestry is Czech, Swedish, and German with "faint traces" of Native American heritage. Her father, Lawrence Doležal, explained that his daughter's experience at Howard University (a historically Black college) and her involvement in social justice work led her to be "assimilated into [Black] culture so strongly that that's where she transferred her identity." One of the great ironies in this story is that while at Howard, Rachel sued the university for racial discrimination, alleging that the university denied her a teaching assistant job and a scholarship because she was white. The lawsuit also claimed that a professor in the Art Department kept Doležal from serving as a teaching assistant one semester and removed some of her artwork from a student exhibition because of racial prejudice. In *Black Mirror*, Eric Lott explains, "Much has been made of Doležal's having sued Howard while a student there for discriminating against her whiteness, which makes her turn to Black seem all the more opportunistic. To my mind, there is hardly any contradiction here: both moves are underwritten by white privilege, both seek recognition from her chosen people."

The part of the story her biological parents left out of their press interviews is that theirs is a family at war with each other. Ruthanne and Lawrence Doležal, evangelical Christians, adopted four Black children ("to show their commitment to the pro-life cause," according to her brother). These Black children are siblings to Rachel, and according to her, they were all subjected to abuse growing up, accusations that her parents deny. According to Rachel, it was a brutal upbringing that included sadistic and racist violence:

> I grew up in a very religious family that used corporal punishment as a way to keep their kids from going to hell. . . . I got beaten with wooden boards and spoons a lot and had to do manual labor jobs like digging potatoes or pulling thistles and weeds, whereas my siblings, who were darker . . . were beaten with a baboon whip . . . and sometimes [my parents] would call the cops on them to get [my siblings] in trouble if there was a sibling disagreement in the teen years. Another punishment was to be confined to your room for up to 2–3 months . . . with nothing but a mattress and a Bible. You were let out to use the bathroom and eat.

Even though her parents deny this abuse, the repeated telling of this story reveals much about Rachel. Her reference to a "baboon whip" is a tell about her own internalized racism (she used this term more than once). The instrument she is presumably referring to is known as a "sjambok" and was a favorite weapon of the apartheid-era police in South Africa. In one version of this story, Rachel refers to it as a weapon used "in slavery" and, thus, situates her parents as slave-owning oppressors. Parenting like this can inflict deep, lasting psychological damage on a child and may be the quintessence of the "abuse" of raising a child to be white. Eventually, Rachel got away from her parents and, with her first husband, who was Black, fought to adopt two of those siblings away from her parents. Perhaps her decision to pass as Black was another way for her to get away from her abusive white-raised childhood.

Passing as a different race has a long history in the United States. In Bliss Broyard's 2007 memoir *One Drop*, she writes about her father, literary critic Anatole Broyard. Her father was Creole, with skin light enough to pass as white, and he ultimately severed ties with his darker-skinned kinfolk entirely. But this sort of passing doesn't happen in a vacuum. Anatole, who was also an author and for many years the book review editor at the *New York Times*, made the decision to pass as white as a way to navigate and succeed in a society in which white people set the rules. For his daughter, Bliss Broyard, it wasn't his racial ancestry that she found troubling; it was that he lied about it to her and built an elaborate wall of deceit to hide his past that she uncovered only after his death.

In James McBride's acclaimed 1995 memoir *The Color of Water*, he tells of his discovery at age twenty-six of his mother's racial identity and complicated history. Her 2010 obituary in the *New York Times* described her "seemingly serial incarnations" by listing her names. She was Ruchel Zylska (when she was born in a Polish shtetl), Rachel Zylska (when she moved to the United States with her parents), Rachel Shilsky (when she was growing up in Virginia), Ruth Shilsky (when she moved to New York City), Ruth McBride (in Harlem), and, for the last fifty-one years, Ruth McBride Jordan (in Red Hook, Brooklyn, and later Ewing, New Jersey, where she died at age eighty-eight). Ruth McBride Jordan didn't lie about her past, she mostly just didn't want to talk about it. McBride narrates his mother's demeanor:

"Whenever she stepped out of the house with us she went into a sort of mental zone where her attention span went no farther than the five kids trailing her. She had absolutely no interest in a world that seemed incredibly agitated by our presence. The stares and remarks, the glances and cackles that we heard as we walked about the world went right over her head." Ruth McBride Jordan simply left people to presume or guess about her racial identity, and they often decided she was "light skinned," which if pressed on the issue is what she would say. It wasn't until James McBride, the eighth of her twelve children, coaxed her into telling her story that the complex truth emerged. Ruth McBride Jordan told her son James that she "crossed over" into the Black community, much as she had converted to Christianity from Judaism. For her, crossing over meant living in a predominantly Black neighborhood, marrying two Black men, raising Black children, and serving in a Black church. As a child, when James or one of his eleven siblings would ask her if they were Black or white, Ruth would answer, "You're a human being." What color is God was often the follow-up question. Her reply: "God is the color of water." The story McBride tells about his mother is ultimately one of colorblindness, and it proved to be wildly popular with the American reading public, selling more than two million copies and remaining on the *New York Times* best-seller list for more than a hundred weeks.

Conservatives and liberals alike were quick to jump into the discussion of Rachel Doležal's attempt at passing to argue that if race is socially constructed, then she should be able to craft her life in whatever socially constructed box she wanted. Further, people with a rudimentary familiarity with the social sciences noted that "self-identification" is the way researchers from census takers to pollsters have assessed racial identity for several decades now, so who can argue with her selection? This set of reasoning aligns with literary critic Walter Benn Michael's take on social constructionist arguments, which he claims are tacitly biological. In his view, one can't "secretly" be your former race if you're effectively passing as some other race—you're just in your new racial definition of yourself. To suggest otherwise is to imply a "realness" to race that is inherent and biological, in the blood, if you will. So, the reporter, her family, all the people who wanted to "expose" Doležal (or Jones/Seltzer) are playing into a kind of one-drop-rule logic that insists on the biological inherency of race. However, Eric Lott explains it is not so easy to decouple Doležal's attempt at passing from the legacy of blackface minstrelsy. He writes, "In assuming the privilege to speak for and as a Black woman, she is nothing if not, at least in part, white once more."

In several interviews, Doležal used the word *transracial* to describe two different experiences: her siblings' experience of being adopted by white parents (in common usage), and her own shift in racial identity between childhood and adulthood (not commonly used). This prompted another public debate that attempted to equate her conflated use of the term *transracial* with the experience of transgender people. In subsequent interviews, Doležal even compared herself to trans celebrity Caitlyn Jenner. It's difficult to parse how much of the public discussion that ensued was a genuine attempt at understanding and how much of it was a disinformation campaign intended to sow chaos.

The trolls of 4chan saw the argument "if transgender, then transracial" as an opportunity to create confusion and own the libs by starting the hashtag #WrongSkin. One such troll account, @AbuShakur (created June 2015), includes a banner photo of a Black Power fist and a profile picture of white man in a kufi hat, with this description: "Born Tom Briggs (my slave name), I'm now Abu Shakur, one of the leading black voices of our generation. #civilrights #blacklivesmatter #transracial #wrongskin." The pinned tweet on this account features a photo of Martin Luther King Jr. with a caption that reads: "End cis-black privilege. All black affirmative action & black scholarships need to include transracial blacks. Stop the hate!" The tweet above the image reads: "Help us end cis-black privilege. #RachelDolezal #WrongSkin #Transracial." This kind of account is typical of the sort that appeared in 2015, and to be clear, there is no "cis-black privilege" and no one, beyond this troll, is calling for an end to it. As convoluted as it may seem, the ultimate goal of these kinds of accounts is to push narratives that erode the goals of racial justice and civil rights by questioning the very ideas of race, systemic racism, and white privilege. The sleight of hand in the #WrongSkin hashtag is to suggest that there is a straightforward "if this, then that" comparison between "transracial" and "transgender."

The reality is that it's not possible to make a simple, uncomplicated analogy between the two. Scholar Lisa Bow published a peer-reviewed academic article in 2009, long before the #WrongSkin hashtag, about what she calls the "twinning icons of segregation," racially segregated drinking fountains and gender-segregated restrooms, to discuss similarities of racial and gender oppression. She also considers examples that confound these simple comparisons. Bow's argument is, in the plainest terms, that people can "pass" along racial lines (e.g., Anatole Broyard, Ruth McBride Jordan) just as people have "passed" as a different gender (e.g., Billy Tipton; Anne Lister/Gentleman Jack). And people who exist outside binaries of Black/white or male/female are what she calls the "interstitial," those who take up space in between and through their existence remind us that those opposing categories are neither natural nor inevitable. Although there may be some similarities between transracial and transgender as concepts—in segregation of physical space—that doesn't magically do away with the social structure that shapes these identities. Cisgender people (those of us whose gender identity as adults corresponds to the sex we were assigned at birth) dominate the world, just as white people dominate the United States and colonial societies. Simple "if this, then that" analogies are inadequate to the task of understanding what it means to pass in terms of race or transition from one gender to another. Despite some similarities, gender, sexuality, and race are different. A key difference is in the love and theft of minstrelsy.

"There was a moment [when] I thought that she genuinely loves Black people but took it a little too far," writer Ijeoma Oluo said about Rachel Doležal after she interviewed her in 2017. Doležal had just published her book *In Full Color*, and she agreed to the interview in order to promote the book, but she endures Oluo's presence with barely hidden contempt. Oluo searches for an opening to ask her how her racial fluidity is anything more than a function of her privilege as a white person. When she poses the question, Doležal becomes even more irritated with her and suggests that Black people who are critical of her haven't read enough of the right kinds of books to understand how race is socially constructed. Oluo describes her experience of the interview this way: "Throughout our conversation, I get the increasing impression that, for someone who claims to love blackness, Rachel Doležal has little more than contempt for many Black people and their own Black identities."

By the time there is a Netflix documentary about Rachel Doležal, she has taken the West African name Nkechi Amare Diallo. Yet, the film, *The Rachel Divide* directed by Laura Brownson, which opened in April 2018 at the Tribeca Film Festival in New York City, uses her previous name. Cultural critic Doreen St. Felix writing in *The New Yorker* called the film "the cumulative biography of a lie." The documentary chronicles the damage this lie has done in her community, including footage of LaToya Brackett and Kitara Johnson, former associates of Doležal/Diallo's at the NAACP, who make it plain how much her stunt has set back their efforts for racial justice in Spokane.

The film also includes archival footage of a Black Lives Matter rally in which she makes her two sons lie in police chalk outlines, a scene eerily reminiscent of a viral photo of a weeping Black child, Devonte Hart, being forced into an embrace with a police officer by his white mother. The filmmaker gives one of her sons, Franklin, room to breathe in the film. Through his eyes, the viewer becomes aware of Rachel/Nkechi's painful destructiveness as a white mother of Black sons, especially as the film circles back to her ongoing charges of bias crimes. When she posts a picture on Instagram of a banana on the hood of her car as evidence of harassment, her son

Franklin wonders aloud if all the incidents are made up. "Why don't you just let it go away?" he asks. By the end of the film, it's clear that there is some deep, unmet need driving Doležal/Diallo, but we still don't know why her pain has presented itself in this racialized way and she does not have the capacity nor the insight to articulate those reasons for herself or for the film.

As I followed her story, I wondered if the phenomenon of Doležal/Diallo was sui generis, a white woman with a one-of-a-kind backstory who happened to emerge near the end of the second term of the first Black president of the United States, when a survey found that half of all Americans believed we were living in a "postracial" America. Perhaps there was something about this one woman's desire for racial fluidity that spoke to something we, or at least half of us, wanted to believe to be true about our world. And then, Jessica Krug happened.

In September 2020, a blog post written by Jessica Krug, then a professor of African and African American studies at Georgetown University, appeared online and quickly drew national attention. In it, she revealed that her life was "rooted in the toxic napalm of lies," and went on to explain, "I have built my life on a violent anti-Black lie, and I have lied in every breath I have taken." Krug revealed that she was raised white in a suburb of Kansas City by Jewish parents, yet spent most of her adult life pretending to be Afro-Latina with an array of fictitious origins: North African, African American, and "Caribbean rooted Bronx Blackness." There was also a more activist persona she created, Jess La Bombalera, with vaguely Puerto Rican and East Harlem roots who, in a recorded video, excoriated the people responsible for gentrifying East Harlem, including Melissa Mark-Viverito, a Puerto Rican woman and former speaker of the city council. In the essay, Krug makes clear that her deception was "the very epitome of violence, of thievery and appropriation." In both tone and language, her essay reads less like an apology and more like a suicide note. In a way, it is a kind of career-suicide note. At one point she writes, "I can't fix this." She mentions "trauma" and "mental health demons." Toward the end of the essay, she says, "I have not lived a double life. There is no parallel form of my adulthood connected to white people or a white community or an alternative white identity. I have lived this lie, fully, completely, with no exit plan or strategy." Six days after she published that essay, Krug was forced to resign from her tenured position at George Washington University.

In the days between when her essay appeared and her resignation, what unfolded fit the pattern of what happened five years earlier with Rachel Doležal. The internet erupted with hot takes like "Doležal 2.0" and "Rachel Doležal had a sister?" Reporters looked for family members to comment (Krug's parents are deceased) and found a sister-in-law, who asked not to be identified by name and who said that Krug and her brother had been estranged for twenty years, but added she is as "white as Snow White." One news site featured an interactive graphic in the middle of their story about Krug, a metered poll that posed the question: "Do you believe race is a social construct?" with two possible answers: "Yes, all humans are one race," and "No, biological differences are real." Lessons learned from Doležal 1.0, distilled into an infographic for the 2.0 version.

As details of her life emerged, it became clear that Krug moved up throughout her academic career by taking advantage of programs designed specifically for Black and Latinx scholars, from the prestigious Ronald McNair Scholars Program (for undergraduates) to the Fellows Program at the Schomburg Center for Research in Black Culture in Harlem (for those with a PhD). Anthropologist Yarimar Bonilla, who was a fellow at the Schomburg at the same time as Krug, described her behavior in a series of tweets: "She always dressed/acted inappropriately—she'd show up to a 10am scholars' seminar dressed for a salsa club." Bonilla said her affect was "strident" and "woker-than-thou." Many people, including a man Krug met for a Tinder date, said that she frequently chastised Black and Latinx people for not being radical enough in their politics. In a way, Krug confessed this, too, when she wrote, "I gaslit you." Bonilla named Krug's game when she said she "cringed at her minstrel show."

Opinion pieces flowed from every outlet. Evette Dionne, writing at BitchMedia, observed, "Everything about Krug's behavior—from her defensiveness and the calculated theft of opportunities from actual Black scholars to her inherent feeling of superiority—screams of whiteness." Lauren Michele Jackson writing about the Krug debacle in *The New Yorker* turned the gaze back onto all the "white supremacy . . . inside the university," and how those with the lightest skin are the ones who are "promoted, professionally and ideologically, within the field" of African and African American studies. Jackson pointed out that, in an early version of a story about Krug, the *New York Times* described her accent in the "Jess La Bombalera" video as a "Latina accent," when in fact, it is a cringe-worthy mashup of several accents. And this suggests how white women like Krug get by with a con like this, because of us, white people in the academy who "failed to recognize the gap not between real and faux, so much, as between something thrown-on and something lived-in. That inattentiveness was Krug's escape hatch."

Sociologist Robyn Autry was among the very few who considered how whiteness and gender shaped all these women's lives. Autry urged readers to consider "what it is about white femininity that keeps producing this phenomenon." And, indeed, there is something here. Autry speculates that perhaps it is "a twisted attempt to be seen and heard." Certainly, the desire of white women to be seen and heard and to take up space is part of these acts. Yet, when it comes to the fantasies of Jones/Seltzer, Doležal/Diallo, and Krug, these are gendered and racialized performances that appear very closely tied to a disturbed sense of self.

I suspect there is something deeper and more pathological underneath these individual white women's fantasies and with the wider swath of white feminine performances of Otherness from blackfishing to more elaborate con jobs. Psychotherapist Natasha Stovall reminds us that "whiteness appears in no therapy manuals," yet when we unpack some of white women's behavior, it looks a lot like psychopathology.

That question doctors ask when evaluating someone for psych hospital-ization, "Are you a danger to yourself or others?" is one we need to ask white people. Stovall writes, "We are a danger to ourselves and others, from the defensive neurosis of white fragility to the paranoid brutality of mass incarceration and Jim Crow, down the psychotic-sadistic rabbit hole of chattel slavery, through the looking glass to the stone cold de-lusion of racial superiority itself." In a 2009 peer-reviewed article called "Whiteness as Pathological Narcissism," psychologists Arianne Miller and Lawrence Josephs write that there is a "vulnerability to states of narcissistic decompensation characterized by white shame and rage." I wonder how much of what we have seen play out with these women's fantasies of Otherness is a response to, or a narcissistic defense against, feelings of shame and rage at their own whiteness.

Of course, I'm fully aware of how psychology has been used as a weapon against women who step out of line from the patriarchy (and I've had my own experience with this), but I want to suggest that for some of us it can become so painful to exist as "white women" that we begin to look for escape routes. Sometimes, we think that our escape is bound up with saving other people who we believe are suffering just a few neighborhoods over from us. Or we imagine a path out of a household where our white parents thought love was the crack of a sjambok. And sometimes, once you begin to see how white supremacy operates, and you see that your white woman body is in-tegral to its smooth, destructive functioning, you would just prefer to exist some other way, be some other category of human being, rather than "white" and "woman."

Once you are "woke" to white-supremacist culture, being a white woman is a difficult subject position to maintain, because how are you going to love yourself once you acknowledge that you are part of the system of white supremacy? And maybe you can't figure that out, and because all of it is so painful, you think, well, maybe a little bor-rowing will be alright. Maybe if I put on this wig, or put my hair in box braids, or wear African prints, then I will get a little relief from this pain. And then that borrowing slides into thievery and into a whole Ponzi scheme of stolen Otherness that you tell yourself is fine as long as you just keep it moving. Then one day everybody wants to see all your receipts and you are caught short, so you write a long blog post and resign your tenured job that you always knew wouldn't be a forever thing.

For women who experience whiteness as a kind of emptiness, they may see taking on another racial identity as a form of self-care. Even though this performance harms the very communities they want to join and the very people they say they love. It is possible to move and live in another racial community, as Ruth McBride Jordan did. However, lying to and gaslighting people about one's racial community of origin undermines trust and lacks integrity, and in the end the act is unsustainable.

This particular moment in the first part of the twenty-first century is an especially challenging one in which to slide over into another racial community without anyone noticing or asking questions about your previous life. As media studies scholar Lisa Nakamura has so deftly explained, we live in a visual digital culture governed by a "racio-visual logic." Today, we fully expect to see photos, including childhood photos, of people and to discern something about race in those images. If someone were, in this racio-visual culture, to attempt to launch a career as a public figure, say, as an author or local NAACP lead or academic, and believe that they would not be asked to reveal childhood photos somewhere along the way suggests a sort of misunderstanding of current social norms, and perhaps even a kind of grandiosity or a sense that those social norms don't apply to them. Whiteness and narcissism both involve using fantasy to distort reality in order to maintain a sense of superiority and to stave off deep feelings of shame and inadequacy.

People with extreme narcissism (we all have some) hold distorted perceptions of the world and themselves. This is part of why narcissists tend to ignore facts, gaslight those around them, lie, and rationalize their behaviors in ways that can seem outlandish to others. The fact that Margaret Jones/Seltzer, or Rachel Doležal/Diallo, or Jessica Krug believed that they could slip easily into prominent roles speaking for and through Blackness and not have their past revealed speaks to the extreme narcissism of whiteness. And the fact that each of them in their own way believed they were "helping" by "doing good" speaks to the destructiveness of being a white woman with fantasies of Blackness.

## "WHO CLAIMS *YOU*?"

For many white Americans, there is something appealing about being a "little bit Cherokee," as there was for me growing up. Some observers call it the "Cherokee syndrome." In the 2010 census, more than 819,000 Americans self-identified as Cherokee—but the combined population of the three federally recognized Cherokee tribes (the Cherokee Nation and United Keetoowah Band of Cherokee in Oklahoma, and the Eastern Band of Cherokee in North Carolina) includes fewer than 400,000 people. Even Ruthanne Doležal claims to have "faint traces" of Native American ancestry, an assertion that went mostly uninterrogated in the furor about her daughter. White women like Andrea Smith and Elizabeth Warren have experienced vociferous pushback for their claims to Cherokee ancestry, but rather than seeing these claims as individual outliers, it may be the quintessential white American move.

In the summer of 2015, someone started an anonymous Tumblr called "Andrea Smith is not Cherokee." Smith is a professor in the Department of Ethnic Studies at University of California, Riverside, who has for many years built a career as a "Native woman," researching, writing, and publishing work about violence against women of color. She is a cofounder of INCITE! Women of Color Against Violence and has been involved with the Chicago chapter of Women of All Red Nations (WARN). And, when she was denied tenure by the University of Michigan in 2008, students and faculty rallied around her, suggesting this was a case of discrimination based on her Native identity. Smith has specifically claimed Cherokee ancestry, and on two occasions hired David Cornsilk, an expert who runs Cherokee Genealogy Services, to help her prove her claims. In an interview, Cornsilk told a reporter about his findings: "Her ancestry through her mother was first and showed no connection to the Cherokee tribe. Her second effort came in 1998 or around then with 'new claims' on her father's lineage, which also did not pan out." Cornsilk went on to say that Smith told him "her employment depended on finding proof of Indian heritage." In July 2015, several Indigenous women scholars published an open letter calling on Smith to stop claiming Cherokee ancestry. In the letter, they noted that even though Smith had promised to no longer identify as Cherokee, "yet in her subsequent appearances and publications she continues to assert herself as a non-specific 'Native woman' or a 'woman of color' scholar to anti-racist activist communities in ways that we believe have destructive intellectual and political consequences."

In response, Andrea Smith closed all of her social media accounts and issued a public statement reasserting her claim, saying her enrollment status (in the Cherokee Nation) "does not impact my Cherokee identity." Enrollment status refers to a person who has an enrolled lineal ancestor listed on the Dawes Rolls. The Dawes Rolls, also referred to as the Final Rolls of Citizens and Freedmen of the Five Civilized Tribes (Cherokee, Chickasaw, Choctaw, Creek, and Seminole), were created by the United States Dawes Commission. The Dawes Commission was authorized by Congress in 1893 to execute the General Allotment Act of 1887. The rolls were used to assign allotments of land to people in the Five Tribes and to provide an equitable division of all monies obtained from sales of other lands. As historian Angie Debo recounts in her classic 1940 text *And Still the Waters Run: The Betrayal of the Five Civilized Tribes*, when word spread that people could get land by getting on the Dawes Rolls, people showed up in droves claiming to be Native, and most claimed to be Cherokee.

Debo writes about the family myths that proliferated after this about being "rejected from the rolls" for a spurious reason or "refusing to enroll" on principle (this was a story my father told me about why we weren't on the Dawes Rolls), when in fact, the reason they were not enrolled was simply that they were not Native American. As an expert in ethnic studies, Andrea Smith must surely be aware of this controversy, so to dismiss enrollment as a trivial concern when it comes to her Cherokee ancestry seems disingenuous at the very least.

About people she calls "pretendians," Jacqueline Keeler (Dakota) says, "I realize now how much being American Indian or Native American is a brand or a desirable commodity to the millions who want to be us." Keeler, a writer and the editor of *Pollen Nation*, a Native-led magazine, says this does real damage because "these people are centering themselves in our issues, they are heading Native American departments, they are telling Native students what they can and can't study—it's to protect their own position. And so it does change our ability to advocate for ourselves when we are constantly being replaced by frauds, white people, or other people of different backgrounds pretending to be us." Making sense of this desire among white people to claim Native American ancestry is crucial for understanding white supremacy.

The urtext for the American mix of white supremacy and Native American commodification may well be Asa Carter. In the 1950s, Carter was a member of the Ku Klux Klan and a fervent supporter of segregationist George Wallace, then governor of Alabama. Asa Carter occasionally worked as a speechwriter for Wallace and penned the infamous "Segregation Now, Segregation Tomorrow, and Segregation Forever" speech that Wallace delivered in defense of racial segregation. He became disillusioned with Wallace once the governor turned away from his more ardent segregationist supporters and tried to strike a more centrist tone.

Carter left Alabama, moved to Texas, and reinvented himself as a novelist. Originally, he took the nom de plume "Bedford Forrest

Carter," a direct homage to KKK founder Nathan Bedford Forrest. Then he dropped "Bedford" and as Forrest Carter wrote a novel called *Gone to Texas*, which later became the film *The Outlaw Josie Wales*, starring Clint Eastwood. The plot of the novel and film is a Confederate revenge fantasy.

Forrest Carter's second book was *The Education of Little Tree*. It was published in 1976 as a memoir about his upbringing by his Native American grandparents. Except none of it was true. Carter's memoir has been exposed as a lie over and over again, but it still makes recommended reading lists from time to time (including Oprah's). Part of why the fraud of *Little Tree* persists is because Carter struck a nerve among white readers. In 1997, Paramount even made the book into a film. As ethnic studies scholar Shari Huhndorf explains the narrative: "In the film version, Granpa—still the repository of Indian knowledge—is now racially white. Early on, he explains: 'I was born white . . . but when I met your Granma . . . we was married, and I begun to see the world through Cherokee eyes.' He becomes, in the words of another character, a 'white Injun.'" In her 2001 book *Going Native*, Huhndorf names the resonance between this notion of Indian knowledge without actual Indigenous people and current New Age practices so popular with white people. In *The Education of Little Tree*, Granpa sets out for the woods with Willow John, the Native character who was "the magic," so that he can learn "all there was to know about being an Indian." As Huhndorf puts it, "Countless New Agers [have] followed Little Tree's path by journeying into the woods in search of Native wisdom." Like Gwyneth Paltrow selling "earthing" to the subscribers of Goop, Indianness has been transformed in American popular culture into an abstraction, into pure knowledge, an essence divested of the histories and the presence of Native people and for sale to white women.

In 2016, when Senator Elizabeth Warren was goaded into taking a DNA test to prove her claims of Native American ancestry, she unwittingly endorsed a way of thinking about race, DNA, and ancestry that reinforces white supremacy. The notion that an individual can discover their tribal affiliation through a DNA test reinforces the white-supremacist notion of "race" as a biological trait tied to a specific gene, discoverable from a cheek swab of saliva. It's the same idea at the core of the Ancestry.com advertisements on television that encourage people to "discover the heroes in your family." This simplistic view of how genetic markers work strengthens retrograde notions about "blood quantum" and race.

"Because we are all genetically related, there are no tribe-specific markers, i.e., no Cherokee, Pequot, or Lakota markers," writes Kim TallBear, a professor of Native studies at the University of Alberta. Her research has established that there are no genetic markers of Native ancestry. In her book *Native American DNA: Tribal Belonging and the False Sense of Genetic Science*, TallBear observes that tribal membership is a legal category, not a genetic one. She points out that it is impossible to disentangle individual genetic information from the constellations of family relations, reservation histories, tribal rules, and government regulations in which genes are formed. Warren likely grew up hearing stories about her Native American ancestors, like I did. White parents who tell their children about a connection to a mythic Native American past, like my parents did, are perhaps unconsciously using it to lay claim to territory and to a sense of belonging. It is a way of asserting: we are the true First Peoples. And a fictive Native American past is a comforting way of sidestepping the disturbing reality of a white settler colonial ancestry that continues to pay benefits in the present.

Material benefits are part of the allure. The ability to assert a Native American identity on official forms can result in access to additional resources. For instance, in the late nineties, a company owned by the brother-in-law of Kevin McCarthy (R-Calif.) won more than $7.6 million in no-bid contracts at US military installations in California based on a flimsy claim of Native American identity. At

Harvard Law School, Warren was celebrated as the first minority woman to receive tenure. This was based on her own claims of Native American identity on employment forms, although she and Harvard Law have denied that her assertion of Native identity had anything to do with her promotion. Then there are the more intangible benefits to claiming Cherokee identity.

"I believe that there is a retreat from white guilt that is happening here," writes anthropologist Circe Sturm in her book *Becoming Indian: The Struggle over Cherokee Identity.* "Whiteness is responsible for indigenous dispossession and the lack of societal connection that characterizes modernity," she said in an interview. Sturm calls people who claim Cherokee identity without any evidence or prior tribal affiliation "race shifters," people who are seeking connection to an identity outside whiteness. Sturm found that these people associated whiteness with emptiness, a lack of spirituality and connection, while they associated Indianness with spirituality, community, and wholeness. According to Sturm, "Whiteness itself is the malady, Indianness the cure." Claiming an Indigenous identity, however flimsy the evidence, relieves some of the discomfort of being a white settler. But simply claiming an identity doesn't automatically shift your identity, nor does it make you part of a community. "It's not about what identity you claim," says Kim TallBear, "it's about who claims *you.*"

## NICE WHITE LADIES AS MONSTERS

It is becoming increasingly uncomfortable to be a white woman in the United States, and perhaps rightly so. Stand-up comedian Bill Burr, in the opening monologue for an episode of *Saturday Night Live* in October 2020, included a funny riff about how white women "swung their Gucci-booted feet over the fence of oppression and stuck themselves at the front of the line" of what he called "the woke movement." He continued, "I've never heard so much complaining in my life, with my SUV and my heated seats. You have no idea what it's like to be me!" He called out white women who have stood by "us toxic white males through centuries of our crimes against humanity. You rolled around in the blood money. And occasionally, when you wanted to sneak off and have sex with a Black dude, and you got caught, you would say it wasn't consensual. Yeah, that's what you did! So why don't you shut up, sit down next to me, and take your talkin-to." Predictably, perhaps, white women took to Twitter to excoriate Burr, and in many ways they proved his point about the fragility of nice white ladies. I chuckled at Burr's monologue at first, until he got to the part about "shut up, sit down next to me." I am still enough of a feminist to want to give a big middle finger salute to a white guy telling me to sit down and shut up, but then it occurred to me that this is the conundrum that white women face when a critique of our racism gets mixed with old-fashioned misogyny. It can be hard to know how to respond.

In a reversal of the common displays of blackface at Halloween, 2020 marked the first year that "Karen" masks appeared for sale. Jason Adcock, a Los Angeles–based artist, sells his Karen Halloween masks on Etsy. "I was starting on this year's Halloween projects and kept seeing 'Karens' pop up in my news feed and thought, 'Damn this is the real monster of 2020,'" Adcock, who is white, said. Adcock makes two versions of the Karen mask. One, with the face twisted into an angry expression, complete with bulging red eyes and a blonde wig cut in a bob. The second mask is similar but is covered in warts and looks sick. The artist calls this one KAREN-19, a reference to the white women who have been captured on video in anti-mask rants during the COVID-19 pandemic. The emergence of Karen masks signals a moment in the culture when nice white ladies have become monsters, at least as white, cisgender, straight men would have it.

The usual monsters in American culture have been the Dark Other, typically Black men, and sometimes other men of color. There are many examples in the popular culture landscape, but perhaps the most obvious one exists in the King Kong movies. Versions of this film have been made in 1933, 1976, 1986, 2005, and 2017, so there is something about this story that resonates with audiences. There are differences among the films, but the main storyline remains the same. The story is set on the fictional Skull Island, located off Sumatra in the Indian Ocean—although its inhabitants are generally coded as African, they are sometimes Asian. King Kong himself is the dark, mysterious Other—a brutal, vicious beast who destroys all in his path and who is chiefly a threat to a nice blonde lady. The King Kong franchise is in the business of selling a story about the monstrous, brutish male sexuality of Black men. This is a story that has real-world consequences for actual Black human beings, including boys like Tamir Rice, Trayvon Martin, and Michael Brown.

When Darren Wilson testified about killing Michael Brown in Ferguson, Missouri, in August 2014, he described the eighteen-year-old as a "demon," a literal monster with terrible resilience and incredible strength. "When I grabbed him the only way I can describe it is I felt like a 5-year-old holding onto Hulk Hogan," said the six-foot-four, 210-pound Wilson of the six-foot-five, 290-pound Brown. "Hulk Hogan, that's how big he felt and how small I felt just from grasping his arm." It is men like Darren Wilson who seem to have the power to decide who the monsters are among us. White women have stood alongside white men to call Black men monsters, and now the ground is shifting beneath us and we are joining the ranks of the monstrous. In cultural studies, there is a school of thought known as "monster theory," and it can be useful for understanding this turn.

Monster theory takes seriously all the monsters in literature and films and tries to understand what they tell us about ourselves. Part of what makes monsters scary is that they don't fit into one category; a vampire, for example, is neither living nor dead. Monsters exist on the fringes of society and they make us uncomfortable. Often, monsters represent borders—between one state of being and another. And monsters often signal some kind of change, a being on the cusp of becoming something else. Now that we, white women, have become monsters, perhaps this is the moment we can begin to transform into something else, find a new way of being in the world that doesn't rely on the destruction of others. In this moment when those who hold the most power in society would create us as monsters along with all Others, perhaps we can reject the false promise of nice white lady-hood and embrace being fully human, along with everybody else.

## CONCLUSION

When we consider why white women love and steal Otherness, we see a desire for attention, a self-interested opportunism, and a perverse kind of entitlement to be heard. We see this on a smaller scale with cultural appropriation, but more bewildering are the heists of Jones/Seltzer, Doležal/Diallo, and Krug's impersonations. These all-in performances of racial Otherness suggest a psychological delusion that may warrant clinical diagnosis. They certainly animate the discussions of the overlap between whiteness and narcissism. What fascinates me about these cases, if we can call them cases of psychopathology, is what they suggest about how unbearable it is for some of us to be white women. It is not coincidental that these cases emerged in social contexts that value, even demand, what now gets called cultural competency, or a knowledge of other experiences beyond whiteness. More than that, the milieus from which Jones/Seltzer, Doležal/Diallo, and Krug emerged—publishing, social activism, academia—require not only authenticity but also a match between identity and authority. In a changing world where whiteness no longer automatically means authority to speak, especially in fields that are figuring out how to value diverse voices, whiteness can feel like a liability.

When I was in graduate school in the late 1980s and early 1990s, I was fascinated by the early Women's Club movement among African American women. Partly, my interest in Ida B. Wells-Barnett led me there, and then I discovered a series of conferences that W. E. B. Du Bois hosted at Atlanta Clark University, which many of the women in this movement, such as Mary Church Terrell, attended. I spent some time going through historical archives and was seriously considering this as my dissertation topic. I hesitated, though, because I worried that I, a white woman, would have a hard time explaining my interest in the National Association of Colored Women's Clubs (NACW), as it was known. In hindsight, I realize I needn't have worried because lots of white people do work in African American studies and build robust careers in the field. However, instead of offering that sort of advice to me, a white woman professor of mine at the time (since retired) gave me some very different guidance. She suggested that if I wanted to pursue this line of research, perhaps I should grow my hair out very long and claim Native American ancestry. "It will be easier for you in the academy," she counseled. I declined her suggestion, but clearly not everyone does. Since the revelation about Jessica Krug, another woman from the same graduate program in history at University of Wisconsin–Madison has had to adjust her claims about her racial identity to clearly indicate she is white.

What fascinates me about white women's love and theft of Other racial identities is that these are happening, in historical terms, at roughly the same time that there is this increased focus on Karens, when the culture is turning on white women as monsters. It makes me reflect on my father's disavowal of his (our) own monstrous past as settler colonialists by creating and clutching to his belief in a Native American past. So convinced was he of his Cherokee past that, in the last few years of his life, he made the trip each summer to attend the Red Earth Festival in Oklahoma. And I think of my mother's horror at the monstrous white baby (me) who had emerged from her, whom she didn't want. Perhaps she was reminded of her own white monstrosity, or of her mother's, when what she wanted to see was her "Indian baby" and my father's (supposed) Cherokee Otherness.

# 5

# PROTECTING
# WHITE FAMILIES

In late June 2020 peaceful protesters carrying "Black Lives Matter" signs walked into the Central West End neighborhood in St. Louis on the way to a protest at the mayor's house. They were protesting the mayor, Lyda Krewson, because she had retaliated against those demanding the city defund the police by reading their names and addresses on Facebook Live. As the protesters made their way to Mayor Krewson's house they walked by another home, referred to by *St. Louis Magazine* as a "restored Midwestern palazzo." Standing in front of the palazzo were the owners, Patricia ("Patty") McCloskey and her husband, Mark, both with firearms. Mark held an AR-15, while Patty gripped a small silver handgun, her finger on the trigger, the safety in the off position. At various times, the McCloskeys, both personal injury lawyers with an adult daughter, pointed their guns at the people walking past their palazzo. Although some found their actions extreme, even laughable, the McCloskeys got support from the White House, where the Tweeter-in-Chief wrote: "God Bless the couple in St. Louis who stood their ground and defended their property. God Bless the Second Amendment." The McCloskeys were charged with two counts of unlawful use of a weapon (they pleaded not guilty), but felony charges did not prevent them from being featured speakers at the 2020 Republican National Convention.

Our first reaction may be to recoil or mock the image of Patty McCloskey in her capri pants holding a pistol, standing next to her AR-15-toting husband, but if we look more closely, we can see that she is in many ways the apogee of nice white ladyhood. McCloskey is a well-educated (summa cum laude graduate of Pennsylvania State University and SMU Law School), professionally employed (practicing attorney), upper-middle-class, heterosexually married wife and mother who, on that day in June, was using a weapon to protect her white-owned property and her white family. The protection of the two, property and family, are thoroughly intertwined for white women. Property is central to white wealth in the United States, and families are the conduit through which whiteness and white wealth flows. Like Patty McCloskey, it is white women's alliance with white men that anchors their position at the center of creating, maintaining, and reproducing whiteness and white families, and solidifying white wealth. Long before they stood armed in front of their palazzo, I'm sure the McCloskeys had a lovely wedding.

## "FAIRY TALE WEDDINGS" AND CREATING ALL-WHITE FAMILIES

On a late July morning a few months after my own wedding in 1981, I got up early to watch what was called the "ultimate fairy tale wedding" of Lady Diana Spencer to Prince Charles of England. Perhaps I identified with Diana, just a few months older than me, marrying a man who did not love her for reasons she didn't fully understand. Perhaps I was taken in by the hype for the royal wedding, which even in the small East Texas town where I lived, was hard to escape. Whatever the reason, I turned on my little color television set at five a.m. and watched along with 750 million other people around the world as Jane Pauley and Tom Brokaw narrated the entire wedding, from the horse-drawn carriage ride to the kiss on the balcony. At the time I wasn't aware of the mark that event would leave on Western culture, but later I would recognize that there was something in the elaborate, transnational spectacle of the royal wedding that was telling a story about whiteness.

As scholar Elizabeth Freeman puts it, the "mass witness to the royal nuptials . . . reanimated the white wedding as a technology for remaking Anglo-Saxon Protestant whiteness into a benign form of cultural specificity." In other words, by all of us watching the royal wedding and buying into the "ultimate fairy tale," we helped to reinforce their whiteness and their heterosexuality as taken for granted, as natural, as not worth commenting on, when it is, in fact, a quite specific identity that merits scrutiny, critique, and analysis. The royal wedding was an event that helped remake a particular kind of whiteness—Anglo-Saxon, Protestant, upper-class—into an ideal. Diana went on to fulfill her role, delivering an "heir and a spare," and, in turn, became a catalyst in transforming white motherhood globally. As it turned out, I wasn't very good at fulfilling the role of wife or mother. When I came out as queer about a decade later, it was at a time and place when that meant stepping outside the nuclear family and any expectations of re-creating that. But I'm getting ahead of myself.

When I married the first time at nineteen years old, like most girl children raised in this culture, I was susceptible to what scholar Chrys Ingraham calls the "wedding-ideological-complex" promulgated by bridal magazines. By now, most of the bridal magazines I grew up with have shuttered their print versions, but new ones emerged to take their place, like *Martha Stewart Weddings*, and traditional lifestyle magazines such as *Harper's Bazaar*, *Town and Country*, and *Vogue* ramped up their bridal features to sell feel-good copy about weddings. Those magazines have been joined by a bevy of wedding-themed television shows: *Say Yes to the Dress, Bridezillas, My Big Redneck Wedding, Platinum Weddings, Rich Bride/Poor Bride*, and the Disney-themed *Fairy Tale Weddings*. Today, these cable television shows exist alongside blogs and websites like The Knot, YouTube channels, Pinterest boards, and Instagram accounts geared toward an audience of mostly young, white, cisgender, straight women.

All the work that goes into producing a wedding suggests a longing not so much for marriage but for public forms of ceremony, pageantry, and celebration. For me, planning the theatricality of a wedding in which I was the bride and therefore the center of attention was a ritual that marked my entrance into adulthood. As is so often the case in weddings like mine, the husband was beside the point; he just had to stand there, hit his mark, and say his lines. I have often wondered how the trajectory of young women's lives might be different if there were some alternate ritual that marked the entrance to adulthood. Staging a play perhaps, a production to plan with costumes, lighting, and sets to arrange, guests to invite, and a party afterward, with dancing, congratulatory speeches, and gifts. Instead, we have the wedding services industry.

A white wedding is usually a reference to the color of the bride's gown, but it has many other meanings. It is a custom that many trace back to Queen Victoria's decision to wear a dress made of white lace at her wedding to Prince Albert in 1840. At a time when clothes laundering technologies were rudimentary and labor intensive, a white dress was an opportunity for conspicuous consumption: an elaborate, expensive dress that could be ruined easily by any sort of spill. Then the white gown became a symbol of innocence and virginal purity, prompting brides and etiquette experts to wrestle with whether it was appropriate for a woman who was not a virgin to wear white; for many decades it was considered a breach of etiquette for the bride to wear white at her second wedding. Although white weddings have been lightly skewered in popular films like *The Hangover, Bridesmaids*, and *Destination Wedding*, the gendered dream of the "perfect day" continues to generate something like $76 billion a year in revenue for the wedding services industry. The average amount spent on a wedding in the United States is around $35,000, with some costing upward of $200,000. In her 2002 book *The Wedding Complex*, Elisabeth Freeman writes that weddings—as performances, fantasies, and rituals of transformation—have the potential to be a way to reimagine, play with, and celebrate forms of social intimacy other than Anglo-Saxon monogamous heterosexuality. But if you put the term *bride* into a search engine, the images that appear are of mostly fair-skinned, thin, and cisgender female bodies in long white gowns.

The whiteness that undergirds the wedding services industry is clear in the continued acceptance of "plantation weddings." Hundreds of former plantations continue to make money as wedding venues that beckon customers with ad copy about "beautiful emerald farmlands" and homes with "Southern charm," but with no mention of the history of forced labor or brutal violence that took place at those sites. In 2019, the advocacy group Color of Change demanded that wedding platforms that host advertisements for plantation venues stop carrying them. Only The Knot and Pinterest responded, but rather than remove the ads, they offered perfunctory declarations about revisions to their policies. The Knot said it would still allow plantations to advertise as wedding venues but promised to "limit the adjectives that can be used to describe a venue." Pinterest said it would "work to deindex plantation content so it doesn't appear in online search results," but plantations remain easy to find on the site. Martha Stewart Weddings and other platforms never even responded to the demand from Color of Change. Although not every bride, and certainly not even most brides, want to host their wedding at a former enslaved labor camp, the fact is that the wedding industry caters to the buying habits of their largest demographic and the one that sees nothing wrong with plantations as wedding venues: white heterosexual women. Catering to that demographic upholds a particular version of whiteness and a tux-and-gown-cake-topper version of relationships.

Weddings have traditionally been a celebration of heterosexuality. But as sociologist Jane Ward points out in her insightful 2020 book

*The Tragedy of Heterosexuality*, the American construction of modern heterosexuality is inseparable from white-supremacist gender norms. Drawing on a variety of evidence from what she calls the "heterosexual repair industry," from early-twentieth-century eugenicists, sexologists, and social reformers writing about marriage to contemporary "seduction classes" geared toward men, Ward makes a convincing case that heterosexuality is a difficult accomplishment, a shaky alliance in need of a propaganda campaign, and a project with white-supremacist goals. Underneath the taken-for-granted notions about "natural" attraction between men and women, Ward exposes the actual antipathy, sexual violence, and visceral repulsion just below the surface of the idea of "normal heterosexuality." It is this antagonism that heterosexual repair experts are employed to ameliorate.

Whiteness is built into the ways heterosexuality is socialized as natural and normal in Western culture. The original self-help books for straight couples, written in the late nineteenth and early twentieth centuries, were written by proponents of the eugenics movement, a faux scientific project meant to encourage reproduction among the white middle class, while discouraging the poor or those of any class who were Black, Indigenous, or immigrants from having children. These early marriage books illustrate Ward's point that defining healthy heterosexual marriage in the United States was also a white-supremacist project designed to help white families flourish and to eliminate others. In the twenty-first century, American and British seduction coaches invite and normalize the fetishization of white women's bodies. They all but promise white women to male trainees, men for whom sexual access to "hot blondes" symbolizes heteromasculine success. Within this constellation of mutually reinforcing whiteness and heterosexuality, the traditional white wedding is the confirmation ceremony that celebrates the triumph of both.

Of course, weddings have changed. Now, you can special order those plastic doll cake toppers with two grooms, two brides, and you can specify any skin tone. When the US Supreme Court extended the right to marry to same-sex couples in 2015, it meant that gay and lesbian couples could have access to a host of civil rights previously reserved for heterosexually married people. Predictably, gay and lesbian unions have been a windfall to the wedding services industry. Between June 2015 and March 2020, same-sex couples spent $3.2 billion on their weddings, but not without controversy. Jack Phillips, a wedding cake baker, objected vociferously to providing his services to same-sex couples on religious grounds and took his grievance to the US Supreme Court. In the 2018 case of *Masterpiece Cakeshop v. Colorado Civil Rights Commission*, the justices ruled that businesses do not have the right to discriminate. But conservatives like Jack Phillips miss a crucial fact about gay and lesbian marriage: it strengthens the traditional nuclear family. As writer Jonathan Rauch has observed, "The intent of same-sex marriage is not to establish new family structures but to reaffirm the old one."

That "old" nuclear family is not a timeless form but rather a historical anomaly that rose to prominence in the 1950s and was only possible through government subsidies. One of the problems with the nuclear family, according to historian Stephanie Coontz, is that it is "almost by definition too small to carry all of life's burdens." The nuclear family, she goes on to say, "harms your ability to call on a larger network of social support that you might need personally from the stresses of life." Yet, same-sex couples have rushed to re-create this 1950s version of the family. The civil rights strategy that drove the push for gay marriage, as Urvashi Vaid notes in her visionary 1995 book *Virtual Equality*, leads inevitably to assimilation because it is based on the proposition that "homosexuals are really just like heterosexuals." Rather than the liberation of all people and their sexuality that fueled the early Gay Liberation Front or the feminism of Adrienne Rich that proclaimed all women were on the "lesbian continuum," now the notion of an internal, fixed, and immutable gay identity has so triumphed that the idea we are all "born that way," to use Lady Gaga's phrase, has become orthodoxy. Lost in this shift toward the stable inner core of identity is the radical potential of fluid sexuality and queer kinship networks.

The overall marriage trend in the United States is what sociologists call "endogamy," that is, marrying someone of the same race. Endogamy is shaped by structural factors like racial segregation in housing, education, and jobs, because those are sorting mechanisms for potential mates. Traditionally, the neighborhood we live in, the schools we attend, the occupation we labor in are how we meet, date, and marry. In the United States, this tendency toward endogamy is strongest among white people. A recent report from the Pew Research Center found that 31 percent of Asians, 26 percent of Hispanics, and 16 percent of Blacks "married out"—that is, married someone of another race—while just 9 percent of whites did. Same-sex couples are slightly more likely to be in interracial relationships than straight couples. A study from UCLA's Williams Institute found that roughly 20 percent of same-sex couples were interracial or interethnic, compared with 18 percent of straight unmarried couples, and 9 percent of straight married couples.

While structural factors work against "marrying out" of one's race, the shift to online dating could, with the algorithmically sorted pool of potential mates and endless possibilities of swiping right, open up a wider range of people to date and marry, and thus change those patterns of endogamy. But it hasn't done that. According to data from OK Cupid, the online dating service, white people still prefer to date other white people. Based on the rates of replies to queries on the app, gay white men and straight white women in particular demonstrated a strong preference for dating only other white people.

For white women, racial identity can be solidified or destabilized through marriage. The Expatriation Act of 1907 held that a US-born woman who married a noncitizen was automatically stripped of her US citizenship. This overlapped with whiteness as a standard for citizenship. Starting at least as early as 1790, one had to prove they were a "free white person" to be eligible for US citizenship. This white rationale for citizenship was applied to immigrant men who came from China, Syria, Japan, and India, and a series of Supreme Court decisions over several decades held that none were "white enough" to qualify for naturalization. But it was only US-born women who could lose their citizenship through marriage. Thus, as theologian Thandeka points out in her 2007 book *Learning to Be White*, it is not unreasonable to say that a white woman could, through her marriage, lose her whiteness along with her citizenship. According to legal scholar Cheryl Harris, the law has accorded "holders" of whiteness the same privileges and benefits accorded holders of other types of property. Harris contends that whiteness is, according to the legal definition, a kind of property. For white women, choosing to marry someone white is a way to secure their investment in whiteness.

As rituals, the fairy tale weddings we're sold and that we actively re-create following the limited range of choices from the wedding services industry do not offer the possibility of reimagining identity or playing with forms of social intimacy. Instead of pageantry that celebrates the range of human sexuality and gender identity and honors alternative kinship forms created by Black, Indigenous, and queer people, we've settled for a commercial version of the classic bride saying "yes to the dress" in ways that naturalize whiteness, heteronormativity, and the nuclear family. White women are not only victims of the "wedding-ideological complex," we are also a driving force behind it and, along with white men, the co-beneficiaries of the systems it normalizes. White women, through the technology of the fairy tale wedding, are active participants in creating and reproducing white families that then become fortresses, like the McCloskeys' Midwestern palazzo, which must be protected.

## WHITE MOTHERS PROTECTING WHITE FAMILIES

"We'll be out until no protester needs protecting," one of the women who organized the group Wall of Moms told a reporter in late July 2020. The group of more than thirty women, most wearing all white and donning bike helmets, linked arms and made themselves into a barrier between federal officers and the protesters demonstrating against systemic racism. The women stood for a couple of hours outside the courthouse before the police used tear gas and flash-bangs to disperse the crowd. The hashtag #wallofmoms began trending on social media, and people shared their support of the women's actions, including the person who posted: "The mothers of Portland have had enough. It's not just the 'anarchists' anymore, Mr. President. #wallofmoms."

In another image from the same protests, a white woman holds a sign that reads ALL MOTHERS WERE SUMMONED WHEN GEORGE FLOYD CALLED OUT FOR HIS MOTHER. The women involved in this action were galvanized around their identity as moms, as fierce protectors of their families, and by extension George Floyd, and all Black people killed by police. The action evokes the observation of civil rights leader Ella Baker: "Until the killing of Black men, Black mothers' sons, becomes as important to the rest of the country as the killing of a white mother's son, we who believe in freedom cannot rest until this happens." The images shared online suggested that the protesters in the Wall of Moms were mostly white women, but their whiteness was largely unspoken in their organizing and in the reporting about them. Erased by the Wall of Moms are the Black mothers who care first and most fiercely about their children murdered by police.

The mobilization of women as mother/protectors is popular across the political spectrum. In the United States, such movements date back at least as early as 1872 and Julia Ward Howe's call for a "Mother's Day for Peace," which was an antiwar protest. The identity of mother is frequently used to galvanize grassroots political action for and against a wide range of political causes: against drunk driving (Mothers Against Drunk Driving), gun violence (Moms Demand Action), and police brutality (Mothers of the Movement) and for equal pay, paid sick leave, and affordable healthcare (Moms Rising).

In 2008, during her run for vice president of the United States, Sarah Palin often referred to herself as "a mama grizzly," by which she meant a mother who "rises up" to protect her children when she sees them threatened. The mama grizzly is, in Palin's conceptualization, fearless in protecting her family and thus an especially lethal adversary against any foe. Palin has attempted to use the mama grizzly idea to launch a movement of conservative women, but it's an image that appeals more broadly. After interviewing one of the organizers of the Wall of Moms action, MSNBC news anchor Ali Velshi remarked that the action reminded him of "the warning we all get when we're around wild animals: don't piss off the moms." Organizing around the identity of mother/protector assumes a universal experience of motherhood that ignores differences of race, class, citizenship, and geopolitics. Evoking the mama grizzly and wild animals who are pissed off suggests that motherhood is elemental, instinctual, and natural.

Yet, the motherhood being invoked here isn't the only thing being naturalized in rhetorical gestures like "mama grizzly." It's also whiteness. The fiercely protective "good mother" is a cultural designation reserved exclusively for white, middle- and upper-class women. Black, Indigenous, and other women of color, as well as poor or working-class women, are framed as dangerous, neglectful, and irresponsible mothers. Take, for instance, the way press coverage differs for women charged with a child's death. Scholar Sarah Carney examined the minute details of newspaper accounts of women accused in a child's death, including reports on their hair color and length, affect (sullen), clothing, friends and family who can testify about what a good mother she is, which babies' funerals were worthy of coverage, and which women's narratives were followed through from trial to verdict. Typically, women of color are regarded simply as monsters, whereas white women are—especially if middle class and heterosexually married—afforded some measure of redemption in the media, whether as a victim of male violence, poorly prescribed pharmaceuticals, or postpartum depression.

For example, in 2001, Andrea Yates, a white mother in a suburb of Houston, in the span of an hour one summer afternoon, drowned all five of her children in the bathtub and then laid them out on the bed. The case received extensive coverage that focused on Yates's severe postpartum depression, casting the mass murder of her children in a sympathetic light. There were multiple interviews with family and friends about her fitness as a mother, and there was extensive coverage from arrest to trial to the guilty verdict.

In 2014, another mother in Arizona, Shanesha Taylor, was unemployed and had landed a job interview. Unable to find childcare, Taylor, a Black mother of a two-year-old and a six-month-old, left her children in the car while she went to the interview. The children were overheated, but survived. News coverage of the incident was intense and brief, relentlessly focusing on Taylor's "questionable parenting," with little context or empathy about her circumstances and zero interviews with family or friends about what kind of mother she was otherwise. Taylor reached a plea agreement that allowed her to stay out of prison, and Yates will spend the rest of her life in a Texas state psychiatric prison.  Yet, white mothers like Yates are assumed to have good, caring intentions even if they murder their children; and Black mothers like Taylor always have the quality of their mothering questioned.

Legal scholar Kimberlé Crenshaw points out that Black women are packaged as bad women in cultural narratives about good women. Sociologist Patricia Hill Collins writes that "the prostitution of Black women allowed white women to be the opposite; Black 'whores' make White 'virgins' possible." This splitting of "good women" from "bad women" is crucial to a nation-building project, argues social psychologist Michelle Fine. When the government refuses to attend to human needs and rights, the ideology of the family expands to fill the void, and white women are at the center of that ideology. The notion of the good woman/mother is used to buttress the need for maternal sacrifice in hard times; the neglectful bad woman/mother is there to discipline and punish all other women lest we fall and become her.

During the late 1980s and early 1990s, under the Bush and Clinton presidencies, the state withdrew a wide range of material support for people through policies like "welfare to workfare," in large measure by pushing the Reagan-generated lie of the "welfare queen." Simultaneously, these administrations—one Republican and one Democrat—gained political power by promoting the notion of family values. Ironically, family values in this framework are linked with individualism.

Political scientist Lawrence Mead, an intellectual architect of welfare reform in the 1990s and still active in shaping policy, believes that the reason for poverty and most crime is the collapse of the family and the structure it provides. Mead, in a 2020 article in an academic journal, writes that "Hispanic immigrants suffer much worse family decline after they come to America than they had in Mexico. Most of them, like most Blacks, have not yet replaced those older external controls with the internalized inhibitions of individualist culture. Their problem is no longer oppression, but freedom." In Mead's view, the West, by which he means white people in the United States and Europe, "has simply chosen a more ambitious way of life than the non-West, where minorities originate." White people in the West, have "an enterprising temperament," and at the heart of that is individualism, which according to Mead: "led to constant change and improvements, then to unparalleled wealth, and finally to world power." Mead's culture of poverty theory, with good, ambitious, wealthy, driven-by-individualism, nuclear-family-constituted people of the West on one side, and bad, collectivist, poor, lacking-in-structure people of the non-West on the other, is, to me, a classic case of splitting.

*Splitting*, in the psychological sense, is a common defense mechanism that we humans deploy. We use it when we are unable to bring together positive and negative qualities of ourselves or others into a cohesive, realistic whole. At an individual level, it means we tend to think in extremes: someone is either all good or all bad, with no middle ground. This way of thinking also has collective consequences. Whether it's the West/non-West split of Mead's thesis or the good mother/bad mother designation, collectively we oscillate—or split— from mother adoration (good mothers) to mother demonization (bad mothers). Perhaps this splitting is an inevitable psychological response when our mothers are our assigned primary caregivers at the same time that our mothers are socially, economically, and culturally devalued and disadvantaged as women. Part of the splitting rests on the configuration of motherhood as a full-time, exclusive endeavor— an idea steeped in whiteness.

In her 2019 book *Mothering While Black*, scholar Dawn Dow challenges the view of motherhood as an exclusive endeavor. In her research, Dow highlights the fact that employment outside the home is intrinsically linked to what it means to be a mother in the African American community. The women Dow spoke with also revealed race-based parenting concerns about how they could encourage development of their children's racial identity and their comfort and skill at navigating race in social interactions. As sociologist Annette Lareau explains in her book *Unequal Childhoods*, the racial segregation of neighborhoods, schools, and playgrounds means that these worlds of mothering rarely overlap. Dow's research also found evidence of what her informants call a "white motherhood society." As one respondent told Dow: "The main thing about being a Black mom that is probably important to say is not feeling included in white motherhood society. . . . It feels like when I go to the playground there is the 'them' and there is the 'us.' . . . I have friends who have left playgroups because the white women look at us funny or like you don't exist."

In 2020, this playground dynamic surfaced in Facebook "mom groups" as Black Lives Matter protests focused attention on systemic racism. As the *New York Times* reported, in Los Angeles, San Francisco, and New York, Facebook groups for moms had temporarily shuttered following backlash from members over their handling of discussions about race. Said the report, "Groups in the New York area, including those for the Upper West Side, Brooklyn, and Jersey

City, are struggling to figure out how to make women of color feel welcome. All-white moderation teams are facing a public reckoning." What Dow's research and the fallout in predominantly white Facebook mom groups suggests is that the work of forming, reproducing, and maintaining families rests mainly with women and it is demarcated by whiteness.

The images of Princess Diana—whose wedding I rose early to watch—reshaped how we think about white womanhood transnationally. Cultural studies scholar Raka Shome, in her 2014 book *Diana and Beyond: White Femininity, National Identity, and Contemporary Media Culture*, writes about the way white women are constructed as "ideal mothers," then used to conjure the idea of a multicultural global family. In the 1990s, as Diana moved to establish her own identity separate from her marriage, she began to craft a new image for herself by being photographed with children all over the world. These photographs typically feature angelic lighting on Diana as she holds frail, sickly children with dark skin, thus replaying the religious imagery of *Madonna and Child*. The imagery suggests something eternal, spiritual, and innately maternal in Diana.

This theme, in which Diana is seen as having some intrinsic power to save and to heal, is also dominant in other representations of white women. This trope is repeated when Nicole Kidman, Susan Sarandon, Angelina Jolie, and other white women celebrities are named UN "goodwill" ambassadors and photographed with Black and Brown children around the world. And repeated again when Madonna, Meg Ryan, Katherine Heigl, and Angelina Jolie (again) adopt Black and Brown children from abroad. The popularized imagery places a particular kind of woman at the center of what Shome calls "global motherhood" in which white womanhood is the source of goodness, nurturing, health, even life itself.

Some kinds of women are not celebrated as global mothers in popular culture, women whose bodies are viewed as lacking desirability and civility, such as the "white trash" woman, the lesbian woman, the nonwhite woman, the non-Western woman. These women do not glow as Diana did and therefore cannot "further life" or the purity associated with an idealized white, reproductive body.

This idea of global motherhood is rooted in colonialism. As historian Margaret Jacobs writes in her book about settler colonialism, *White Mother to a Dark Race*, it was white women who played a key role in the policies of Indigenous child removal in both Australia and the American West. Government officials, missionaries, and reformers justified the removal of Indigenous children from their parents in particularly gendered ways that focused on the supposed deficiencies of Indigenous mothers, the alleged barbarity of Indigenous men, and the lack of a patriarchal nuclear family. Once again, the heterosexual white family is the ideal used as a kind of weapon to enact violence against Indigenous people. In this effort to "mother" Indigenous children, white women were often deemed the most appropriate agents to carry out these child-removal policies. And it was white women who maneuvered to influence public policy affecting Indigenous people. Then, it was white women who eagerly volunteered to serve as surrogate mothers to Indigenous children removed from their families.

Today, white evangelical women reenact this history by leading the movement to adopt children from developing countries, including those separated from their families along the southern border of the United States. As journalist Kathryn Joyce reveals in her book *The Child Catchers*, the white evangelical adoption movement has made adopting children from other countries part of their mission to "save" children, both from poverty and from an un-Christian existence. This has led to what Joyce calls a "massive rise in transracial adoptions," particularly among white evangelicals in the southern United States. Like the Indigenous child-removal policies of a century ago, the evangelical adoption movement is led by white women. Whether in the American West and Australia of the late nineteenth century or the contemporary United States among white evangelicals, white women are configured as best equipped to mother children born to women who are Indigenous or from the Global South.

My argument here is not chiefly about white women's bodies and skin color. It is about whiteness, a concept created in part to justify colonialism, and how it endures as a social construct in order to maintain white global dominance. And the enforcement of whiteness is gendered; white women have a specific and insidious role in justifying and enacting intergenerational white dominance. In other words, whiteness does stuff—it allows certain policies and practices that keep reaping benefits for white people. And when nice white ladies fail to recognize that we have been assigned a role in reproducing whiteness, we are passively ensuring that structural racism continues.

White families are the underlying technology that enables white supremacy to reproduce itself from one generation to the next, and white women are crucial to enacting and sugar-coating this process. When white women are tasked with deciding what's best for their white children, whatever the consequences for Black and Brown children, they are protecting and handing down unearned advantages through white families.

## HOARDING WEALTH AND EDUCATION

White people dominate the annual *Forbes* list of the richest Americans. Today, white families are twice as likely to be millionaires as they were a generation ago. The richest one hundred families control more wealth than all the Black people in America. In the United States, we worship the idea of wealth and, at some level, we have bought into the myth that the richest families worked harder or were smarter than everyone else and that's why they have so much wealth. But the current members of the ten richest families didn't earn all that money themselves. All ten are on that list because they inherited wealth from a rich, white family member.

White women are key to creating and maintaining white families and to hoarding wealth, education, and other resources within those all-white families. According to the Brookings Institution, in 2020 the average wealth of a white family was $929,800; that's 6.7 times greater than Black average wealth ($138,100). This trend continues even during recessions. From 2007 to 2013, a time when there was a financial crisis in the United States, the median net worth for white families declined by 26 percent while Black families experienced a 44 percent decline. In fact, the gap between white family wealth and Black family wealth is higher today than at the start of the twentieth century.

Wealth and income are related, but not perfectly correlated. Two households can have the same income, but the household with more accumulated wealth from past income or inheritances, or just from owning rather than renting a home, will have more wealth. The racial wealth gap remains even for families with the same income. For those in the top 10 percent by income (only 3.6 percent Black), the racial wealth gap is still quite large: median net worth for white families in this income group is $1,789,300 versus $343,160 for Black families. A racial gap exists in every income group except the bottom 20 percent (23.5 percent Black), where median net worth is zero for everyone.

In their study of racial wealth disparities in the United States, economists Darrick Hamilton and Sandy Darity find that inheritances and other intergenerational transfers account for "more of the racial wealth gap than any other demographic and socioeconomic indicators." In addition, white families are less likely than Black families to lose their footing in the labor force through layoffs or other cuts, and white families are less likely than Black families to be relied upon by extended family, friends, and neighbors for financial support. Part of the explanation for this is that white families have long had the support of the federal government to rely upon.

In 1862, for instance, President Lincoln signed the Homestead Act, which gave 160-acre plots to some Americans. Any citizen could get this free land from the US government, as could any "intended citizen," which was a way of enticing white foreigners to immigrate for the land. There were restrictions: the claimants could not have "borne arms against the U.S. government," in other words, they could not be former Confederate soldiers. And they were required to build a dwelling and cultivate the land. The Civil War ended in 1865 with the Emancipation Proclamation, and, as Nikole Hannah-Jones writes, Black people implored federal officials to take the land confiscated from enslavers who had taken up arms against their own country and grant it to those who had worked it for generations. They were asking to, as the historian Robin D. G. Kelley puts it, "inherit the earth they had turned into wealth for idle white people." Instead, the federal government extended the program of giving 160-acre plots to white families, while it left Black families with nothing.

The Homestead Act was applied to Oklahoma in 1889, and this is where I begin to know my family's history. My great-grandfather, along with approximately a hundred thousand white men, made "the run" to stake his claim on his 160 acres. The land had been part of the resettled Cherokee Nation, but from the time the Homestead Act was signed in 1862 until it was expanded into Oklahoma, there was a propaganda campaign to redistribute Cherokee land to white families. For example, on February 26, 1885, the *Kansas City Times* published the following editorial:

> There is something due these homeless white men. They are at least entitled to lands which are lying idle. . . . If the Indians had reduced these lands to farms or otherwise utilized and improved them, there might be some force in the clamor about protecting the poor red man against white cupidity and robbery; but they have not cultivated one acre in a thousand—and the government has kept them in food and clothing like so many helpless and dependent children.

In this rendering, white men are the aggrieved victims who must get help from the government to intercede on their behalf. It should be noted here that *homeless* in this context does not mean living outside or on the streets, as it often does today. *Homeless* here refers to white men who did not own their own homes with accompanying acreage for farming. The editorial finishes with this: "If the dream of making the Indian race agricultural and self-supporting is ever to be realized it must not come through great possessions of real estate, but through a better conception of what land was made for and how a living is to be obtained from it." Thus, President Lincoln's land grant program was specifically crafted to enrich white families who were seen as more deserving than either the recently freed Black Americans, who should just be grateful for their freedom and not expect restitution, or the Indians, who were regarded as "helpless and dependent children" who did not understand "what land was made for."

The land grant program continued until 1934. Altogether the federal government gave away some 246 million acres, in 160-acre tracts, nearly 10 percent of all the land in the nation, to more than 1.5 million white families, both native-born and foreign. As one researcher points out, some 46 million American adults today, nearly 20 percent of all American adults, like me, descend from those homesteaders. In our family, there was no wealth passed down from those original 160 acres, squandered as it was within a generation. But that, too, is a distinct kind of privilege: to get a substantial leg up from the federal government and then piss it all away in twenty or so years.

One substantial way to reduce the gap between the richest white families and everyone else would be through a significant tax on large inherited estates. Estate taxes are supposedly race-neutral policies, when in fact the accumulation of white wealth at the expense of Black families has been anything but race-neutral. As Nikole Hannah-Jones writes in the *New York Times Magazine*, "While Black Americans were being systematically, generationally deprived of the ability to build wealth, while also being robbed of the little they had managed to gain, white Americans were not only free to earn money and accumulate wealth with exclusive access to the best jobs, best schools, best credit terms, but they were also getting substantial government help in doing so."

Hannah-Jones, along with scholars like Sandy Darity and the writer Ta-Nehisi Coates and many others, have called for financial reparations to Black people to redress this generational and government-subsidized theft. Nevertheless, making it easier for the wealthiest white families to pass on their assets is a core value of the political elite in the United States. In 2017, Congress passed the Tax Cuts and Jobs Act (TCJA), a bill that cut $1.9 trillion in taxes that primarily benefited the wealthy. Prior to this legislation, the limit on inheritance that could be passed on without taxation was $5,490,000. Under the TCJA, the federal estate tax exemption was doubled. As of January 1, 2018, the exemption was $11,180,000. According to *Forbes*, this means that "With careful planning, married couples can gift up to $22,360,000 exempt from federal estate and gift taxes."

It's not only wealth that white families hoard but also education. "So we, so we just—so we just have to say we made a donation to your foundation and that's it, end of story?" the actress Lori Loughlin asked Rick Singer, a fixer who had promised to get her two daughters into the college of their choice, University of Southern California, for a fee paid to his fraudulent Key Worldwide Foundation. According to a federal affidavit in the case, Loughlin and her husband paid $500,000 in bribes to get their two daughters into USC. In a recording made by the FBI, the Newport Beach–based Singer said to a prospective client, "What we do is help the wealthiest families in the US get their kids into school."

Loughlin, along with another celebrity, Felicity Huffman, and about fifty other people, were indicted in a scheme that operated from 2011 through February 2019. In most cases, the parents paid Singer between $250,000 and $400,000 per student. "These parents are a catalog of wealth and privilege," said Andrew Lelling, the US district attorney who brought the charges against these parents. "They include, for example, CEOs of private and public companies, successful securities and real estate investors, two well-known actresses, a famous fashion designer, and the co-chairman of a global law firm."

Unspoken in most of the reporting on this story, which became known as the College Admissions Scandal, was the fact that these were not only wealthy parents, but white parents, and that it was most often the moms, like Lori Loughlin and Felicity Huffman, who were reaching out, scheduling visits, following up with email, and making the arrangements for payment to Singer. In other words, they were doing the kind of work that many moms do caring for their children, but in this instance the "motherwork" of these white, wealthy women was to hire someone to bribe testing officials, falsify the records of their children's achievements, and pay off athletic coaches to recruit their children. Most of the children were unaware that their parents had arranged for the cheating, which only served to disguise the machinations of unearned privilege from the very ones who benefited from it. Although these events appeared to shock many, white women's role in hoarding education is not new and extends well beyond rigging college admissions.

White Americans tend to play up moments of racial progress— chief among these is *Brown v. Board of Education*—but schools in the United States are more racially segregated today than they were in 1954. According to one recent report, more than half of the nation's children attend school in racially concentrated districts, where over 75 percent of students are either white or nonwhite. And this is no accident. As Pulitzer Prize–winning reporter Nikole Hannah-Jones has documented, white parents have rolled up their sleeves to fight with verve against the desegregation of school districts across the United States, even in self-proclaimed liberal communities.

Hannah-Jones discovered recordings of public school district hearings in Missouri in which white parents were fighting against the desegregation of schools, but, as Hannah-Jones observes, "race barely comes up that night, except when white parents insist it is not the issue." At the hearing, after a Black mother names the racism keeping her child out of the school, a white mother walks to the microphone and says, "We have both—my husband and I both have worked and lived in underprivileged areas in our jobs. This is not a race issue. And I just want to say to—if she's even still here—the first woman who came up here and cried that it was a race issue, I'm sorry, that's her prejudice calling me a racist because my skin is white and I'm concerned about my children's education and safety." The crowd in the auditorium of mostly white parents erupts in cheering and clapping, and then the woman finishes: "This is not a race issue. This is a commitment to education issue." This woman is not that different from the woman on the Upper West Side of Manhattan or from the mothers in Boston who fought school desegregation there in the 1970s. As Elizabeth McRae documents in her 2018 book *Mothers of Massive Resistance*, white women have been at the vanguard of defending racial segregation in schools. It is one of the chief ways that white families hoard resources for their children at the expense of all other children.

Wide gaps in school funding are directly linked to housing segregation, but it doesn't have to be this way. In his study of suburban schools, *Inequality in the Promised Land*, R. L'Heureux Lewis-McCoy documents the way white families cultivate school district staff and policymakers in order to make changes that accrue benefits to their families, from impeding desegregation plans to blocking financial resources targeted at poor and Black families. Lewis-McCoy refers to this as "opportunity hoarding" for the children in one community at the expense of all the children. When white people think they might lose these fights, they vote with moving vans and leave the districts. And it's not only conservatives or people on the right.

White women who think of themselves as liberal or progressive publicly declare their support for policies like school desegregation but then refuse to send their white children to integrated schools. Reporter Chana Joffe-Walt documents this in her 2020 podcast *Nice*

*White Parents,* in which liberal white people in New York City voice all the right platitudes about racial equity in schools but then balk when it comes time to enroll their children in public schools with majority Black and Brown students. "I just didn't want to subject my kids to that," says one of the nice white moms Joffe-Walt interviews. Jeremiah, a fifteen-year-old student and a keen observer of race, gender, and education, says in an interview, "For white moms, integration is just, you know, it's popular now, like yoga." Jeremiah, who is Black, goes on to point out that "when integration is no longer beneficial to white families, it will go right back to where it was." He clearly understands that the white parents involved at his school are only invested in his future when it suits them.

I watched this play out in my own life when a judge issued a ruling in *Cisneros v. Corpus Christi Independent School District* for the schools to be desegregated so that I would be riding a school bus come September 1974. My father refused to comply with the judge's order. Within two weeks of that ruling, my father did what white people usually do: he voted with a moving van and relocated our family to what was then the whitest possible suburb just north of Houston. My mother, Shirley, did not want to move back to Houston, where her abusive mother was a local phone call away, but (as women tend to be in nuclear families) she was completely dependent on my father financially and emotionally, so she simply packed our things into that Mayflower moving van like a good wife.

## MOMS PASSING ON WHITENESS

My mother had a saying that she used all the time. It's one of those Texas phrases that I grew up hearing, but not really paying attention to, like: "That ol' boy would rather climb a tree and tell a lie than stand on the ground and tell the truth." It's a more decorative way of calling someone a liar. The expression my mother used whenever I was being ungrateful and had no reason to complain was this: "You'd bitch if you were hung with a new rope, wouldn't you?" I heard this phrase my whole life and hadn't thought about it since I left Texas in the early 1990s. It's certainly not a phrase I use now. But it came to me in a dream recently, when I could hear my mother's voice reminding me of my ingratitude: "You'd bitch if you were hung with a new rope, wouldn't you?"

Was a new rope supposed to make one glad about being hung? I heard these words as if for the first time in 2020 in my late fifties after years of research into white supremacy, and realized this expression was a lynching reference. A gesture toward lynching passed down from one generation to the next, as a commonplace. It is saying: We are the people of the rope. We expect you to be grateful if the rope is new. Moms pass on whiteness, and my mother was doing it in subtle ways I may never fully fathom.

My mother learned this expression about the rope somewhere, probably from her mother, who learned it from hers. I wonder about the lessons my mother was taught about whiteness growing up in the 1930s and 1940s in Central Texas. In Kristina DuRocher's 2011 book *Raising Racists*, she documents the way white parents in the Jim Crow South taught their children what they believed to be an ideal vision of whiteness. Parents brought their children up to believe that hygiene and purity were important values and that it was only possible to achieve these by keeping themselves physically separate from Black people and anything associated with Blackness at all costs.

Traces of this got passed down to me when my mother told me, as a very young child, to never put coins in my mouth because a Black person "might have touched the coins" before they got to me. In the 1960s, I was visiting Big Granny's house when she paid a Black man to mow her lawn one hot summer day. When he was finished, she offered him a cold glass of water. Then, she came back into the house and put the glass in a pot of boiling water to "clean it" after he drank from it. In this formulation handed down to me, Blackness is a powerful and toxic contaminant that can be transferred, virus-like, on unclean surfaces.

And white parents in the Jim Crow South shared their belief in the power of whiteness by bringing their children to routinely brutal public rituals of human torture and murder, which you can see in lynching photographs that include white children in the crowds. Scholar Grace Hale argues in her book *Making Whiteness: Segregation in the South, 1890–1940*, regular lynchings functioned to strengthen segregation by helping to create "a collective, all-powerful whiteness." Certainly, these were powerful lessons for the children who were there, and a source of connection between and among white family members. The postcards with photographs of lynchings circulated among white people and within white families after these gruesome events as a way to solidify family bonds.

A postcard, of the kind that was for sale in dime stores across the Jim Crow South, features the burned and mutilated body of Jesse Washington, who was lynched in Waco, Texas, in 1916. The back of the postcard bears an inscription: "This is the barbecue we had last night. My picture is to the left with a cross over it. Your sone [*sic*] Joe." As scholar Koritha Mitchell writes, "Sending this postcard, Joe presumably assures his parents that, with their guidance, he has become a man who understands his place in society and his obligation to keep Blacks in theirs."

Postcards commemorating active participation in racial violence were woven into the kind of whiteness that my mother was raised with during the Jim Crow era in Central Texas. Her version of whiteness was different from the kind she raised me with, but she still passed on vestiges of the form she knew. The version of whiteness that I learned from my homemaker mother descended from Scotch-Irish people, while being raised in South Texas at the tail end of the civil rights movement and on the cusp of the women's movement, was a very specific type of whiteness. But it's in no way the last or only form.

Today, of course, there are parents who are raising their children not to be racist but to be "color blind," or even "color conscious," as Margaret Hagerman points out in her 2018 book *White Kids: Growing Up Privileged in a Racially Divided America*. Hagerman explores two predominantly white communities, which she calls Sheridan and Evergreen, and does a deep, ethnographic dive into the kinds of race talk that these upper-middle-class white parents engage in with their children. Many of the parents say they "moved there for the schools: [and] to escape the problems of Petersfield," the nearby town with more Black students. These parents describe their choice as wanting "the best education possible" for their children. In one interview, Hagerman asks one of the mothers, Mrs. Avery, while sitting in her large, modern kitchen, if she thinks about the diversity in her children's lives: "They get very little racial diversity in Sheridan . . . we try to take different opportunities to expose them to different things. I look for those examples to teach them because they are not living it every single day." When Hagerman probes for specific examples, Avery explains:

I tell the kids stories about [how] depend[ing] on the color of your skin . . . well, *The Help*, Alicia and I read the book. . . . I have probably more of a knowledge base about that stuff than Alicia does, but both of us were reading the book . . . and you're just horrified. You're like, "Oh my god! Seriously? That is what they dealt with?" . . . We all went to see the movie . . . there are parts of it where your mouth is just hanging open because you just can't quite believe what you are seeing . . . and [Alicia] will say, "Oh my gosh, thank god I didn't live then! Thank god we live *now*, where it doesn't really matter what the color of your skin is."

The second community Hagerman studies, Evergreen, has some racial diversity but is still predominantly white, and parents there are more committed to raising color-conscious or even antiracist children. In Evergreen, when she poses the question, "Do you think racism is a problem in your school?" and then follows up by asking the same about the country as a whole, a young person named Conor responds:

> I think [racism] is a way bigger problem than people realize. It's nowhere near what it used to be . . . it's just different and white people don't realize it. . . . I think it's still there. It's just not as present and people want to hide it. Because they are scared to talk about it.

Hagerman is making a nuanced counterargument to the idea that white children, like sponges, adopt the dominant racial views, and it's an important point to make. But unacknowledged here is that the moms of both Sheridan and Evergreen are still passing down whiteness. And if whiteness *is* property, as legal scholar Cheryl Harris argues, then that is the most valuable inheritance they can offer their children, whether color blind or color conscious. Although Hagerman forces the whiteness in Sheridan and Evergreen to become visible, most of the time whiteness is unremarked upon, hidden in plain view, as it is on TV.

Lisa Rinna, one of the women featured on the reality-based television show *The Real Housewives of Beverly Hills*, has two daughters, Amelia Gray Hamlin and Delilah Belle Hamlin. In 2020, Amelia Gray searches for her own apartment in California after a failure to launch her college life in New York City. In one episode, Amelia Gray, her mother, and a real estate agent discuss a prospective apartment. In listing her preferred amenities, Amelia Gray begins by sharing that she has "major anxiety," and thus recasts the amenities she wants into accommodations she needs for her wellness. "My thing is security, I need to have a doorman." Her mother interrupts, "Even though that comes with a price tag of like, $5,000." Amelia Gray continues with her list as the agent dutifully scribbles it all down: "I love a pretty kitchen island. I love marble. I love white. I'd love a sub-zero refrigerator. Something with big windows to make me happy. My mood is easily changed by my surroundings. Everything needs to be there, like the pool, with the cabanas." There are several times when the camera cuts to Lisa Rinna for exasperated-mother reactions. At the end of the scene, Lisa Rinna says, "I've created a monster."

But she hasn't; she's raised her daughter to be a nice white lady in the fashion, in the style, and with the affective valences of the *Real Housewives of Beverly Hills*. In her daughter, Rinna has created the "spoiled rich white girl" that Venus Xtravaganza said she dreamed of becoming in the 1990 documentary *Paris Is Burning*. Lisa Rinna's mothering and Amelia Gray's internalization of it are part of what creates "suburban housewives" as a political category of white women voters.

"Most white Americans believe they were born white, yet their own stories of early racial experiences describe persons who were bred white," writes Thandeka, the theologian and author of *Learning to Be White*. She contends that there are ways that learning to be white is a form of child abuse. She is not being metaphorical. Drawing on psychoanalytic theorist Alice Miller's *Prisoners of Childhood*, Thandeka argues that the child raised to be white must go through a process of self-alienation in which they must disavow their feelings of connection toward racialized others. Eventually, such children learn to "repress, deny and split off from consciousness feelings that, if expressed, would provoke racial attacks from the adults in their own community." In this process, parents teach children to cut off their empathy toward racialized others as a condition of identifying with and bonding with their caregivers.

She writes that this process is inherently destructive to the child's psyche: "The Euro-American child learns to feel ashamed of its own differences from its community's white racial values." This process of self-alienation can leave the child with a sense of "emptiness, futility, and homelessness," feelings that are a hallmark of child abuse. She contends that the price of admission for becoming white is exacting and includes humiliation, lost self-esteem, and a general feeling of self-contempt. Of course, there are benefits to whiteness, but Thandeka argues, there are costs, too, entailed in "making, acquiring, and protecting this personal investment in white racial identity."

In 2010, news accounts revealed that a couple in New Jersey gave their children Nazi-inspired names: Adolf Hitler Campbell and JoyceLynn Aryan Nation Campbell. A debate ensued about whether or not naming these children in this fashion was a form of child abuse, and surely it is. But when trying to apply Thandeka's argument more broadly than the New Jersey couple's outlandish behavior, I couldn't agree. The idea that raising children to be white is child abuse seemed like an example of "white tears," another way to put the focus on white people's feelings, this time as children.

I began to change my mind about this idea at a workshop called "Shame and Resilience for White People" presented by clinical psychologists Robin Schlenger and Alana Tappin. This was the first of these kinds of workshops I've attended that directly addressed whiteness through the issue of shame and child abuse. In the workshop, we talked about the ways we were taught to revere white elders who were racist, a subject I had wrestled with but to no satisfactory end. There was something about the context of the workshop and the set of exercises we engaged in that gave me the permission I needed to look at my own childhood differently. What it enabled me to see was that my grandfather, my father's father, had abused me in two ways: as a child molester and as a member of the Klan. Although my father was empathetic in his response when he learned of the first kind of abuse, he compounded the latter form of abuse by saying Granddad's membership in the KKK was "not a big deal." I grappled with these facts as an adult, and though I was grateful for the abundance of resources for dealing with sexual abuse, this workshop was the first time that anyone had been equipped to help me deal with the peculiar form of abuse that comes from having ancestors who were in the Klan. Historians estimate that membership in the KKK in the 1920s ranged from two million to four million. Even if you take the lower estimate, and figure that those people all had only two children, that means there are tens of millions of us, maybe a hundred million of us, who are descendants of the Klan, and there are a meager few who have faced this head-on and dealt with the trauma of it.

In some ways, the notion that passing on whiteness is a form of child abuse is an idea that I had been seeing over and over again in my classroom. When I teach Introduction to Sociology, I teach about the process of socialization, whereby we humans learn to internalize the rules of our culture and make them our own. In recent years I've been using a documentary, along with assigned readings and lectures, to teach this concept to my beginning sociology students. The 2010 film by Stephanie Wang-Breal, *Wo Ai Ni Mommy*, follows the life of Fang Sui Yong, an eight-year-old Chinese girl from Guangzhou, China, who is adopted by Donna Sadowsky, a white, Jewish woman from Long Island. The film follows her during the first year of her adoption, and we watch as Fang Sui Yong is transformed into Faith Sadowsky. It is a painful process to watch. At one point, Fang Sui/Faith sits on the floor of her bedroom on Long Island and cries inconsolably as the filmmaker translates, through the girl's sobs, for Donna Sadowsky: "I want to go home . . . now!" It is anguishing to witness, and some of my students felt what they saw onscreen was child abuse. But time passes and by the final scene the girl that was Fang Sui Young is gone, and the girl who has become Faith Sadowsky pedals gleefully down the driveway of her suburban home in her Barbie-branded toy convertible, every inch an American girl. When the filmmaker asks Faith whether she sees herself as Chinese or American, she smiles and says, "American."

One reading of the film is that it depicts the process of socialization into a new culture, and that's what I want my students to take away from viewing it. Another reading is about how agonizingly difficult it is to move from one culture to another and learn a new language, mannerisms, customs, and religion (the Sadowskys are Jewish and we see Faith attend her brother's bar mitzvah); so many of my students are immigrants or the children of immigrants, I want them to feel seen in Faith Sadowsky's struggle to adjust. Some of my students, like the subject of the film, are themselves from China and were adopted by white, well-meaning moms and dads here in the United States, and I hope that the film plants a seed in them to explore more about what it means to be from China and have white parents, a subject the film briefly explores. But I kept thinking about my students who named what they saw onscreen as "abuse." Is that what we're watching? How could that be when Faith's adoptive mother, Donna, plainly loves her so much?

Of course, I realize now that abuse comes from the same people who tell us that they love us. In fact, it seldom comes any other way. A different reading of the film, then, is through the lens of Thandeka's observation: what we are watching is the trauma associated with becoming white. Of course, Faith Sadowsky will always be Chinese, but her socialization into her new life on Long Island means that she has learned not only to be American but also a particular kind of whiteness. The whiteness she learned from her suburban Nassau County white Jewish mother in the early 2000s has a different flavor than the one I learned from my suburban Harris County white Scotch-Irish mother a generation removed from Jim Crow. But, it seems to me, what Faith Sadowsky and I share is that our survival, our very lives, depended on identifying with primary caregivers who were passing on their destructive belief in whiteness. This is the trauma Thandeka points to at the center of becoming white. It is the trauma that white moms pass on to their children, wrapped in love and care.

## WHITE SAVIOR MOMS

When actress Meg Ryan adopted a baby from China, she referred to the process as a "metaphysical kind of labor." And when pop star Madonna adopted baby David from a clinic in Malawi, she said she was "transfixed" by him. The idea that white moms can rescue the children of the world is one that travels. In July 2005, celebrity Angelina

Jolie announced that she was adopting a baby girl from Ethiopia. In October of that same year, Ann Watt of Ohio was inspired by Jolie. She told a reporter: "I remember being at the store and seeing Angelina on the cover of, I think it was *People* magazine, and I said 'Oh my gosh! We can do this!'" Watt's husband, Jason Hillard, was onboard with the plan, saying, "We're inviting a whole new genealogy to our family line. We invite culture and diversity into our family and those are things that inspired [us] to adopt." Jolie's role as white savior mom, promoted in *People* magazine and circulated throughout celebrity news outlets, resonated with Ann Watt, and the script of a white mom rescuing a Brown child from another country gets repeated.

The trope of white motherhood gets replayed on the big screen as well. The 2009 film *The Blind Side* is a quasi-biographical portrayal of Michael Oher (Quinton Aaron), a football player for the Carolina Panthers. The main storyline is the evolution of the young African American man's relationship with the Tuohys, an upper-middle-class white family who take him in when he is a teenager. The film was enormously successful at the box office, grossing more than $309 million, and was nominated for Best Picture. Sandra Bullock won Best Actress for her portrayal of Leigh Anne Tuohy, the white mother who is the center of the film. And, in a life-imitating-art turn, Bullock went on in real life to adopt Louis, a Black baby boy, in 2010 and Laila, a Black baby girl, in 2015.

Although many people have pointed out the very obvious fact that this is a white savior film (e.g., Hernan and Gordon's *Screen Saviors: Hollywood Fictions of Whiteness*), there is something very specific going on here in the portrayal of a white savior mom. In one pivotal scene, Leigh Anne/Sandra Bullock is teaching Michael/Quinton Aaron about football, because he is not hitting the other players hard enough. She tells him: "This team is your family, Michael. You have to protect them." This is a key part of the story, toughening up the gentle fictional Michael to be a ferocious football player, but one the actual Michael Oher says never happened. The point of the scene is not merely about football, it is about reinforcing the lesson that protecting white families is what's most important.

Later in the film, when one of Michael's neighbors back on "the other side of town" calls Leigh Anne "snowflake," then threatens Michael, saying, "Tell him to sleep with one eye open, you hear me, bitch?" She turns and walks back up to him and says, "No, you hear me, *bitch*. You threaten my son, you threaten me. You so much as cross into downtown, you will be sorry. I'm in a prayer group with the DA. I'm a member of the NRA and I'm *always* packing." She turns to leave again, and the neighbor asks, "What you got in there, a .22? Or a Saturday Night Special?" She replies: "Uh-huh, and it shoots just fine all the other days, too," and taps her purse, and exits. Here, Leigh Anne/Sandra Bullock is performing the mama grizzly, defending her son and using the kind of Smith & Wesson feminism my father taught me. The gun makes her feel powerful in confronting the Black man she encounters and is taught to fear. She then threatens this Black man with violence if he "so much as cross[es] into downtown."

The threat of violence from this white savior mom is not only directed at the Black man outside but also directed toward Michael, inside her home. Near the end of the film, Michael has graduated from high school and is about to begin college, and the whole family is on campus, wishing him well, when two young white women walk by. A faint smile crosses Michael's face. "Michael Oher, you listen to me, alright?" Leigh Anne/Sandra Bullock says, "I want you to have fun, but if you get a girl pregnant out of wedlock, I will crawl in the car, drive up here to Oxford, and I will cut off your penis." The Tuohy's younger son, comic relief for most of the film, quips: "She means it." Michael/Quinton Aaron says, "Yes, ma'am," and keeps smiling. Her mention of castration for sexual contact with a white woman is, like my mother's expression about a new rope, a lynching reference. That it is allowed to pass in this film as a joke is evidence of how inured we are to threats of violent white supremacy when they come from a nice white lady like Leigh Anne/Sandra Bullock.

The film exemplifies two sides to the popularized white mother role. The notion of the white savior mom as the source of life and healing for children like Michael Oher reinforces a false notion that white women are somehow especially capable as mothers. Specifically in this film, a white mother is somehow (through her extreme privilege) inherently more capable than a Black mother. And this saviorism also carries with it a threat of violence.

The reproduction of whiteness itself is destructive, and when it is not possible to pass on whiteness, then saviorism collapses. In 2014, a young white mother from Ohio began a YouTube channel and later an Instagram account that featured wholesome, family-themed videos and images of her and her children. Over the next several years, she became what one news outlet called a "mid-level Mom influencer" who boasted several high-profile sponsors of her content. In 2017, she began to share regular posts about the two-and-a-half-year-old child she and her husband adopted from China. She shared details about the child's autism diagnosis—often in posts sponsored by advertisers—and she wrote about what a struggle it was to be a parent to a special-needs child. Then on Mother's Day in May 2020, she wrote that it had been one of the "hardest days ever." Fans on her social media accounts worried that they hadn't seen the little boy in some time. Then, she revealed that she and her husband had "re-homed" the boy. That is, they had returned the child they adopted and sent him to live with another family that could "better care for his needs." On her YouTube channel, she explained: "After multiple assessments, after multiple evaluations, numerous medical professionals have felt that he needed a different fit in his medical needs, he needed more" than they could give him. In the video, which amassed more than five hundred thousand views before she closed down her accounts, the couple assured their viewers that the toddler was "thriving" and asked for "grace, support, and privacy." Unlike Michael Oher, who Leigh Anne could mold into a star athlete, it wasn't possible to easily pass on whiteness to a boy from China with autism, so back he went, like a defective appliance.

The damage that white savior moms can do is perhaps clearest in Devonte Hart and his siblings. In late 2014, a photo taken by Johnny Nguyen of a then twelve-year-old Devonte went viral. In the image, Devonte, small for his age, is embraced by a large, white police sergeant at a Black Lives Matter rally in Portland, Oregon. The occasion for the protest was the decision in Ferguson, Missouri, not to indict Darren Wilson, the cop who shot and killed Michael Brown, a youth just six years older than Devonte. The photo, which quickly became known as "the hug felt 'round the world," circulated as a supposedly touching image of "hope, harmony, and healing." However, it takes only a modest amount of emotional acumen to see that Devonte looks terrified. Jennifer Hart, his adoptive mother, described what happened in the photo on her Facebook account:

> Last night I encouraged Devonte to face his concerns and fear [of the police]. It was one of the most emotionally charged experiences I've had as a mother. He trembled holding a Free Hugs sign as he bravely stood alone in front of the police barricade. Tears rushing from his eyes and soaking his sweater, he gazed upon them not knowing how they would react. After a while, one of the officers approached him and extended his hand. Their interaction was uncomfortable at first. I kept my distance and allowed him space to truly have his own experience.

While Devonte "trembled" and "cried" in front of a police barricade, Jennifer Hart "kept her distance," snapped photos for her Instagram and Facebook feeds, and had "one of the most emotionally charged" experiences of being a mother.

Devonte was one of six children that Jennifer and Sara Hart adopted. The two white women met in South Dakota, became a couple in the early 2000s, and married in Connecticut in 2009. In 2004, they fostered a fifteen-year-old girl that they later dropped off at her therapist's and relinquished to another family. "I remember being devastated," the now twenty-something young woman recalls. "They didn't even say goodbye." Shortly afterward, in 2006 and 2008, the Harts adopted two sets of siblings, Markis, Hannah, and Abigail and Devonte, Jeremiah, and Ciera, all from Texas. On Devonte's twelfth birthday, Jennifer Hart, a prolific Facebook and Instagram poster, described her adopted son this way on social media:

> Devonte Hart entered the world 12 years ago with drugs pumping through his tiny newborn body. By the time he was 4 years old he had smoked, consumed alcohol, handled guns, been shot at, and suffered severe abuse and neglect. He knew only a handful of words, including fuck and shit, and he struggled to identify the names of food, body parts, and everyday objects. Devonte was a violent toddler and his health was weighed down by a heavy list of disabilities.

Each social media post had the same storyline: these moms had rescued these kids, and now they were thriving against all odds. As family friend Ian Sperling put it, "You saved them, awesome!" The supposedly good mothering of the white moms who adopted Devonte relies on the allegedly bad mothering of his Black mother and other caregivers. But the reality is that Devonte was abused in both the homes he knew, only one form of abuse was hidden from public view except from the state, and the other had a carefully curated social media profile that accumulated likes and followers that helped his abusers evade state control.

The six children in the Hart household were starved, physically beaten, and subjected to sensory deprivation techniques similar to those used on prisoners who are tortured. A friend of the family reported that Jen ran the family "like a regimented boot camp," not letting the kids cry and punishing them for laughing too loudly.

Also, according to the same person, "True kindness, love, and respect for the kids was largely absent." Withholding food as punishment was common. One witness to the family dynamic said the kids would eat freely while Jen wasn't around, but once she entered the room they would deny they'd eaten at all. When Jennifer ordered a pizza, she said the kids could each only have one, small slice. When she noticed the next day that someone had eaten more, she forced all six children to lie blindfolded on an air mattress for five hours. In one social media image of Devonte, Jeremiah, and Ciera painting ("Mini Jackson Pollocks," the caption reads) with their shirts off, the children appear emaciated. The photo is also striking because the children are not smiling for the camera, as they are in so many images Jennifer posted. As one anonymous informant to the Oregon Department of Human Services put it, "Jen does this thing for her Facebook page, where the kids pose and are made to look like one big happy family, but after the photo event, they go back to looking lifeless." The same person also said that the children appeared to be "scared to death of Jen."

Reports later revealed that Sergeant Bret Barnum, pictured with Devonte in "the hug," had liked a Facebook post that showed a Portland Police badge emblazoned with the words "I am Darren Wilson." Although Barnum denied that he was a supporter of Wilson specifically but rather police in general, it raised questions about the viral image. For the opportunity to take a photo, Devonte was forced to embrace someone he was legitimately terrified of and who had endorsed the very brutality that Black Lives Matter protesters were demonstrating against. The photo of "the hug" is arguably an image of child abuse, and it is abuse perpetrated by a white savior mom against a twelve-year-old Black child. That image was an early warning about the abuse Devonte and his siblings were, right then, suffering. But few paid attention, distracted as we were by myths of white racial innocence and motherly goodness, and feel-good images that we could "heart," "like," and share.

In late 2017, Hannah Hart, then twelve years old, slipped out her bedroom window in rural Washington State and over to a neighbor's house and knocked on their door around one thirty a.m. "You gotta help. Please protect me! Don't make me go back!" she said to the woman who answered the door. "They're racists, and they abuse us!" Jennifer and Sarah Hart found Hannah, and minimized her claims of abuse by telling the neighbor that Hannah, and all their children, were adopted and "drug babies" and that Hannah's biological mother had been bipolar. Devonte began to sneak over to the same neighbors and ask for food that he would smuggle back home for his siblings.

Eventually, the neighbors alerted Child Protective Services (CPS). The Harts had lived in Minnesota when they adopted the children from Texas, then moved to Oregon and eventually to just outside of Woodland, Washington, each time evading state-level child protection authorities. When Washington CPS knocked on the Harts' door on March 23, 2018, no one answered, even though the family was home. According to data collected from the GPS unit in the family's SUV, that night around eight thirty p.m. Jennifer and Sarah Hart put all six children into the vehicle and drove away. Over the next two days, the Harts drove more than five hundred miles until they reached Leggett, in Northern California. Sometime during the night or early morning of March 25, Jennifer Hart revved the engine and drove her SUV off a cliff along Highway 1 in Mendocino County, killing all eight people inside. There were five bodies recovered at the scene, the two women inside the vehicle, and three of the children—Markis, Jeremiah, and Abigail. Hannah's and Ciera's bodies later washed ashore. Devonte's body was never found.

Devonte and his adopted siblings are part of a pattern: Cassandra Killpack, Michael Tinning, Hannah Grace-Rose Williams, Lydia Schatz, Timothy Boss, and Ahmad King are just some of the Black children killed by their white adoptive mothers and parents. According to child advocate and scholar Stacey Patton, the Hart tragedy and the cases of children of color killed by their white adoptive parents demonstrate that we need to "interrogate . . . the passing down of intergenerational white sadism." Those of us who are raised to be white are often impaired by that very upbringing when it comes to trying to understand intergenerational white sadism. We are trapped in what philosopher Charles W. Mills describes as an "epistemology of ignorance," unable to understand the world we ourselves have created. This becomes clear in the documentary film *A Thread of Deceit: The Hart Family Tragedy* (2020), by Chris Kobin and Rachel Meyer, in which the children's heartbreaking deaths at the hands of their white mothers gets retold as a story about the way the moms were misunderstood on social media following the murder-suicide. Through interviews with members of Devonte's and Jeremiah and Ciera's biological families in the Third Ward neighborhood of Houston, the film invites the viewer to see the children as better off with their white moms than if they had stayed in Houston, in poverty and surrounded by other Black people. Jennifer and Sarah Hart were misunderstood, but not in the way the filmmakers intended. What Jennifer and Sarah Hart did to the children they adopted was to engage in a form of intergenerational white sadism that fed their egos even as it destroyed the bodies and lives of those children.

The Harts' story is a violent one, to be sure. Jennifer and Sarah Hart were clearly disturbed. And transracial adoption—especially of six children—is an anomaly when it comes to how white women become mothers. That said, the Harts' story can still tell us something about whiteness and motherhood.

The process of passing on whiteness is one that is often left to white women who are mothers and do the bulk of child-rearing work. Through mothering, white women teach their children who is "safe" (the police) and who is deserving of empathy, food, and justice (not racialized Others). It is these practices, among many others, that constitute the web of customs, habits, and mores that are passed down when someone is raised white. This way of being in the world goes deeper than simply bias or prejudice. It is rooted in who we feel connected to, where we feel safe, and how we move through the world. And it is this process of being raised white that equips us for participating in the system of white supremacy because we have been taught it is natural and that we are innocent.

## CONCLUSION

The white nuclear family is one of the most powerful forces for reproducing white supremacy, and I found this out when I stepped outside of it. Once I publicly declared myself a lesbian, I divested from supporting the idea of the nuclear family. I neither wanted to create my own nor continue protecting the one I'd grown up in. I finished my PhD dissertation about the KKK and groups like it, and after studying with Patricia Hill Collins, I figured that I needed to write about my "positionality," the term she uses that means researchers should write about their relationship to the thing they're studying. My relationship to my grandfather, the child molester and Klan member, seemed a relevant detail to note in the preface of the book that grew out of my dissertation research. When I wrote about some of this, and sent those pages off to my father, I naively hoped he would be proud of me. Instead, his response was to have me involuntarily committed to a psych ward for seventy-two hours.

Since that time, I've built my life mostly around chosen family, what the anthropologist Carol B. Stack calls "fictive kin." And, when my life fell apart in 2018 after my relationship ended, I turned first to my family at the queer church. Metropolitan Community Church of New York was also the last spiritual home on this earth for Sylvia Rivera, the trans activist, Stonewall pioneer, and beloved Puerto Rican elder. Before MCCNY, Rivera spent much of her life on the streets of the West Village. When she died in 2002, she made Rev. Pat Baumgardner promise that she would establish a shelter for queer homeless young people in the basement of the church. Reverend Pat followed through, and young people who are pushed out of their homes by parents who are transphobic, homophobic, and otherwise unloving now have a place to stay. But the dozen or so beds at Sylvia Rivera's Place provide refuge for only a small portion of the estimated twenty thousand homeless young people on the streets of New York City each night, over a third of them identifying as LGBTQ. This is a failure of nuclear families.

It's not merely the individual prejudice of specific families, though that is certainly a problem. Many of these young people living on the streets are there because they've aged out of the foster care system, abandoned by or removed from their parents years before they came out as queer. Think of it this way: in a society where health insurance is connected to having a job, those without a job are without health insurance. Having a family is like having a job, it connects you to all kinds of other benefits. Living in a system of racial capitalism like we have in the United States means that having a white family can be like having a very good job with direct deposit, a gym membership, and a corporate credit card, but an abusive boss. Without a white family to turn to, I wondered in some of my bleakest days if I'd be staying at the shelter, too. As grateful as I was to have MCCNY, I needed something more. In my season of anguish, I reached out to my brother and reintroduced myself. We hadn't spoken much since he sprung me from the lockup our father had engineered. I was glad to be able to layer in some biological family to the fabric of the new life I was stitching together.

What I am beginning to see is that to undo white womanhood we have to conceive of other forms of kinship outside the model of the nuclear family. We have to reimagine alternative forms of kinship that blend queerness and (some) familial ties together in ways that challenge systems of domination. I think that undoing the damage of white womanhood is possible if we can take the affective impulse of the Wall of Moms, acknowledge the work that whiteness is doing here, and direct that energy toward undoing structural, systemic harm. Otherwise, we risk repeating the destructiveness of whiteness, passing on the trauma and sadism to the next generation, and the next and so on. We have to take a long, generational view toward undoing white womanhood. If we don't, we'll be left with our family fortress, like Patty McCloskey, standing barefoot in our capri pants on the porch of our palazzo holding a silver handgun, defending the all-white families we've created, our white-owned property, and whiteness itself, like nice white ladies do.

# 6

# THE LIE THAT IS
# KILLING ALL OF US

In 2009, Diane Schuler, thirty-six, described by some as a "perfect PTA mom," spent a long weekend at the Hunter Lake Campground about two hours north of New York City with her husband, Danny Schuler, their two kids, and her brother's three daughters. On Sunday, July 26, Danny left the campground in his pickup truck towing their boat, while Diane loaded the Ford Windstar minivan with the five children, and both vehicles headed back to Long Island, where the families lived. At around noon, Diane Schuler called her brother, Warren Hance, and told him she was disoriented. About an hour later, eight-year-old Emma Hance called her father on her aunt's cell phone and said, "There's something wrong with Aunt Diane." Somehow, no one is quite sure how, Diane Schuler drove the minivan onto the Taconic Parkway going against traffic. At one thirty p.m. on a bright, summer afternoon, after driving two miles at a speed of approximately eighty miles per hour in the wrong direction, Diane

Schuler crashed head-on into another vehicle, killing herself and seven other people, including four children.

"There's nothing that leads us to believe this was suicide," said one of the crash investigators. A week later, the Westchester County coroner's office released the toxicology report. Diane Schuler had a blood alcohol level of 0.19 (more than twice the legal limit of 0.08) and had high levels of THC, the psychoactive chemical found in marijuana. A magnum 1.75-liter bottle of vodka was discovered under a seat in the minivan. Some press accounts expressed outrage; How COULD SHE? blared the headline on the *New York Post*. Yet, despite the evidence that Diane Schuler's body contained the equivalent of ten drinks and that she had smoked weed within fifteen minutes of the crash, family members expressed disbelief.

"This is the absolute last thing that we ever would have expected," Warren and Jackie Hance, her brother and sister-in-law and parents to three children killed in the crash, said in a statement about the toxicology report. Danny Schuler, her surviving husband, has maintained that his wife did not having a drinking problem and only rarely used pot. Even media reports a full decade later are unable to acknowledge the facts of the case: 10 YEARS LATER, MYSTERY SHROUDS TACONIC WRONG-WAY CRASH read the headline in July 2019, when a Lower Hudson Valley news outlet ran a follow-up story. That the press reports, even ten years later, could say "mystery shrouds" the crash that killed eight people, when the toxicology reports unequivocally showed that Diane Schuler was severely intoxicated, is a testament to the power of the belief in white women's inherent purity, nurturing, and goodness. Surely, there must have been some other explanation besides drinking and drugs since she was a "perfect PTA mom," goes the rationalization.

Diane Schuler's death would have been counted by the Centers for Disease Control and Prevention (CDC) as one of the thousands of deaths in 2009 that occurred as a result of "unintentional injuries," and these include all kinds of accidents, such as motor vehicle crashes, falls, fires, drownings, poisonings, and choking. In 2017, there were 29.4 million emergency room visits and 39.5 million visits to physicians' offices because of these kinds of injuries, according to the CDC. In 2018, roughly 167,100 people died from unintentional injuries, making them the third leading cause of death in the United States overall, accounting for 6 percent of all deaths. Among white women and young girls, unintentional injuries are the number one cause of death from age one through age forty-four, accounting for some 36 percent of their deaths. While certainly few are as dramatic as the Schuler crash on the Taconic Parkway, the others are no less tragic and preventable. Eight-year-old Emma Hance's last words to her father, "There's something wrong with Aunt Diane," ring true beyond the terrible circumstances of that summer afternoon in 2009. There's something wrong with white womanhood, and it is killing us.

## DYING OF WHITENESS

"On the night of November 21, 2014, Becca Campbell, a twenty-six-year-old woman from Florissant, Missouri, died of whiteness," writes Jonathan Metzl. On November 17, just days before Campbell's death, Missouri governor Jay Nixon declared a state of emergency in Ferguson and signed an executive order activating the National Guard. Becca Campbell, a young mother of two small children, bought a gun in response to unrest in nearby Ferguson, Missouri, following the police killing of teenager Michael Brown. Campbell was in a car with a male friend who was driving as they left a pub in downtown St. Louis where she worked as a server. The friend reported that Campbell pulled a gun out of her purse and jokingly waved it around. According to him, she said, "I'm ready for Ferguson!" This playfulness took his attention off the road. He then rear-ended the car in front of him. When he did, the impact caused Campbell's hand to clench, including her finger around the trigger. The bullet entered her head, killing her instantly.

Rather than merely a horrible accident, Campbell's death is emblematic of a particular kind of death that's on the rise among white people, Metzl writes in his 2019 book *Dying of Whiteness*. The key insight Metzl offers is that certain policies have become so intertwined with white identity that the policies themselves serve as racial identities. Once this association between a policy and white racial identity gets locked in, some white people are willing to die to support those policies even when they cause harm and shorten their lives. You can begin to see this in the long-term trends on life spans and how we die.

Longevity is one of the measures of a prosperous society. In the United States, persistent racial disparities in life expectancy have been documented; white people generally live longer (averaging 79 years) than Black people (75 years). Even with those gaps, for decades, the overall trend in the United States has been toward longer life spans across all racial groups. However, in recent years, public health researchers have found that life spans for white Americans are shortening. This decline is in contrast to the continuing upward trend for other racial and ethnic groups (Hispanics averaging 82 years; Asians, 86 years). That is, even as life spans continue to increase for other racial and ethnic groups, they're decreasing for white Americans. And it's anomalous in historical terms. The last time there was a decline in overall life expectancy in the United States was between 1915 and 1918, during both a global flu pandemic and a world war. The decline in white life spans is so vexing that one global health researcher, Michael Marmot, director of the Institute of Health Equity in London, compared it to "the catastrophic seven-year drop for Russian men in the years after the collapse of the Soviet Union."

The steepest declines have been for white women without a high school diploma, who lost five years of expected life span between 1990 and 2008. In 2012, public health researchers found that life expectancy for white women without a high school diploma was 73.5 years, compared with 83.9 years for white women with a college degree or more. For white men, the gap was even bigger: 67.5

years for the least-educated white men compared with 80.4 for those with a college degree or better. David Cutler of Harvard University found declines in life expectancy for white women baffling, and said, "There's this enormous issue of why. It's very puzzling and we don't have a great explanation."

It's this conundrum about shortening white life spans that's at the center of *Dying of Whiteness*. Metzl uses case studies of political issues with a core of support among white voters in three different states in the American Midwest to make his argument. These are the expansion of gun rights in Missouri after the #BlackLivesMatter uprising in Ferguson; Tennessee's decision to opt out of the Affordable Care Act (ACA); and the GOP experiment in Kansas that implemented extreme funding cuts to a host of public goods, including education. In these cases, white people swayed by a particular ideology are embracing policies that guarantee both their ill health and an early death. Metzl, trained as both a physician and a sociologist, analyzes population health statistics from a number of databases and news reports. He also conducted in-depth interviews in each state from 2013 to 2018 and spoke with middle-class, working-class, and working-poor people about what he calls the "urgent and contested political issues facing the American electorate, including health care, guns, taxes, education, and the scope of government."

Perhaps the most telling example comes from the Tennessee data. Here, we meet a man Metzl calls Trevor, described as a forty-one-year-old cab driver who is chronically ill with hepatitis C and has no health insurance. If Trevor had lived one state over, in Kentucky, which adopted the Affordable Care Act, he would have had access to lifesaving and expensive medications called polymerase inhibitors or been eligible for a lifesaving liver transplant. But, because he lives in Tennessee, a state that has repeatedly blocked the Obama-era health care reform, Trevor faces an early, and painful, death. When Metzl interviews Trevor at his home, the man offers this justification for his refusal: "Ain't no way I would ever support Obamacare or sign up for it. I would rather die." Metzl asks a follow-up question about why he feels this way, and Trevor says, "We don't need any more government in our lives. And in any case, no way I want my tax dollars paying for Mexicans or welfare queens."

This sentiment, expressed over and over again by Metzl's respondents, is one answer to the mystery about white death. It is an illustration of what, a century ago, scholar W. E. B. Du Bois first identified as the "mental wage of whiteness." In the contemporary milieu, the wages of whiteness have been combined with what historian Timothy Snyder has called "sadopopulism," in which political leaders win support from already subjugated citizens only to implement policies that are designed to hurt them.

In the Missouri case study, Metzl considers the state's repeal of a permit-to-purchase (PTP) handgun law, making guns easier to buy and legal to openly carry. Metzl analyzes gun suicide rates by race and gender and finds that white men in Missouri are seven times more likely to turn their firearms on themselves than to be fatally shot by intruders. Yet, Metzl finds little support for regulating guns in Missouri, even in suicide support groups. When he asks a white woman from Missouri who has lost a loved one to suicide what guns mean to her, the reply is swift: "Freedom. Liberty. Patriotism. That's why we just voted for Trump. No way we were going to let 'Crooked Hillary' take those things away from us." In further analysis of the resulting impact on what epidemiologists refer to as potential years of lives lost, he finds that "loosening gun policies in Missouri went hand in hand with the loss of over 10,500 years of productive white male life in the state." Metzl connects the allure of "armed white maleness" with a system of rights, privileges, and power that eases the pain of social dislocation that many whites feel. And this system of rights, privilege, and power is also how Becca Campbell ended up with a handgun on that night in November 2014.

It would have been exceptionally difficult for Becca Campbell or anyone in Missouri to purchase, conceal, or transport a handgun just a decade earlier. But in the years and months leading up to her death, a series of pro-gun laws made it much easier for citizens to own firearms and carry them in public. In fact, just two months before, Missouri lawmakers passed a law that allowed citizens to carry concealed handguns at schools, annulled most city and regional gun restrictions, and allowed just about anyone over the age of nineteen to carry a concealed weapon without a permit. Among Missouri's pro-gun laws were so-called Castle doctrine statutes that permitted gun owners to shoot perceived intruders in their homes, like the law my father taught me growing up in Texas. These new Missouri laws made anyone who used a gun against an intruder "free from legal prosecution for the consequences of the force used." Gun sales spiked in St. Louis ahead of the Darren Wilson verdict, and particularly among "new, inexperienced gun owners," like Becca Campbell. In the months after Campbell died, legislation would extend Castle doctrine protections to a person's car. These kinds of laws are, in the broader sense, tied into the kind of political rhetoric that promises to "Make America Great Again," restoring an era of supposedly unquestioned white rule. Yet, when read through the lens of health, such policies have boomeranged back to deliver widespread harm to the white population. Between 2008 and 2013, white people from Missouri unintentionally shot and killed themselves, their friends, and their family members ten times more frequently than they shot any other racial or ethnic group.

## SUICIDE AND OTHER DEATHS OF DESPAIR AMONG WHITE WOMEN

In April 2020, Dr. Lorna Breen left New York City, where she had worked in the emergency room of New York-Presbyterian/Columbia University hospital treating COVID-19 patients, and returned to her parents' home in Charlottesville, Virginia. Breen, forty-nine years old, was described by work colleagues as a "lively presence, outgoing, and extroverted" who enjoyed salsa dancing, snowboarding, and travel. She had no history of mental illness. On April 26, while staying at her parents' home, Dr. Lorna Breen ended her own life. Those close to her said that she had been overwhelmed by the pressure to save the many people with COVID-19 who came into the emergency room where she worked. "She tried to do her job, and it killed her," her father, Phillip Breen, said.

White women who are medical doctors take their own life at twice the rate of other women who work, according to a large study of twenty-six US states over the span of nine years. "White female physicians have a higher suicide rate than other working white females in the USA regardless of age," concluded the study's authors, who used a national database of deaths to compare numbers of suicides among doctors, dentists, and all other occupations. But it's not just white women doctors. Suicide is more widespread among white women, compared to white men, and the trend goes beyond just those who work as physicians.

According to a Centers for Disease Control and Prevention study, suicide rates in the United States increased by 40 percent between 1999 and 2016. In 2016, there were more than twice as many suicides as homicides, and 84 percent of people who killed themselves were white. Recent reports indicate the trend in suicide rates is going up for women. Specifically, suicide rates are on the rise for white women despite their structural advantages. The biggest change was among women in late middle age. "For females between the ages of 45 and 64, the suicide rate increased by 60 percent," said Dr. Holly Hedegaard, an epidemiologist.

The pattern in suicides is not the same for all women, and this is a place where trying to explain a phenomenon in gender-only terms hinders, rather than helps, our understanding. Researchers have discovered something called the "suicide paradox" in which Black women are much less likely to die by their own hand than are white women. The role of social networks and religion in Black women's lives may act as a protective factor. One study pointed to two additional factors that mitigate against life-ending self-harm. First, Black women's encounters with long-standing race, gender, and sometimes class oppression have forced many Black women to develop resilience. Second, Black women are highly regarded within their support systems, so their levels of responsibility and commitment to others may help to protect them from taking their own lives. I want to be careful here to acknowledge the very real suffering that Black women, specifically, endure at the intersections of gender, race, and sometimes class oppression. There is a centuries-old lie that Black women feel less pain, and that myth often invites more mistreatment, such as the horrific gynecological experiments Dr. Marion Sims conducted without anesthesia on enslaved women. In part because of this history, Black women often have been required to cultivate a network of social support and forge connections to larger communities in ways that white women have not.

Of course, white people, including white women, get to skip all those life stressors associated with systemic racism, and that pays off in physical health advantages. Housing and employment discrimination, daily microaggressions, and the biases of healthcare providers and systems erode health and chip away at life expectancy. However, despite the racial privilege that insulates white people from those stressors, they report poorer mental health than African Americans. National data suggest that white people experience a higher number of psychiatric disorders over a lifetime than members of other racial groups. And, since the mid-1990s, reports of chronic pain and mental distress among middle-aged whites have increased.

It's this last fact, about the increase in reports of chronic pain and mental distress among white people, that may be part of the explanation for the rise in white women's suicide rates. Prescription drugs, including opioids, are more readily available in white populations than in communities of color. African Americans, in particular, are routinely denied access to pain medication, while whites have ready access to it. For example, African Americans are 34 percent less likely than whites to be prescribed opioids for back pain, abdominal pain, and migraines and 14 percent less likely to be prescribed such medications for pain from traumatic injuries or surgery. Pharmacies in poor white neighborhoods are fifty-four times more likely to have "adequate supplies" of opioids than pharmacies in similar neighborhoods where people of color live. Given the easier access to prescription pain medicine for whites—and the corollary restricted access to pain relief for African Americans—it is perhaps not surprising that rates of overdose death from prescription opioids are higher among white people than Black people. The rate of increase is shocking, however: deaths of women from prescription opioids increased more than 400 percent between 1999 and 2010. These statistics are reported in gender-only form, not broken out by race, but it is safe to assume that the majority of this increase is among white women.

Princeton economists Angus Deaton and Anne Case in their 2020 book *Deaths of Despair and the Future of Capitalism* write that "heavy drinking, overeating, social isolation, drugs, and suicide are plausible outcomes of processes that have cumulatively undermined the meaning of life for white working-class people." Those processes include globalization, the decline of unions, and resulting downward mobility. What Case and Deaton found is that the places with higher rates of deaths of despair are the same places with higher levels of unemployment. This holds true even when you look separately at rates of suicide, drug overdoses, and alcohol-related liver disease. Each one of these goes up where joblessness increases. This explains some of what's happening with the white working class; when jobs go away, so does hope for living. But even the rigorous and valuable work of Case and Deaton doesn't explain the even steeper rise in deaths among white women.

Could it be that these deaths of despair are, at least in part, a response to the kind of psychic numbness that James Baldwin talked about? Baldwin wrote that the "price of the ticket" required to become white is to give up one's full humanity. To cope with this dissociation, we rely on soul-numbing technologies—drinking, drugs, overeating—all while anaesthetizing ourselves with the latest "binge-worthy" television. Perhaps these are all ways to try to forget the price we've paid for whiteness and the awful bargain we've struck.

## SHIRLEY

Suicide has divided my life. When I was twenty-one and she was forty-eight, my mother, Shirley, took her own life. That one night in March of 1983 will always be the moment that splits my life into before and after.

Since then, I have been consumed by a desire to understand the phenomenon of death turned toward the self. I wonder, sometimes, if I became a sociologist because one of the key texts in the field is *Suicide* by Émile Durkheim. I felt at home in a field that was committed to understanding the broad patterns of these kinds of deaths. Even now, some thirty-seven years later, I will read any news story that involves suicide, whether it's about someone well known, like Kate Spade or Robin Williams, or a local story about someone I've never heard of. I line up the details of each news report of suicide with the details of my mother's: she drank most of a fifth of vodka and took five bottles of prescription pills before she went to bed that night in March, laying down next to her husband, my father, who was already asleep. At around three a.m., her body went into convulsions, and my father woke and called for an ambulance. She was dead by the time the ambulance arrived. She left a note that simply said, "I love you all —S." Our family was set adrift then and never recovered from her violent decision to leave us.

Shirley grew up in a household of abuse and neglect, and did her best to recover from that psychologically, but could never shake the profound sense of worthlessness she inherited from her mother. This came through in our discussions about housework, her chief occupation. When she was growing up, Shirley's mother forced her to stay home from school to clean house, while her two siblings, one older and one younger, went off to school. If Shirley didn't clean well enough or fast enough, her mother would beat her until she bled. When, as a child, I would ask Shirley to teach me how to do some of the housework she regularly did for my father and me, she would refuse, saying, "You don't need to know this, don't be like me. You'll have someone do this for you." Her highest aspiration for me was to marry up in class as she had done, heterosexually of course, and to subcontract out the domestic labor she thought was beneath me. This plan was an especially problematic one, resting as it did on multiple and overlapping systems of domination and submission, including my own. It was also a response to the sadomasochism of her upbringing. In the end, she turned that on herself.

While I will always be sifting through the psychological wreckage that my mother's self-destructiveness left for me, it's the broad patterns of suicide that fascinate me. I wasn't a feminist when my mother died, but I could already see the way the role of nice white ladyhood had shortened her life. A teen marriage, a high school dropout, a child, a divorce, a second marriage to my father—a step up the class ladder—and another child (me), she seemed to have overcome every struggle to finally win the promised golden prize of becoming a suburban housewife. Then, the reality of doing housework every day settled in, and the prize looked less unambiguously benevolent. Shirley's life began to echo this archetype in the culture of the depressed, suburban housewife—from poet Sylvia Plath to April Wheeler (*Revolutionary Road*) to Betty Draper (*Mad Men*)—the theme repeats. It is a narrative about the lives of women who have come to the end of the rewards of the white woman ideal and have found the promised prize to be empty, isolating, and unfulfilling. I've come to see the end of Shirley's life as collateral damage from whiteness as much as gender. This self-destructive behavior isn't bounded by or easily explained by economic hardship. It's also relatively affluent white women, like my mother, like Diane Schuler, like Dr. Lorna Breen, who are dying. I've felt the pull of those same forces, like an undertow, trying to drown me, too. I wonder about the ways I haven't escaped.

At Shirley's funeral, her mother said, through big sobs and to no one in particular, "How could Shirley do this? She had everything! That new car, that big house, all that jewelry! Why wasn't she happy?"

*How could she* not be happy.

## THE PROMISE OF HAPPINESS

For white women who are taught to be nice above all else, there's something insidious about this promise of happiness, which is often presumed to be the reward for niceness. Feminist writer Sara Ahmed is critical of the way happiness has become a moral imperative. We *must* be happy. When happiness is promised as a "reward for certain ways of life," then happiness becomes a form of social control. Even if that happiness doesn't arrive along with that certain kind of life, it is still implied as waiting somewhere just beyond the next turn. Ahmed's 2010 book *The Promise of Happiness* explores those figures who are stereotypically unhappy—feminist killjoys, queers, immigrants. For Ahmed, there is joy and a whole range of other ways of being in the world, which become possible when we refuse the social control that is embedded in the promise of happiness. I think this is part of how I escaped the undertow that pulled Shirley away from us; I refused the assigned script, turned away from the social ideal, and thus avoided much of the social control that went with these. But I still feel the pressure to strive toward an acceptable form of happiness, often dressed in New Age drag as "positivity" or in corporate-branded pink ribbons.

The leading cause of death for white women between the ages of forty-five and eighty-four is cancer, and we are supposed to be happy about it or, at the very least, cheerful. Barbara Ehrenreich, in her book *Bright-Sided: How Positive Thinking Is Undermining America*, describes the nonstop cheer she had to confront when she was diagnosed with breast cancer. She writes that dissent against this kind of obligatory cheerfulness was regarded as a kind of "treason" by those around her. And the "smile or die" ethos surrounding cancer she observed is particularly harsh for women who are, in other arenas, constantly street-harassed to smile for the pleasure of men. More than this, not displaying positivity was regarded with a kind of superstition that it would make her more vulnerable to cancer, when in fact research suggests just the opposite.

A series of studies over the past few decades show that suppressing your emotions can and does affect your body and your mind. One 2013 study by the Harvard School of Public Health and the University of Rochester showed that people who bottled up their emotions increased their chance of premature death from all causes by more than 30 percent, with their risk of being diagnosed with cancer increasing by 70 percent. One scientist involved in the study said, "Looking on the bright side of life might not be helpful in difficult times, with studies showing suppressing emotions can negatively affect your health."

Over 268,000 women die of breast cancer each year in the United States, with white women having the highest rate of diagnosis (432 per 100,000), followed by Black (391), Hispanic (340), American Indian/Alaska Native (306), and Asian and Pacific Islander (305). But Black women have the highest mortality rates from cancer. In statistics from the CDC for 2016, Black women have a mortality rate of 64 per 1,000 compared to 46 for white women and 31 for Hispanic women. Positivity in the face of hundreds of thousands of women dying each year is, like mindfulness, a kind of racket. Collectively, we should be furious about the underlying causes of cancer and organizing across racial and class differences to fight the toxins in our environment, in our food supply, in our water, and in the products we buy that are largely to blame for cancers. Instead, we get a pink-ribbon-industrial-complex that celebrates the corporations that are, more often than not, the source of these carcinogens that are making us sick in the first place.

The Ford Motor Company has a cobranding agreement with the Komen Foundation to promote Ford Warriors in Pink, which is "dedicated to helping those touched by breast cancer, through actions that support, inspire, and empower patients, survivors and co-survivors throughout their journey." In 2008–2009, Ford sold a Pink Warrior Mustang, a sports car with pink accent stripes. And the current website for Pink Warriors offers more modest purchases—scarves, ties, and face masks—all branded with Pink Warrior colors as "gear that gives" and promotes the "$138 million donated since 1993." As Samantha King points out in her book *Pink Ribbons, Inc.*, companies like Ford benefit from the gauzy association with the "fight" against breast cancer, while the donations collected are not necessarily doing anything to end the scourge of cancer on women's lives and as their products continue to harm the environment and women's bodies. In a perverse and perfectly capitalistic twist, the same companies then turn around and profit once more from bedecking us in pink as we march, run, and race "for the cure."

As women, and particularly white women, we think the bargain is this: be nice, channel light and love, and everything will work out. But the real bargain is actually: be nice and don't speak up because our collective silence, and specifically the silence of white women, facilitates the continued smooth operation of oppressive systems. It's the situation Princess Diana found herself in, isn't it? Be a good princess, deliver the heir and a spare, and you'll be happy. But she wasn't, and when she spoke up about it, she very nearly toppled the oppressive monarchy that held her captive. Once she escaped that gilded cage, she was caught by another. The paparazzi's quest for a photograph of her angelic whiteness led to a chase through the streets of Paris and a car crash late one August night in 1997, another death due to unintentional injuries. To the extent that we've been sold on the idea that happiness will be our reward for niceness, or that looking on the bright side will help us cope, we've been sold a load of horseshit, as they say in Texas.

## THE LIE OF WHITENESS, AND THE TRUTH OF IT

Whiteness is both a lie and the truth. It is a paradox that white people are being forced to grapple with at this moment in multiple ways.
Many of us are coming to terms with what it means to claim a white
racial identity, how we contribute to the current reality of white supremacy, and how we can come to terms with ancestors who were
settlers and colonizers. In 2020, many white people were reawak-
ened to just how profoundly white identity was connected to system-
ically racialized violence and death, from witnessing a white cop kill
George Floyd, to seeing how much more deadly COVID-19 was for
Black and Brown communities than white communities, to taking in
the global scale of the Black Lives Matter protests. For some, the pre-
dictions of a white demographic minority, the declining white birth
rate, and the mere presence of immigrant neighbors represented painful challenges to the very essence of white identity. For others, race
remained a topic they felt too uncomfortable with and ill equipped to
address, so they preferred to avoid the subject entirely.

When Barack Obama became president, many people proclaimed
that the fact that a Black man was elected to the highest office was
proof that we were living in a "postracial America." The idea that
President Obama represented a transcendence of race seemed to
appeal to a certain type of white person. Like the Dean Armitage
(Bradley Whitford) character in Jordan Peele's 2017 film *Get Out*,
who says, "By the way, I would have voted for Obama for a third
term, if I could. Best president in my lifetime, hands down," even as
he plots the kidnapping and murder of Black people closer to home.

Around the time of Obama's first inauguration in January 2009,
the postracial idea circulated in the press, with headlines like, OUR
POSTRACIAL PRESIDENT, in the *New York Daily News*, and one that
proclaimed THE END OF WHITE AMERICA in the *Atlantic*. For the
latter, writer Hua Hsu explored the idea of our postracialness and
interviewed sociologist Matt Wray, who observed that many of his
students at Temple University were troubled by what he called a

racial identity crisis: "They don't care about socioeconomics; they care about culture. And to be white is to be culturally broke." Wray's quote from 2009 seems prescient now. He went on to say, "The classic thing white students say when you ask them to talk about who they are is, 'I don't have a culture.' They might be privileged, they might be loaded socioeconomically, but they feel bankrupt when it comes to culture. . . . They feel disadvantaged, and they feel marginalized. They don't have a culture that's cool or oppositional."

A short nine years later, the headlines were much different. In August 2018, the *New York Times* ran a piece by Pankaj Mishra with the headline THE RELIGION OF WHITENESS BECOMES A SUICIDE CULT, in which he detailed the destructiveness of white-supremacist policies that were conceived of, developed, and implemented by the Trump administration. This careening from "postracial" to "culturally broke" to "suicide cult" is more than a reflection of the vicissitudes of presidential politics; it also maps onto something about whiteness.

"The discovery of personal whiteness is a very modern thing," W. E. B. Du Bois wrote in a 1920 essay called "The Souls of White Folk." Du Bois points out that this "personal" whiteness is also global. Du Bois's assessment foreshadowed the development in the latter half of the twentieth century of a globally networked whiteness, forged out of the formation of transnational identities and national exclusions, and circulated over the internet. But this personal and global whiteness—this identity that people have made a "religion" of, in Du Bois's terms, and that so many are willing to die for, in Metzl's telling—is also a myth.

"As long as you think you're white, there's no hope for you," Baldwin wrote in his 1984 essay "On Being White . . . and Other Lies" for *Esquire* magazine. This, then, is the paradox of whiteness. It is an identity that, once embraced, makes the reality of life easier within racial capitalism; and it is a fiction that, once embraced, can undermine one's physical health, shorten one's life span, corrode one's mental health, and perhaps even damage one's soul. Baldwin also wrote about what he called the "moral erosion" that has made it "quite impossible for those who think of themselves as white in this country to have any moral authority at all—privately, or publicly." He then went on to describe what that moral erosion looked like, as white people "sit, stunned, before their TV sets, swallowing garbage that they know to be garbage, and—in a profound and unconscious effort to justify this torpor that disguises a profound and bitter panic."

Baldwin named the moral and material cost of maintaining whiteness for white people: self-destruction. The lie of whiteness holds out a promise that being white will save us from social isolation and disconnection through materialism, individualism, and the satisfaction of superiority. A century ago, the specter of Black, Indigenous, and other people of color having "too many" children sparked apocalyptic visions of "race suicide"—called "white genocide" today—among political elites and populist voters alike and prompted efforts at shoring up white heterosexuality and marriage. The metaphor of "race suicide" has had very real consequences for women's lives because it created the conditions for the forced sterilization of Black, Indigenous, and Latina women and pressed white women into eugenic service to literally reproduce the white race. Upholding the lie of whiteness is deadly for all of us.

## THERE'S SOMETHING WRONG WITH "KARENS"

There is something wrong with us, the white women who become "Karens." We are not so different from Derek Chauvin, the police officer who we all watched kneel on George Floyd's neck as he cried out for his mother. What is so clear in that video is the sadomasochism, the pleasure Chauvin takes in inflicting pain on Floyd. He is defiant, even. Chauvin is part of the "armed white maleness" that Metzl points out is endemic to the United States. Amy Cooper, aka "Central Park Karen," displays a differently gendered version of this phenomenon, still rooted in sadomasochism.

In the Central Park video taken of Amy Cooper, it appears that she is intentional about bringing "death by cop" to Christian Cooper when she says, "I'm going to tell them that an African American man is threatening my life." And we can hear her artlessly throw her voice into a higher register with the 911 dispatcher to explain that she is in danger. As Christian Cooper records her, she nonchalantly strangles her dog while she looks defiantly back at his cell phone camera. Derek Chauvin's face has the same defiance as he stares down Darnella Frazier, the seventeen-year-old Black girl who recorded George Floyd's death. It is the same look of murderous intent and expansive entitlement seen in the faces of white people in the crowds in lynching photographs. The knowing cruelty persists.

In the events that followed the Central Park video going viral, Amy Cooper lost both her job at Franklin Templeton and her dog. The shelter where she adopted the dog made her return her pet. A week later, she got the dog back, but not her job. In an interview with CNN, Amy Cooper said she wanted to "publicly apologize to everyone," adding, "I'm not a racist. I did not mean to harm that man in any way." She also said she didn't mean any harm to the African American community. Her statement is so disconnected from reality, and the very real harm she threatened to cause and did cause, that it suggests something terribly wrong.

For his part, Christian Cooper has been magnanimous in response to her threat to him. "I think her apology is sincere," he told CNN's Don Lemon. "I'm not sure that in that apology she recognizes that while she may not be or consider herself a racist, that particular act was definitely racist." In a humanizing turn, he goes on to express compassion for Amy Cooper and calls out the violent threats against her. "I find it strange that people who were upset that . . . that she tried to bring death by cop down on my head, would then turn around and try to put death threats on her head. Where is the logic in that?" he said. "Where does that make any kind of sense?"

It doesn't make any sense. And for him to care for Amy Cooper's well-being in the midst of all this speaks to Christian Cooper's greater humanity, his higher spiritual development, even. Mr. Cooper created art out of his experience, producing a graphic novel about a Black teenager who looks at birds through binoculars and instead sees the faces of Black people who have been killed by the police. Ms. Cooper has disappeared from public view and has not, as far as anyone knows, created art out of her experience.

How do we make sense of Amy and the other Karens, the white women behaving badly in this particularly oppressive way? More than that, how do we make sense of her response, almost identical to the response that so often follows these incidents: "I'm not a racist. And I didn't mean to cause harm in any way."

I don't think we can make sense of it until we understand the sadomasochism at the heart of whiteness. In sociologist Lynn Chancer's classic text *Sadomasochism in Everyday Life*, she argues that sexual sadomasochism is only the best-known manifestation of what is actually a much more broadly based social phenomenon. Chancer moves from personal relationships to interactions in school and the workplace to explain how capitalism and patriarchy create a social psychology awash in rituals of dominance and submission. The evidence of this proposition seems clear in the stories of Harvey Weinstein and Roger Ailes, in which extensive reporting and court documents revealed the way that these powerful white men routinized the dominance and submission of women in the workplace.

As a culture, we seem to be entertained by rituals of humiliation. Many of the reality-based television shows we consume, such as *The Swan, Who's Your Daddy?*, and *The Apprentice*, are steeped in patterns of dominance and humiliation. As *New York Times* reporter Alessandra Stanley puts it, "Humiliation is the unifying principle behind a successful reality show." Novelist Salman Rushdie contends that such forms of entertainment are reinventing "gladiatorial combat" in which the TV set is the Colosseum and the contestants are both gladiators and lions; their job is to eat one another until only one remains alive. "But how long . . . before real lions, actual dangers, are introduced to these various forms of fantasy island to feed our hunger for more action, more pain, more vicarious thrills?"

When Lynndie England, the Army Reserve soldier from West Virginia, was photographed holding a leash tied around the neck of an Iraqi man held prisoner, she smiled and gave a thumbs-up. The images of abused, naked Iraqi prisoners at Abu Ghraib were considered humiliating precisely because a woman, a white American woman soldier, was dominating the men. Although the US military disavowed the photographs taken at Abu Ghraib as the result of rogue soldiers, their circulation continued; television news viewers witnessed these images, photographed for the express purpose of showcasing terror.

As scholar Myra Mendible points out, such images reflect a curiously morbid reflection of Western culture's "narcissistic relationship with the camera." For her part, Lynndie England told a BBC reporter that "I hated myself for Abu Ghraib." And this, then, is the self-destructive cycle of sadomasochism: I torture you and then hate myself because I've mistreated you, then I want to hurt you again because I'm so angry at you that you've made me feel this way about myself. It is the underlying dynamic in intimate partner abuse, and when humiliation rituals get played out in and through geopolitics like at Abu Ghraib, it can incite international conflict. White women are not only victims of this dynamic; like Lynndie England, we are also perpetrators.

Education scholars Cheryl Matias and Ricky Lee Allen have explicitly connected sadomasochism to whiteness. They write: "Fearing loneliness, whites masochistically cling to the white polity, expecting to find some wholeness and love there." Here, they draw on Thandeka's theory about the psychological formation of the child who is brought up to believe in their own whiteness. We fear that acknowledging the emptiness of whiteness will leave us ostracized and alone, so we hold on to the fiction of our own superiority, even as it destroys the world and us along with it.

Matias and Allen go on to explain why some people, like Amy Cooper perhaps, become emotionally invested in whiteness. They write, "Facing what they believe to be an unbearable condition, that is, to be without the white 'race' and thus alone and racially vulnerable, whites exhibit neurotic behavior when their contradictions are exposed. Living the lie of whiteness, they become angry, defensive, and agitated when the reality of their racial practice is shown to be incongruent with their racial idealism." There is, in this formulation, something acutely neurotic in the repeated behavior of white women who inflict pain and trauma onto people of color. Underneath all the protestations about the reality of white harm, there are the original selves that gave up their independence to get the conditional love of the white family, a "love" that remains only if we fall in line and maintain the facade of racial superiority and separateness. Inherent in this emotional investment is a false sense of belonging, a defensive sense of self-understanding, and a distorted sense of love tied to a group identification. However unrecognized or suppressed in us, we are trapped in a sadomasochistic relationship with whiteness, with its fear of isolation and loneliness that so compels us to never leave whiteness. In other words, we don't cling to whiteness out of love; rather, we take up whiteness for fear of being expelled, alone, and powerless in the face of white racial domination.

White women like Amy Cooper make life-threatening 911 calls with one hand as they strangle their dogs with the other, and then say they "meant no harm." The disconnect is so profound, and so often repeated, it suggests a psychological compulsion rooted in the unconscious. It could be that Amy Cooper and the other Karens who call 911 on innocent Black people are replaying the intergenerational sadomasochism of whiteness. The routine harm of racialized others through police brutality and the 911 calls that summon it are, like the lynch mobs attended by white families and the postcards that circulated among those families for decades afterward, practices that enable white people to reaffirm their dominant place in society by inflicting pain on others. For some white women, engaging in this domination is the only way they can assuage their unease at not being whole without it.

## CONCLUSION

Historian Diane Miller Sommerville researched suicides for a recent book. She focused on the Civil War era in the United States and found that although suicide was regarded as a weakness at an earlier time, this shifted after the war ended. She writes that for those in the defeated South, "by the end of the 19th century, suicide among whites was . . . a kind of marker of nationalism and white suprem- acy." Better to end one's life than live under the tyranny of the North, the thinking went. For white women, suicide was the heroic martyr's choice. In Thomas Dixon's 1905 novel *The Clansman*, Marion Lenoir, a fifteen-year-old white girl and love interest of the main character, Ben Cameron, a white man, is brutally raped by Gus, a Black man. She then commits suicide by leaping off a cliff. Her mother, Jeannie Lenoir, joins her daughter in a suicidal plunge off the same cliff. We, white women, have been dying of whiteness and by our own hand for a long time, it seems.

Whiteness is the lie that is killing us, and the lie is gendered. Dy- ing from the despair of whiteness doesn't look the same for all white women. For Becca Campbell, whiteness showed up in Missouri's gun laws and Castle doctrine, which made sure she had the right to carry a loaded gun as a response to the protests after a Black teenager, Mi- chael Brown, was killed by police. For Dr. Lorna Breen, it material- ized as an elite career in New York City, but her desire to save patients was no match for a global pandemic disproportionately killing Black and Brown people, and her despair ended her life. Whiteness has an unrecognized role in the rising number of white women who are dying from suicide, opioid overdose, and alcohol-related liver disease.

For Shirley, my mother who grew up poor in Texas, who never graduated high school, then who married above her parents' class, white ladyhood offered the promise of being a happy homemaker, and that was no life at all. The bargain that Princess Diana agreed to was just as bankrupt, though with a more gilded, and intensely pub- lic, cage. And the 268,000 and more women with breast cancer who are cajoled into cheerfulness as they struggle with a brutal disease are suffering from the added pressure of a performative cheerfulness most often required of white women.

"Whiteness is nothing if not unconscious," writes clinical psychologist Natasha Stovall. She goes on to add: "White Americans are in the midst of a public mental health crisis—just check the acting out: suicide, addiction, mass shootings." She's right. As many scholars have already pointed out, the mass shootings are overwhelmingly committed by white men. WHY IS IT ALWAYS A WHITE GUY, reads a headline from *Salon* magazine in 2013 after another mass shooting. In it, the author explains the way whiteness and masculinity are connected and how that connection results in violence. In her award-winning book *White Rage*, scholar Carol Anderson writes about the people so invested in whiteness that they could not bear to see a Black man as president.

Could it be that white women express their rage differently from how white men do, from the safe remove of a 911 call? And when that fails, perhaps they turn that rage inward, on themselves. Accustomed to the language of gender and resigned to seeing ourselves as victims of oppression, white women can recognize the way gender shapes our lives. Yet, because whiteness remains unconscious for so many of us and because we, as nice white ladies, resist seeing ourselves as perpetrators of oppression, we do not as easily see the way it shapes our lives.

Filmmaker Liz Garbus in her documentary *There's Something Wrong with Aunt Diane* enlists the help of a forensic psychologist, Dr. Harold Bursztajn, to understand what led up to that crash on the Taconic Parkway. Bursztajn conducts a psychological autopsy on Schuler, trying to make sense of small clues that point to a larger truth. We learn that when she was nine years old, Diane's mother left her family and Diane then took on the role of caretaker to her three brothers and her father. "This could be very traumatic for a young girl," he says at one point, but the viewer is left wanting to know more about what was really going on inside the mind of Diane Schuler.

Watching Bursztajn's struggle in that film might feel familiar to anyone who has sorted through the detritus of a sudden death that leaves more questions than answers. When that happens, one is left with the forensics of the case, and you speculate and spin possible scenarios from little bits of evidence. In the Schuler case, relatives speculate: Maybe she had a stroke? Maybe she had severe tooth pain? Maybe the toothache led to a stroke? Anything but the facts revealed in the toxicology report: she had a blood alcohol level of 0.19 and THC in her system at the time of the crash. This is what psychologists call denial, both Diane Schuler's denial of her own psychic pain, which she was self-medicating to manage, and her family's denial about her condition.

We are also practiced at denial about the pain that white women can cause. The shock of the photographs from Abu Ghraib was a response to the cruelty captured in those images and to seeing Lynndie England, a white woman, as the tormentor. Underneath that is an assumption that England, a working-class white woman, couldn't possibly torture those men. It is the same impulse as in the headlines about the Taconic crash, How COULD SHE? Although England expresses remorse about her actions, she cannot offer insight about her actions because she does not have any. Amy Cooper, aka Central Park Karen, does not smile for the camera but nevertheless proceeds unimpeded to threaten "death by cop" against the Black man recording her as she strangles her dog. She, too, apologizes but, like England, cannot offer insight about her actions because she does not have any. We can only speculate about what motivates Lynndie England or Amy Cooper because their own lack of self-awareness leaves us, again, with the forensics of the case afterward, speculating on what led up to these terrible series of events. We have to find a way out of the dead end on offer within white womanhood.

In his novel *The Virgin Suicides*, Jeffery Eugenides writes, "In the end, the tortures tearing the Lisbon girls pointed to a simple reasoned refusal to accept the world as it was handed down to them, so full of flaws." The 1993 novel tells the story of five sisters, ages thirteen to seventeen, growing up in the suburban idyll of Gross Pointe, Michigan. One by one, the sisters kill themselves as their ineffectual parents and the lascivious boys that live across the street watch, unable to stop them. One literary scholar writes that the Eugenides novel is about "the difficulty of abandoning European pasts in order to adopt the white American identities required for a life in the suburbs." It's as if the Lisbon sisters saw their future as white suburban women and refused the crushing of self that is required in that version of American identity. I think there was a kind of refusal in my mother's death as well, a refusal to continue to accept the pain and limitations of her white, suburban housewife existence. We have to find a different kind of refusal rather than death by suicide.

As Sara Ahmed suggests, part of how we get free is through a refusal of the promise of a certain kind of happiness. I believe that if Shirley could have figured out ways to refuse the version of happiness that had been packaged and sold to her, she could have made her way out of housewife servitude alive, but she could never imagine a world where she deserved better. Perhaps she never knew that anything else was possible. What I have come to understand is that there is joy and liberation on the other side of refusing happiness. There is a certain kind of joy that is part of what being queer has meant for me: it is a rejection of niceness, a renunciation of ladyhood, and it has saved me. And, to the extent that I have chosen to put my life in community with Black, Indigenous, Latinx, Asian, and immigrant people, I have found ways to divest from the death cult of whiteness. This, too, has been a refusal of happiness and an embrace of joy and liberation.

There is something wrong with us, those of us who cling to being nice white ladies. Yet, refusing white womanhood is no easy task; we cannot simply shrug it off, like we might a cardigan from a twinset on a warm afternoon.

# CONCLUSION

"We're entering a new phase of American whiteness," Nell Irvin Painter told a reporter in early August 2020. She should know. Painter is the author of *The History of White People*, the definitive scholarly tome on the subject. From her perspective as a historian with a centuries-long view of the historical development of whiteness, Painter sees a shift occurring.

"What's happened since the spring and summer of 2020 in the George Floyd and Black Lives Matter demonstrations and protests is that millions of white Americans are waking up to their whiteness and being puzzled," she said. "What I see changing now, there's a big space for people who are understanding that they are raced as white people and aren't quite sure what it means and are learning about it," Painter said. I see this change, too, along with the uncertainty and confusion.

We who are raised white are not practiced at noticing whiteness and even less so at undoing it. However, we are living through extraordinary times of protests and a pandemic that have shaken loose something in the foundations of whiteness. In the summer of 2020, in large cities and about 2,500 small towns across the United States, there were more than 4,700 demonstrations, an average of 140 per day, with turnout ranging from a few dozen to tens of thousands. "I've never seen self-reports of protest participation [this] high for a specific issue over such a short period," sociologist Neal Caren told a reporter. In this moment, some white ladies began to question white dominance rather than rely on it to cushion their existence.

White women have been active agents in perpetuating systems of inequality from which they benefit, as the previous chapters have explained in some detail. Now I want to turn to some of the ways that a small handful of white women have relinquished power, stepped aside from unwanted advantage, and joined with those fighting to dismantle white supremacy. My hope is that their examples, few though they are, will inspire other white women to join in these efforts to tear down this destructive system we've helped create.

The police killings of Breonna Taylor and George Floyd prompted some white women to join with others who were putting their bodies on the front lines of protests. Black Lives Matter protesters in Louisville, Kentucky, have waged a sustained uprising to call for justice in the death of Breonna Taylor, a twenty-six-year-old Black woman who was shot and killed by Louisville police when they entered her home in the middle of the night in March 2020. At one of the protests in late May, a group of white women formed a line, each one locking arms with the woman next to her, creating a barrier between Louisville Metro Police and Black protesters. These white women were responding to instructions from Chanelle Helm, one of the lead organizers for Black Lives Matter Louisville, who through a bullhorn said: "If you are going to be here, you should defend this space." This example of a group of white women following the organizing strategy of a Black woman, Chanelle Helm, demanding justice for another Black woman, Breonna Taylor, is one small instance of the shift we need to make as white women. Listening to and taking the lead from Black women organizers is a good start. For other white women, there has been a renewed awareness that our votes and elections have consequences.

"I just want to apologize to the world. I feel so guilty for having a part in voting this moron in," one unidentified white woman told a reporter in the months before the 2020 election. Another white woman, Juliann Bortz, who lives in Lehigh Valley, Pennsylvania, voted for Barack Obama in the previous election, but in 2016 she thought a "new approach, a business approach" couldn't hurt when she cast a ballot for Trump. "I was wrong. Boy was I wrong," said Bortz. Kris Searcy, a white Kentucky native, said she felt "disgusted" about voting for the GOP in 2016 but that she had had serious misgivings about Hillary Clinton. "I thought Trump would just sit back, [not] be involved in anything [and] get a lot of really smart, intellectual conservatives to come in." It didn't take long for Searcy to have a change of heart. "When I heard his inauguration speech, I just felt sick to my stomach," she recalled. Despite the media attention on white women like these for changing their minds, polling data indicates that most did not. In fact, the percentage of white women who voted for children in cages, a Muslim ban, and "good people on both sides" at a white-supremacist rally increased from 2016 to 2020. It doesn't have to be this way.

Even white women who have joined the extremist white-supremacist movement have the potential for transformation. Corinna Olsen, one of the women profiled in journalist Seyward Darby's book *Sisters in Hate*, grows disillusioned with the movement and defects. We know some of what it takes to deradicalize someone, thanks to the work of women like Angela King, who runs Life After Hate, a nonprofit that helps people leave extremist groups, as she did. It took her years to leave behind her friends in the movement and to detox from white-supremacist ideology. Each individual turned away from extremism contains a complex set of circumstances that need to be better understood so that we might scale these conditions to work on a national level. And we might have this knowledge in hand except that the Trump administration cut funding for programs to counter right-wing extremism and blocked the dissemination of data on the subject. It was only in 2019 that the Department of Homeland Security acknowledged that white supremacy was a national security threat, but that wasn't enough for one white woman.

Elizabeth Neumann, a lifelong Republican, voted for Trump in 2016 and "very reluctantly" worked in the administration. She served in the Department of Homeland Security as assistant secretary of counterterrorism and threat prevention and resigned after three years. In a series of interviews after her resignation, she said that if voices "at the top" of government would speak out against extremist groups, it would help diminish their appeal. "But instead, we have the opposite effect. We have the president not only pretty much refusing to condemn, but throwing fuel on the fire . . . through his rhetoric," Neumann said. Although it would be easy to criticize her for being late to this realization, Neumann's decision to resign and speak out was a principled one that may have helped someone else gather the courage they needed to resist in other ways.

There have been other white women of even greater courage who have made it their life's work to help dismantle white supremacy. These women took heroic risks, often to their own lives, to fight white supremacy. And their lives contain lessons for us today.

## A TINY HANDFUL (OR, A SHORT FUCKING LIST)

When Sarah Grimké was five years old, she saw one of the enslaved people her family owned being whipped. What she witnessed so horrified her, as she would tell the story later, she attempted to board a steamboat so she could go to a place where there was no slavery. Sarah and her sister Angelina were daughters of a wealthy family in Charleston, South Carolina. Both sisters moved north in the 1820s, and as historian Gerda Lerner explains in her classic text *The Grimké Sisters from South Carolina*, the women stepped out of the conventional roles set out for them and into a life of activism that they designed for themselves. They became prominent writers advocating for the abolition of slavery and, later, for women's rights. They spoke out for the right of enslaved people to read, even though that was illegal. Angelina urged her readers to ignore wrongful laws: "Consequences, my friends, belong no more to you than they did to [the] apostles.

Duty is ours and events are God's . . . arise and gird yourselves for this great moral conflict." For their activism, the Grimké sisters were thoroughly ridiculed by most of white society. Fiercely religious, the sisters were rebuked by the Quakers and denounced by Congregationalists, who cited the Bible in reprimanding them for stepping out of "woman's proper sphere" of silence and subordination. This only served to fuel their embrace of feminism.

In the middle of the twentieth century, white women were engaged in the freedom struggle, a handful anyway. Viola Liuzzo, a woman from Chicago who went south to join the struggle and was killed by the Ku Klux Klan, is probably the most well known. And there were other white women who joined the Freedom Rides, including Emmie Schrader Adams, Elaine DeLott Baker, Joan C. Browning, Dorothy Dawson Burlage, Constance Curry, Theresa Del Pozzo, Casey Hayden, Penelope Patch, and Sue Thrasher. All nine of these white women from different places in the North risked their lives to join the Southern Freedom Movement.

"Let's be realistic—if you see a house, you like the house, regardless of where it is, get a white person to buy the house for you and transfer it to you. It's that simple," a real estate agent told Andrew and Charlotte Wade, an African American couple who wanted to buy a house in racially segregated Louisville in 1954. Anne Braden and her husband, Carl, a white couple committed to racial justice, did just that: they bought the house and transferred it over. Then, the Wades moved in. Their desire to buy a home was followed by racist violence and arson that destroyed the house they purchased. And for the Bradens, there were real costs, too. The local authorities charged them with sedition, for attempting to overthrow the government; Carl Braden was convicted and spent a year in federal prison. Anne Braden was ostracized and struggled to find paid work. Yet, she continued her activism until her death in 2006, including training a new generation of activists, such as Carla Wallace, also from Louisville and one of the founders of Showing Up for Racial

Justice (SURJ), a national racial justice organization. But, as an out lesbian, Wallace faced her own struggles against homophobia within antiracist activism.

"I was coming out as a lesbian, so I went to Anne," Carla Wallace told a documentary filmmaker in 2012. "I told her, we're going to launch this [queer rights] organization called the Fairness Campaign and we're going to build it broadly with a vision that has antiracism at its core, and Anne was like 'What?!?'"

Anne Braden, raised white, Southern, and heterosexual, at first could not see the connections between the struggle for racial justice and the struggle for queer rights. But white supremacy has always included, either implicitly or explicitly, a hetero-nuclear family agenda that rests on the destruction of queer lives. "It took the Klan coming to town and a huge mobilization against them," Wallace says, for Braden to realize the way these struggles are related. Afterward, Anne Braden said to Carla Wallace: "Carla, I owe you a tremendous apology. I was wrong." Carla Wallace is part of a long, but very thin, history of white lesbian antiracists like Lillian Smith, Mab Segrest, Suzanne Pharr, and Minnie Bruce Pratt.

"I just can't stress enough how important white women and their privilege and proximity to power are to this," said Stephanie Kimou, founder of PopWorks Africa, an organization that works to dismantle what she calls the "white gaze" in development. A 2018 book by Edgar Villanueva, an expert on social justice philanthropy and an enrolled member of the Lumbee Tribe of North Carolina, *Decolonizing Wealth*, challenges the wealthy to rethink conventional philanthropy. Villanueva points out that "there is still a very small percentage of philanthropic dollars going to communities of color." And perhaps this, too, is changing. In 2020, four years on from a diagnosis of terminal brain cancer and inspired by the Black Lives Matter protests, Susan Sandler, an affluent white San Francisco heiress, gave $200 million to racial justice organizations. That was most of her approximately $215 million net worth, and that gesture is noteworthy. But there is still the estimated $12 trillion it would take to pay reparations to those who had their labor stolen through slavery, and one-time donations are not the same as a systemic transfer of wealth; there are few if any white women advocating for that.

In 2017, Heather Heyer was murdered while protesting the white-supremacist demonstration in Charlottesville, Virginia. Today, young white women like Angela King, Gwen Snyder, Emily Gorsenski, Talia Lavin, and Joan Donovan risk their lives as they fight Proud Boys and neo-Nazis online and in the streets. And perhaps there are many, many more fighting against white supremacy in locations and through organizations that I have not heard of. It's quite possible that my lack of knowledge of the history of white women's resistance to white supremacy has made the scarcity of examples here seem slimmer than it might be otherwise. It could also be that there are not many beyond the tiny few included here.

Poet Claudia Rankine gave a speech, "On Whiteness," at the ArtsEmerson event in Boston in March 2017. When she was awarded the MacArthur grant the previous year, she announced that she would use her stipend to study whiteness. In her talk in Boston, she recounted some of her experiences teaching a class on whiteness at Yale University. "Every class discussion was ghosted by the underground consideration of what it means for Americans to aspire to white dominance," she said. Then, Rankine shared a complaint about the assigned readings from a student who asked why the syllabus didn't reflect more historical examples of "individual white benevolence." Rankine noted that she might have reconfigured the syllabus to include "white abolitionists and white civil rights activists." But, she continued, "in the moment, I was bemused that the student wished me to turn my attention away from the problems of systemic white dominance in order to create a more palatable narrative for her. I couldn't think of a good example of systemic and sustained white advocacy for Blacks in a culture with the trajectory of slavery to Jim Crow to the warehousing of Blacks in prison." The paucity of examples I have listed here is, I suspect, less about my individual dereliction and rather more about our collective failure at doing the work of knee-capping white supremacy and destabilizing whiteness.

## REIMAGINING A FUTURE WHERE WHITENESS MATTERS LESS

It is possible to imagine a future where freedom and abundance are available to everyone and not just people who are raised white. There is a debate about how to get to that future in an academic field known as "whiteness studies." In the thirty or so years that scholars have been publishing books and papers in this field, two camps have emerged about what we should do about whiteness. Some argue that one should declare oneself "not white," as a rhetorical move that would help to chip away at the social construction of whiteness. These scholars often cite James Baldwin and his brilliant 1984 essay "On Being White and Other Lies," in which he writes, "Because they think they are white, they believe, as even no child believes, in the dream of safety." Baldwin's prose is elegant, but in practical terms, this idea of not white has done little to disrupt structural inequality, and it's resulted in some wacky behavior on the part of some raised-white people I've known. Some I've met have simply declared they are not white and thereby race traitors to anyone who will listen, while others cosplay a new racial identity into social media infamy or a Black studies professorship.

In the most nefarious manipulation, the Far Right exploits this idea through the viral slogan "It's okay to be white," which appeared on college campuses in the United States and as a social media meme in 2018–2019. Cable news outlets picked up this story and amplified it further. That had real, political consequences half a world away when the Australian parliament directly responded to the slogan through a resolution meant to condemn any forms of "anti-white racism." Although the resolution was narrowly voted down, the event showed that the Far Right meme "It's okay to be white" had permeated international mainstream culture. Promulgating this slogan was a punk-ass move by the habitués of 4chan to push white-supremacist ideas into the mainstream, and it worked because it played on the flimsiness of the not-white strategy.

In a different take, some scholars argue that we should reclaim whiteness as a positive racial identity. They argue that eliminating whiteness is impractical, so we should embrace it and find what is valuable in it. This idea permeates workshops and trainings where those assembled are split into affinity groups based on people's racial identities. I've participated in these activities in many different settings. Each time, as we sit with our chairs in a circle, we are tasked with coming up with things we "like about being white." Part of this exercise is to help white people grasp the breadth of unearned advantages we accrue on a daily basis. People in such groups inevitably end up sharing observations such as, "I like not being followed in a department store when I go shopping." As the exercise unfolds, we all grow uncomfortable and then report back to the people from the other affinity groups in the workshop. I understand that the discomfort is part of the exercise, but sitting in such groups, I can never shake the awareness of how much these small groups have in common with "white pride" gatherings in their attempt to reclaim whiteness. I do not mean to impugn the motives of well-intentioned people, committed to antiracism, who organize these workshops. Yet, this kind of activity demonstrates the perils of resuscitating whiteness, an identity and practice formed through brutality, domination, and cruelty.

This conundrum about white identity—both the rejection of it and the unease with embracing it—leads to all manner of nonsense, but it mostly takes us down a path where we end up stuck in guilt, shame, reactionary rage or dissociation, numbness, and inaction. And it keeps us focused on whiteness. This is a problem mentioned again and again in whiteness studies: how to do this work and not recenter whiteness. In other words, how do you focus a critical lens on the power of whiteness without white people sucking all the air out of the room?

Being raised white doesn't mean we have to invest in whiteness. In Claudia Rankine's filmed rendition of her play *November*, one of the five Black women actor-narrators says, "You can be human and white. You can be white without going white. You can be in place without taking all the space. What history has taught us is that you can be white and swerve away from the supremacy of whiteness while swerving towards the someone who is not you." What would it mean to swerve away from a whiteness and toward liberation for all of us? Could we swerve away from our own comfort, safety, and pleasure, which is predicated on the pain of others? Could we learn to be white without "going white," can we avoid taking up all the space, is it possible to swerve away from the supremacy of whiteness?

January is an untrustworthy month for flying out of New York City. The best laid itineraries transmogrify into an elaborate map of contingencies, delayed flights, and late arrivals. In the first weeks of 2014, a wave of cold north air dubbed the polar vortex kept me from getting to the University of Michigan in time to give a keynote speech about race and technology for a group of feminist scholars. The airline booked me on a later flight so I could make it in time for another part of the scheduled event: a panel conversation among scholars Alondra Nelson, Lisa Nakamura, Sidonie Smith, and me.

The morning after I finally arrived, I am sitting down to breakfast at a hotel restaurant across from campus when my friend approaches.

"Sister friend!" Alondra announces and joins me with her usual, warm greeting. I slide out of the booth and stand up to give her a hug.

"It's so good to see you! I can't believe we have to come to Ann Arbor to have breakfast together."

"I know, but at least we're here now. Jessie, I have a question for you. I was talking to someone the other day, a historian, who told me all about Jessie Daniel Ames, who was this white woman that organized against lynching in Texas. Are you related? Is that your grandmother?"

"Ha, no! But funny you should ask. I haven't told you this story before, about my name change?"

"Nope. Please, do tell." The waitress comes and pours us both coffee, takes our breakfast orders, and leaves.

"It was during graduate school when I found out my grandfather on my father's side was in the Klan. My family dismissed it as no big deal, but it was upsetting to me." I tense up when I share this part of my story with a friend who is African American, because at the deepest level I worry that they will not want to be my friend anymore, but Alondra is unfazed. She takes in this information with a nonchalant nod.

"After I finished at UT and did the postdoc with Pat Collins, I knew that I had to write a preface to my first book that talked about my family's history and all that." This is shorthand for what we both understand is a longer conversation about Collins's Black feminist theory that encourages sociologists to discuss their "positionality," that is, the way personal history and social position are connected to the research, analysis, and writing process.

"The more I thought about publishing that book with my then last name, Harper, the same last name as my Klan granddaddy, I just knew I had to change it. He was also a child molester, by the way." I don't worry about sharing this information in the same way I do the Klan detail.

Alondra's eyes soften. "Oh, Jessie."

"Yeah, so, anyway, then I realized that I didn't want his name on that book, or on me. I had never liked my first name, Suzanne, which turns out to mean 'white lily,' symbol of white womanhood in the South, so I started looking around for a different name. I didn't want to appropriate someone else's culture, so I started looking for examples of white women who'd stood for racial justice, and let me tell you that's a short fucking list."

"Word." She chuckles.

"I'd read *Revolt Against Chivalry* and thought Jessie Daniel Ames was a pretty righteous white woman, and she was from Texas like me, so that was a bonus. I've never had a middle name, so I just took the first two. And I've been Jessie Daniels ever since then. Did the whole legal name change thing."

Alondra and I spent that day in conversation with Lisa and Sidonie riffing on the body as a way to think through issues of race, gender, and liberation. There is a picture from that event that is one of the few images I have of myself that doesn't make me cringe. It's a full-length shot of all four of us, arms around each other's waists, all smiling. The picture is not substantially different from other photos that fill me with self-loathing; I am still a size 18, not a size 2, and my face carries ancestral traces of my Klan granddaddy and my suicidal mother. But what comes through in this image is the connection between us and the very real, substantive joy at doing the work of liberation. For me, the photograph is a mnemonic for what it looks like to swerve, to be white without going white, to not take up all the space, to swerve away from the supremacy of whiteness.

## EIGHT THINGS WHITE WOMEN CAN DO

One of the ways white women become immobilized in the work of dismantling white supremacy is that we act as if it is an unchangeable law of nature, like gravity. In *Between the World and Me*, Ta-Nehisi Coates writes that white Americans view race as a "feature of the natural world," and thus unchangeable. It is not. It can be changed. It is a human-created system that we help sustain every day, and we can take concrete steps to undo it.

Mikki Kendall writes that white women have got to "move past any idea of being an ally and into being an accomplice in order for it to be meaningful." An ally is someone who stands to the side, helping. I will correct someone when they refer to me as an "ally" in the fight against white supremacy. It's my fight, too. When we've done the work, even a nice white lady can be a trusted accomplice. This list is by no means an exhaustive one when it comes to doing the work, but it's a decent way to begin.

## 1. Take an Inventory

Inventory how you spend your time, energy, and money. If you were raised white, start keeping a diary of where you spend your time each day. How much of your time is spent in white-only spaces, institutions, social groupings? How do these spaces make you feel? Safe or isolated? If you live, work, and socialize in white-only spaces and you're not trying to change them, you are part of the problem.

Go further and take an inventory of where your money comes from and where it goes. Does it flow from white-owned institutions? Probably. Where does your money go after that? Does it stay in white-controlled hands?

To go further, take an inventory of your family history going back several generations and pay attention to the ways your parents, grandparents, and great-grandparents profited from laws and ordinances intended to benefit white people. How are those paying off for you now?

There are a few examples to follow in this practice. The 2008 documentary film *Traces of the Trade: A Story from the Deep North* by Katrina Browne is an intergenerational exploration of slavery's lingering impact on one family. And, Edward Ball has done a similar investigation for his 1998 book *Slaves in the Family*. Sociology professor Jennifer Mueller has her students investigate their personal family histories of wealth acquisition and transfer. They are tasked with asking questions of their family such as: Is there a family history connected to slavery? Did anyone in previous generations inherit property, money, or businesses? Did parents or grandparents receive down payment help for purchasing a home or assistance with college? Did the family take advantage of formal programs that would facilitate wealth/

capital acquisition, like the Homestead Act or the GI Bill? Did anyone use social networks to get jobs, secure loans, open businesses?
Mueller reports her students find the exercise "eye-opening."

The point of this inventory is to help you begin to notice the
whiteness of your surroundings.

## 2. Divest from White Spaces, Institutions, Wealth

Once you start noticing, you can begin to divest from white-controlled spaces and institutions. And, when we do that, we begin to
starve them of the time, energy, and repeat business they need to
survive.

If you are employed in a white-only or white-dominated organization, can you change it from within? If not, consider working
somewhere else. Do you live in a white-only neighborhood? Do your
children go to a white-only school? What are the choices that led
you to those spaces and institutions and how can you change them
now? How are these white-only spaces predicated on the existence of
"wastelands," underresourced areas that are nearby and designed for
Black, Indigenous, and other minoritized people? In your area, who
is working on changing the neighborhood and school to align it with
racial and climate justice? Find these people and organizations and
join the work they are already doing.

If you have more economic resources than you need to cover your
own needs, what do you plan to do with that wealth? If you are passing down wealth from one white generation to another, you are actively contributing to the racial wealth gap. Once your basic needs
are met, do like Susan Sandler and put your money to work for racial
justice rather than keeping it locked in family coffers.

## 3. Reimagine Kinship

Much of the harm white people have inflicted on others is done in the
defense of the family and rehabilitating white men. White women
actively participate in creating all-white families and enclosing their

circle of caring and resources to include only other white people. At the same time, the notion of kinship for everyone else is torn apart by a police state designed for the comfort and putative safety of white people.

White women can begin to reimagine kinship by reconsidering their emotional, economic, and political attachments to white men in their families, whether fathers, brothers, or husbands. Are these entanglements reinforcing your investment in whiteness, or are they helping you divest? For those of us raised white, we need to begin asking questions about where we put our energy, where we invest our time, and who we defend.

Helena Duke, an eighteen-year-old Massachusetts high-schooler who identifies as a lesbian, decided she would no longer defend her white family when she shared a video and identified her mother as one of the rioters at the Capitol on January 6, 2021. "Hi mom," Helena wrote on Twitter, "remember the time you told me I shouldn't go to BLM protests bc they could get violent . . . this you?" Helena claims she was kicked out of the house and has set up a Go-FundMe to help pay for college. It is "queer people—and dykes in particular—[who] are keen observers of the tragedy of heterosexuality," writes Jane Ward. Those who are queer have always been reimagining kinship, because we have had to.

Three years after the video of the killing of Eric Garner in 2014 played on an almost constant loop on local television, a white woman, Alicia Cross, stood at the altar of a Brooklyn church and married Daniel Pantaleo, the officer who choked Garner to death. According to press reports, the couple began dating shortly after the chokehold death of Garner. A friend of the couple told a reporter, "She was there for him when he was going through a tough time," and added that Pantaleo has "every right to live a happy life."

If we are to divest from a system that routinely kills Black people, white women are going to have to reconsider the calculus of who is an attractive partner, of who they are comforting and who they choose to share their life with, because the other side of that calculus is who is considered so expendable they can have the life choked out of them on a city sidewalk.

If you were raised white by people who are avowed racists and you want to imagine a different life for yourself, you have some hard, and potentially dangerous, choices to make. There is a conversation popular online right now that white people need to "talk to your family" about their racism. And, though I agree in a general way with this approach, I want to complicate this by saying that you may not be the best person to talk to your family about their racism. Relationships within families are freighted with all kinds of other baggage about who got the most love and did we get enough. Adding a conversation about white supremacy to the mix may not be the most productive way to have that conversation. That said, if your raised-white family are avowed racists, you need to ask yourself why you are spending your time, your energy, and your one precious life with them. When we expand our thinking away from the narrow boundaries of the families we were born into and we look out to the wider horizon of people we might call kin, people who love us and understand us and are there for us in ways that our families of origin cannot be, then we begin to radically stretch the amount of love we have in our lives.

If you are considering a dialogue with family about white supremacy, be sure you have a safety plan. Are there guns in the house? Is there someone who will come get you if they put you on a psych hold, if you get arrested? If someone in your immediate family has become radicalized by white supremacy, it is imperative that you get away from them and that you have a safety plan in place to do that.

"For many years I alone have defended my husband . . . but my loyalty and love did not save his soul. I will carry the burden of failure through the rest of my days," said Amber Cummings in a 2010 statement to the court when she was being sentenced for murdering her husband two years earlier. Her husband, James Cummings, stockpiled Nazi memorabilia, radioactive materials, and instructions on how to build a dirty bomb that he planned to detonate at the inauguration of President Barack Obama. Before he could do that, Amber Cummings shot him to death while he slept. If Amber hadn't married James Cummings and thought she could save him, then she wouldn't have had to make the terrible choice she did.

## 4. Acknowledge and Repair Harm: Abolition and Reparations

White women have done our share of harm, individually and collectively. When we cause harm, we need to work to repair it. As individuals, we cause harm through microaggressions we might not be aware of; and as a collective, we have benefited from slavery, Jim Crow segregation, and mass incarceration. As just one example, almost every monument to the slavery-defending Confederacy that exists in the United States today (many in the North) is there because of the fund-raising and propaganda efforts of white women who were members of the Daughters of the Confederacy. What if white women began to see it as their obligation to join with those working to remove these monuments and tell the truth about white supremacy instead?

Much of the current system of mass incarceration in the United States has been built in service of white women's supposed safety and comfort. Based on her years of work as a prison abolition organizer, Mariame Kaba writes in her book *We Do This 'Til We Free Us*, "abolitionist politics and practice contend that disposing of people by locking them away in jails and prisons does nothing significant to prevent, reduce or transform harm in the aggregate." Instead of warehousing people in cages, what if white feminists began to join the movement to abolish the prison-industrial complex? What if white women began to see the fight for reparations as an issue that affects Black and Indigenous women and their families and began to include those as part of gender justice?

## 5. Work to Shift White-Supremacist Culture

Our nation and culture was founded in genocide and slavery and the myth of white superiority; because of that there are ways that white supremacy seeps into everyday life. This comes through in ways that we may not recognize if we're unaccustomed to noticing these traces, such as the tendency toward perfectionism, either/or thinking, efficiency, paternalism, fear of open conflict, and valuing individuality over collective goals. These are just a few of the ways white-supremacist culture becomes normalized, and we can work to change those values by identifying them and refusing to reproduce them in our daily lives.

White women in particular wield tremendous power (albeit less than white men) in culture-shaping industries, such as publishing, film and television, social media, museums, librarianship, social work, and education. What if white women began to use their access to power in each of these arenas to elevate voices of people whose stories challenge white supremacy? For instance, what if white women working in film and television began to divest from shows in which cops and DAs are the heroes? What if librarians (overwhelmingly white women) began to host regular events to teach raised-white people how to explore their family history to uncover the way whiteness gave them a generational boost? What if each metro area, midsized city, and small town had a staff of social workers equipped to understand how to deradicalize young people drawn to extremism? What if there were educational programs starting in elementary school and through high school that told the ugly truth about white supremacy and colonialism?  As Kaba observes, "Changing everything might sound daunting, but it also means there are many places to start, infinite opportunities to collaborate, and endless imaginative interventions and experiments to create."

## 6. Learn to Call In Other White Women

We need to learn how to call in other white women when they are actively causing harm. And we need to support one another in the hard work of learning to swerve away from white supremacy. What if it became routine for white women to say to one another, "I don't want to be white with you today," as a way to refuse an invitation to engage in exclusionary practices? What if white women gathered in weekly small groups to read, discuss, and workshop how they were metabolizing the damage of whiteness? What if it became common for these gatherings to be a place where white women talked about shedding their false sense of safety for a more authentic, fully human life that places the value of racial justice at the center? We also need to recognize that sometimes people will resist acknowledging that they are causing harm, will refuse to be held accountable, and then we should move on.

## 7. Change Your Mindset

For those of us raised white, every aspect of our lives is shaped by whiteness. Looking at the world through the white racial frame impairs our ability to see the world clearly and understand it realistically. It takes effort to change our mindset and think outside the white racial frame, and it is possible. As Mariame Kaba reminds us, "When we set about trying to transform society, we must remember that we ourselves will also need to transform."

Part of what transformed me was a job I had in graduate school, transcribing hundreds of interviews with middle-class Black Americans about their experiences with racial discrimination. Because I had to type every word of those interviews, I was in listen-only mode and it transformed me. I moved from being a white liberal, proud of being less racist than my parents, to having a deep appreciation for the pervasiveness of systemic racism, even as the Black people in the interviews I was transcribing tended to downplay the role of discrimination in their lives. Transcribing those interviews with middle-class Black Americans, who, one after another, recounted their multiple degrees, also upended the racist ideas I'd absorbed about Black people's disdain for education and my own family's mediocrity when it came to educational achievement. Since then, I have tried to imagine how I might replicate this experience for other people who are raised white, and there are many pathways out of the white racial frame.

One is to get a degree in Black studies, or another way would be to read memoirs by Black authors or listen to podcasts or watch documentaries. The information is available; the point is to retrain your mindset to move away from the white default that we were taught is normal. It is important to keep in mind that 75 percent of us who are raised white have no friends of color, so we are not learning through relationships. And even for that 25 percent who do have friends of color, it is not their job to educate you. We need to learn how to do deep listening, the kind of listening where you don't object, interrupt, or eagerly await the opportunity to interject "yeah, but . . ." The point is to educate ourselves by listening and not becoming a burden by asking Black people and other people of color to teach us, unless that is something they have volunteered to do.

## 8. Find a Spiritual Practice That Embraces Radical Love and Supports the Work of Dismantling White Supremacy

If you decide to embark on the path of dismantling white supremacy, and I so hope that you do, you are going to need some support. It can be hard to challenge the status quo, and it can be soul destroying to look squarely into the destructiveness that we have caused. I have found that this requires a strength and courage that is not available except in some kind of spiritual practice. For me, that has meant finding a spiritual home at Metropolitan Community Church of New York, my quirky, queer, multiracial, multigendered congregation. If your community of faith does not help you along the road to dismantling white supremacy, I encourage you to find a different spiritual home. I am not here to tell you what to believe about the universe but to encourage you to find some community of people who believe in love and gather with them regularly. Find a spiritual community that is committed to the idea of radical, inclusive love and that supports the work of dismantling white supremacy. When all of this gets to be too much, and it will, go there, gather your strength, rest up, and get back in the fight when you're replenished.

For some, therapy and workgroups with others on the path to dismantling white supremacy offer valuable support. Clinical psychologists such as Robin Schlenger and Alana Tappin offer online classes and workshops geared for white people in this work. Natasha Stovall and Francesca Maximé host a regular discussion via Facebook Live that digs deep into some of the issues discussed here. Journalist Julie Kohler hosts a podcast, *White Picket Fence*, about the politics of being a white woman today. The organization Showing Up for Racial Justice (SURJ) also has a podcast, *BOLD*, and probably has a chapter someplace near you. If they don't have an existing chapter, consider starting one.

All of these resources are meant to help you not get stuck in guilt and defensiveness, because if you're new to this work you will be challenged, will probably be called racist, and will get your feelings hurt. You may have to force yourself not to be defensive but to continue working to do better, even though it will often be painful. Take a deep breath, and keep it moving. You will live. The point of all this support is to keep your focus on how to leverage all your unearned privilege in a way that is of some practical help to others and to alleviate suffering whenever possible.

This work is, I believe, spiritual work and one that requires a lifelong commitment, whenever that begins for you. Racial justice work has always been a spiritual, emancipatory project. This is something that the Grimké sisters and others in the struggle to end slavery knew. Abolitionist and writer Frederick Douglass said: "I prayed for freedom for twenty years, but received no answer, until I prayed with my legs." Whether it is in stepping outside the conventional paths laid down for us, or joining with a protest march, or giving away generational wealth, there is real joy in finding other people on the same path. Although I realize we live in a secular age, that does not preclude experiencing the Divine, which can happen anywhere. I have felt that spark attending a Toshi Reagon concert, getting arrested in a street protest, listening to Amanda Gorman read a poem, and dancing at a dyke bar in Texas—anyplace where people are defying expectations, embracing a collective *we*, and gathering around some greater purpose. That's where you'll encounter hope and transformation. This is what Mariame Kaba means when she says "hope is a practice."

## THE FUNCTION OF FREEDOM

"My feeling is white people have a very, very serious problem and they should start thinking about what they can do about it. Take me out of it," Nobel Laureate Toni Morrison said to TV interviewer Charlie Rose in 1993. The recording of her saying this is online, you can find it easily if you look for it, and it has improved with age. In the context of the interview with Rose, she is clearly calling him out for a misbegotten question that put the burden of racism onto her formidable shoulders, and she isn't having it. She turns the question back onto her interlocutor, who, a couple of decades later, would be accused as a serial sexual harasser (charges he denied). Her emphasis on "they" is strong, pointed, almost sarcastic as her eyes skewer Rose: "they should start thinking about what they can do about it." Her "they" clearly means Charlie Rose needs to start thinking about how he needs to change up his questions. And, for those who can hear the other registers of her voice, she is addressing all the rest of us who are raised white.

"Don't you understand," she says, in off-the-cuff eloquence that makes the point I've been trying to make here, "there is something distorted about the psyche. It's a huge waste and it's a corruption and it's a distortion. It's like it's a profound neurosis that nobody examines for what it is. It feels crazy. It is crazy. It has just as much of a deleterious effect on white people as it does Black people." For those of us raised to be white women, she is telling us that we need to think about what we can undo to address our very, very serious problem and become more fully human.

In my ongoing quest to figure out how to become more fully human, I read, listen, and follow Black women, Indigenous, Latinx, and Asian people, queer and trans folk, and others who are writing as outsiders. In Keeanga Yamatta-Taylor's wonderful collection of essays from 2017, *How We Get Free*, she includes writings and interviews with Black feminists marking the fortieth anniversary of the Combahee River Collective Statement. The statement grew out of a Black feminist, lesbian, socialist organization active in Boston from 1974 to 1980. These women came together to say that neither the white feminist movement nor the civil rights movement were addressing their particular needs as Black women and, more specifically, as Black lesbians. It is a key document for Black feminist thought, and it was life-changing for me when I first read it at least thirty-five years ago. Most of the statement is addressed to an audience of Black women and it lays a foundation for the decades of intersectional analysis that came afterward. There's one line near the end that I read as a direct address: "Eliminating racism in the white women's movement is by definition work for white women to do, but we will continue to speak to and demand accountability on this issue." When I first read this in my late twenties, I thought: *this is work for me to do.*

Over the years since then, I've come to realize that simply opposing racism is not enough if we want to get free. Antiracism is, as Linda Martín Alcoff writes in her 2015 book *The Future of Whiteness*, "a negative agenda, directed at repudiating and overcoming racism; we also need a positive agenda for changing society." We need to work toward something rather than merely disavowing something. A positive agenda for changing society must include working toward love and joy. These are not subjects that sociologists generally take up, but I believe we must consider these in order to address our very,

very serious problem. Toward the end of *How We Get Free*, historian Barbara Ransby writes that revolution is most often motivated by feelings of love:

> And we have to take from that, never hesitate to love your people and the people who struggle alongside you, but also never be afraid to critique and struggle with those you love.

When I read this, my first thought was: *You can't trust white people's love if the goal is to get free.* I thought of Gregory and Travis McMichael, father and son who must surely love one another, who in late May 2020 shot and killed Ahmaud Arbery as he jogged past their Georgia home; and I thought of Lindsay McMichael, their daughter and sister whom they also must surely love, who posted a photo of Arbery's body on her Snapchat account because she's a "true crime fan." I thought about my family, and the sadomasochism that got passed down and called love there. And I thought of my decades of research into the Far Right, including former Grand Dragon of the KKK David Duke, who maintains that he doesn't "hate anyone, I just love white people." Certainly, his is a rhetorical strategy to mainstream white supremacy, but it unwittingly speaks to something true about what happens to love when it gets distorted by whiteness and power. We have to become more authentically human so that we can learn to experience love and joy that are not tainted by whiteness or domination.

The COVID-19 pandemic has begun to make it plain just how interconnected we all are, and it may move some white women to a more expansive circle of caring. In August 2020, a white woman with young children in New York City's public schools spoke with a reporter from WNYC about the mayor's plan to reopen schools. She said that her kids "desperately want back in the building" and she, too, wants them to go back to school, but she said, "What about the kid who lives with their grandma, or someone else who is vulnerable?

I just don't see how we can do it." This is the turn outward, the swerve from her concern for her children only and toward a wider circle of caring to include "the kid who lives with their grandma." This is the beginning of a more collective idea of caring and it is what we must do if we are to undo the damage of white womanhood. For white women to be able to follow Barbara Ransby's admonition to "never hesitate to love your people," we have to expand who our people are beyond the families and social networks we've created of people who look just like us. Each new crisis is calling us in, demanding that we see beyond ourselves and the worlds we've created. In that calling in, there is hope for transformation, renewal, and maybe even revolutionary change.

To make a change, we will have to reckon with our compulsion to be nice at all costs and learn to experience the full range of human emotions, including empathetic pain, anger, and mourning when another Black person is killed by the police or when the pandemic decimates tribal communities. And we need to go beyond "feeling bad" about these events as we might a natural disaster and step into taking action. We who are raised white have been trained to distance ourselves from the pain of others. To begin healing, we will have to open ourselves to what activist-scholar Ann Russo calls "broken heartedness" as a way of acknowledging the harm of white supremacy. If not, then we will have to acknowledge that being nice is a cover for the nasty reality that we take pleasure in the suffering of others. Those white women who profit from or take comfort in others' pain are not to be trusted with sisterhood and must be held accountable for their active role in our collective misery.

To move toward liberation, we will have to shed the half life of heteronormative ladyhood and the ways we have been trained to cater to the patriarchy. Straight culture, as Jane Ward astutely observes, is coded with white-supremacist gender norms and it romanticizes misogyny and violence. The "delicate coexistence of hate and love, the slap and the kiss," she writes, have come to represent the heteroerotic. Rejecting straight, patriarchal culture that fetishizes "hot, thin blondes" could be the most radical form of self-care for white women who no longer want to be nice white ladies. In her brilliant "Dear 8th Grader," feminist writer Mona Eltahawy urges young white girls to resist the patriarchy that "so successfully grooms girls to be polite, well-behaved, not make a scene or raise their voice, and not speak too much [so] that when they grow up and a man disrespects them, they will keep thanking him . . . and never once dare to tell him to shut the fuck up." Sometimes, liberation comes to those who learn to dig deep within to find their inner "shut the fuck up" voice.

It is time to move toward freedom and imagine ourselves as more fully human than the monstrous nice white ladies we risk becoming. Instead, we can stand shoulder-to-shoulder in broken heartedness and rage and love and joy with everyone else who wants a better world for us all. We can learn to be human and white, to be white without going white, to be in a place without taking up all the space. If we can do that, we just might be able to help stop the plunder, warehousing, and death designed for our comfort.

# ACKNOWLEDGMENTS

This book began decades ago when I read about white women, and myself, in Ida B. Wells-Barnett's account of lynching in *The Red Record*. I discovered Wells-Barnett's writing through Hazel Carby. I am indebted to Carby, along with the other scholars, including Patricia Hill Collins, Kimberlé Crenshaw, Angela Y. Davis, Bonnie Thornton Dill, Paula Giddings, Elizabeth Higginbotham, and Audre Lorde, who were at the vanguard of thinking about race, class, gender, and sexuality when I was just at the beginning.

I am grateful to Joe Feagin for introducing me to Vine Deloria and W. E. B. Du Bois and for giving me the opportunity to transcribe all those interviews with middle-class Black Americans. Joe also had the foresight to think that blogging might be a good idea, and together we started Racism Review in 2007. It was at Racism Review where I first launched a series of posts on "The Trouble with White Women and White Feminism," in 2014, and that served as a rough first draft for this book.

Chloe Angyal discovered my writing online and invited me to become a regular columnist at *Huffington Post*. I learned so much from Chloe's sharp editing about how to remove the academic jargon from my writing, and I am still grateful to her for the opportunity.

I am extremely lucky to have wonderful colleagues at CUNY who are smart, generous, and committed to their students and the idea of public education. There are far too many to mention them all, but several have been especially key to my thinking for this book, including Linda Alcoff, Juan Battle, Yarimar Bonilla, Lynn Chancer, Sarah Chinn, Michelle Fine, Jennifer Gaboury, Ruth Wilson Gilmore, Eric Lott, and Diana Rickard. For a time, Jennifer Gaboury, Sarah Chinn, and I were in a writing group, and their comments on early versions of this book proved invaluable. Diana Rickard has been a great writing buddy and guide to all things popular culture. Erica Chito Childs served as chair of the Sociology Department at Hunter College while I was writing this book and was supportive of this work even as it has distracted me from my day job. For that, and for her friendship, I am indebted.

I am grateful to Rebecca Tiger and Peter Bruno, who opened their home to me, fed me, told me funny stories, and brainstormed book titles with me in the midst of writing this book. I am so thankful for them. I credit Rebecca Tiger with introducing me to *monster theory*, which proved useful for me in writing this book.

My friend and colleague R. L'Heureux Lewis-McCoy was the person from whom I learned the term *opportunity hoarding* and for that, I am grateful. On a more personal note, he and his partner Aisha Lewis-McCoy have been steadfast friends through some of my worst days, and I am thankful for their friendship.

I met Minal Hajratwala what feels like a lifetime ago, and since then she has become a friend and a wonderful writing guide. I have taken classes with her, have had the joy of working with her as an editor, and have taken inspiration from her Fiji Finishers group for authors. I am so fortunate to know her.

One of the very best editors and proofreaders, and a damn good listener, Tony Amato, has been a crucial bookhusband for me as I worked on this manuscript. I will always be grateful to him and his partner, Susan Corso, who opened their fabulously queer, spiritual Cupcake Manor to me for writing retreats and pandemic-era porch sits. They offered me love and food and a place to rest when I needed them most.

Mutale Nkonde has been a friend, colleague, and ardent champion of this work since we first met at Data & Society in 2018, and then at the Harvard Berkman Klein Center in 2019. I am so thankful for her enthusiasm for my writing, for her friendship, and for her incredible energy to make things happen.

Kristie Helms Nettles and Kathryn Nettles have been great friends and some of the first people that I tried these ideas out on. I am so grateful to them for their radical hospitality, their good humor, and their courage in picking up what I was laying down.

Nance Bell and Deb Ziegler read a version of this book when it was in process, pushed me to make it better, and for that I am grateful. Just knowing they were reading made the writing easier.

I so appreciate everyone at Metropolitan Community Church of New York for loving me and letting me be a part of this quirky, queer, multiracial, multi-everything family. I am especially grateful to Rev. Elder Pat Bumgardner for her powerful example of love and grace.

Leslie Harf has listened to me talk about most parts of my story, and this book, and helped me find meaning in them. On a weekly basis, she reminds me that I don't have to repeat the past of the white women who came before me, and for that I am indeed grateful.

While I was writing this book, I met writer and psychotherapist Natasha Stovall, and I am so thankful. At a point when I wasn't sure I could finish this book on time, she offered me a place to stay and a week's worth of solitude that made all the difference for me, and for this I am grateful.

I am deeply appreciative for Safiya Umoja Noble and Brendesha Tynes, who, as editors of the book *Intersectional Internet: Race, Sex, Class and Culture Online* (2016), saw enough value in an early version of this work that they included it in their volume.

When there's not a pandemic, I like to go to writing workshops. In 2015, I met Saeed Jones at the Creative Nonfiction Writers Conference in Pittsburgh. When I told him some of my story about my Klan granddaddy, his response was "More confidence! More confidence!" which felt like a blessing and a beautiful, queer incantation for which I am grateful. In the summer of 2016, I was delighted to attend Aspen Summer Words Writers Conference and Literary Festival, where I got to work with Darin Strauss. I learned so much from him about the craft of writing and remain grateful for that experience. In the summer of 2018, I attended the Tin House Summer Workshop, where I had the abundant pleasure of working with Kiese Laymon and an amazing group of other writers, including Alea Adigweme, Kavita Das, Maya Doig-Acuña, Elisabeth Fennell, Cassandra Lopez, Doreen Oliver, Monterica Sade Neil, Rochelle Newman-Carrasco, and Jenna Wortham. I name all these writers here because what Kiese Laymon was able to do in a very short week was to mold us into a writing community that continues, and for that I am grateful. I was able to write this book because I felt I was part of that community of writers. For this, and so much more, I am indebted to Kiese Laymon.

Several people have asked me to come give talks, participate in panels, and otherwise discuss the ideas in this book. As anyone knows who has worked on a project like this over many years, giving talks can be very generative, and I want to thank everyone who has ever invited me into your class, workshop, or panel. I am especially thankful to Alondra Nelson and Merle McGee for inviting me to talk to young femme-identified people about white feminism, and I am grateful to those young people for their attention and thoughtfulness. Over coffee sometime later, Merle McGee suggested I do a graphic novel of these ideas so they would be accessible to a younger audience, and I still plan to do that. I am especially grateful to Alondra Nelson for being the kind of friend who, when your world falls apart, will invite you in and tell you it's okay to sit on your couch and eat Cheez-Its for a year if that's all you can manage.

One day in the spring of 2019, I was thrilled to get an email from actor, writer, and producer Eevin Hartsough, who created a short, comedic film, *Beckys Through History*. It was based on her outrage at the 2016 election and created after finding some of my writing about white women. She invited me to be part of a panel discussion after a screening of the film, and I am grateful to her for that experience.

JV Fuqua, chair of Women and Gender Studies at Queens College, a fellow former Texan, and an old friend, invited me to give a talk as part of Women's History Month in 2019. When I demurred, JV insisted, and for that I will always be grateful because it turned out to be a life-changing event for me. One of the copresenters on that panel was the luscious Amanda Lugg, who has brought joy, love, and laughter into my life and just in the nick of time. Amanda listened to me read each chapter of this book as I finished it. I am so thankful for her.

I want to thank my agent, Katie Kotchman, who said "let's try" when I came to her with a proposal for this book. Finally, I am grateful to my editor at Seal Press, Emi Ikkanda, whose enthusiasm for this book has never wavered.

# NOTES

## Introduction

There is fascinating research on the US Census and race, including Clara E. Rodriguez, *Changing Race: Latinos, the Census, and the History of Ethnicity in the United States* (New York University Press, 2000); Melissa Nobles, *Shades of Citizenship: Race and the Census in Modern Politics* (Stanford University Press, 2000); and Kim M. Williams, *Mark One or More: Civil Rights in Multiracial America* (University of Michigan Press, 2006). The book *Manifest Destinies: The Making of the Mexican American Race* (New York University Press, 2018), by Laura E. Gómez, is especially helpful in thinking through the category of "race" as it applies (and doesn't) to Mexican American people. I first thought about these issues when I read *Ethnic Options: Choosing Identities in America*, by Mary C. Waters (University of California Press, 1990). The numbers cited here are from the *New York Times* reporting in 2014 on the number of people who changed their census category from "Hispanic, Latino or Spanish origin" or "some other race" to "white," available here: https://www.nytimes.com/2014/05/22/upshot/more-hispanics-declaring-themselves-white.html.

The discussion of white women under British colonialism and the Papua New Guinea example are drawn from the second edition of *Beyond the Pale: White Women, Racism, and History*, by Vron Ware, with a foreword by Mikki Kendall (Verso Press, 2015). I read the first edition of Ware's book in 1992, and it sits in my imagination alongside several other books from the 1990s. Karen Brodkin's book

*How the Jews Became White Folks and What That Says About Race in America* (Rutgers University Press, 1998) is essential reading for understanding the process of immigrant assimilation of Eastern European Jews into a white, American culture. Ruth Frankenberg's *White Women, Race Matters: The Social Construction of Whiteness* (University of Minnesota Press, 1993) made a big impression on me and shaped my thinking early on, as did the volume Michelle Fine and Lois Weis edited (along with Linda Powell Pruitt and April Burns): *Off White: Readings on Race, Power and Society* (Routledge, 1996).

Natasha Stovall's article "Whiteness on the Couch" was published in *Longreads* in August 2019 and was crucial to my thinking about white women for this book. It is available here: https://longreads.com/2019/08/12/whiteness-on-the-couch/.

On very young children and race and racism, see Joe R. Feagin and Debra Van Ausdale's book *The First R: How Children Learn Race and Racism* (Rowman & Littlefield Publishers, 2001); Amanda E. Lewis, *Race in the Schoolyard: Negotiating the Colorline in Classrooms and Communities* (Rutgers University Press, 2003); and Mica Pollock, *Colormute: Race Talk Dilemmas in an American School* (Princeton University Press, 2009).

In the early 1990s through about 2012 or 2013, many still believed in the inherent liberatory potential of technology. See, for example, "The Rebirth of the Feminist Manifesto," by Emily Nussbaum, which was published in *New York* magazine, October 28, 2011 (available here: https://nymag.com/news/features/feminist-blogs-2011-11/). In the spring of 2012, the Barnard Center for Research on Women sponsored an event known as #femfuture, described on its website as "#femfuture is an experiment in movement-building that develops solutions for sustainability and impact in 21st century feminism." The event produced a report that suggested a business model for "sustainable" online feminism, and one of the outcomes of the event was a proposed "self-care and leadership retreat." The report, the exclusiveness of the event, and the perceived whiteness of it (in fact, there were two women of color involved) received intense pushback. Then, in 2013 Hugo Schwyzer, self-described male feminist and "the token guy of the lady blogosphere," revealed himself to be an abuser (he tried to kill his ex-girlfriend), and lots of white feminists came to his defense. This is when Mikki Kendall invented the hashtag #SolidarityisforWhiteWomen. And it was in response to this series of events—the pushback against the #femfuture report and the critique of the white feminists' defense of Hugo Schwyzer—that Michelle Goldberg wrote "Toxic Twitter Wars," which was published in *The Nation*, February 17, 2014 (available here: https://www.thenation.com/article/archive/feminisms-toxic-twitter-wars/). Then, in 2014, "Gamer Gate" happened and the white feminists online pivoted to expressing what a terrible, sexist, racist place the internet—and especially Twitter—could be. There is an excellent article by Adrienne Massanari that explains some of what happened: "#Gamergate and The Fappening: How Reddit's Algorithm, Governance, and Culture Support Toxic Technocultures," *New Media & Society* 19, no. 3 (2017): 329–346.

In 2020, diversity trainer Robin DiAngelo's book *White Fragility: Why It's So Hard for White People to Talk About Racism* (Beacon Press, 2018) became a best seller. I first encountered her ideas in a 2011 article in the *International Journal of Critical Pedagogy* (simply titled "White Fragility"). Her accounts of white people who are so frightened of being called racist or of being forced to recognize their complicity in systemic racism that they slam desks, cry, and even appear to have a heart attack always struck me as gendered, that is, responses more typical of white women. Her work has also been critiqued by linguist John McWhorter as "condescending" to Black people. Others have questioned whether DiAngelo's field of diversity training is effective or whether it is simply a way for her to enrich herself.

The Economic Policy Institute report written by Jessica Schieder and Zane Mokhiber was published September 12, 2018, and provides key numbers from the Census reports *Income and*

*Poverty in the United States: 2017* and *The Supplemental Poverty Measure: 2017* (available online here: https://www.epi.org/blog/by -the-numbers-income-and-poverty-2017/).

I first wrote about the advantage to white women from affirmative action in 2014 on Racism Review, my blog with Joe Feagin, in a post titled "White Women and Affirmative Action: Prime Beneficiaries and Opponents" (available here: http://www.racismreview .com/blog/2014/03/11/white-women-affirmative-action/). The information about IBM and the lawsuits against the University of Texas are discussed in the article "Affirmative Action Has Helped White Women More Than Anyone," by Sally Kohn, June 17, 2013, *Time* magazine (available here: https://time.com/4884132 /affirmative-action-civil-rights-white-women/).

It is a persistent feature of whiteness to minimize the harm of racism and overestimate progress. A report by Michael W. Kraus, Julian M. Rucker, and Jennifer A. Richeson, "Americans Misperceive Racial Economic Equality" (*Proceedings of the National Academy of Sciences of the United States of America*, September 26, 2017) offers empirical evidence of one aspect of this. I learned of this research through the reporting of Nikole Hannah-Jones.

Each year, *Forbes* magazine publishes several different versions of "the richest" list. The list of the richest families in the United States includes some well-known names, such as Walton, Koch, Mars, Cargill-MacMillan, Cox, Pritzker, Johnson, Hearst, Duncan, Newhouse, and Lauder—all of them white and all of them passing on their wealth to their white families. (The list is available here: https://www .forbes.com/families/list/). The tax cut passed in 2020 will effectively make these rich white families even richer while pushing the US economy into a deficit (see, for example: https://www.washington post.com/business/2020/01/28/us-deficit-eclipse-1-trillion-2020-cbo -says-fiscal-imbalance-continues-widen/). For more on the way white families hoard wealth, commonly referred to as "the racial wealth gap," see this 2016 report by Danyelle Solomon and Jamal Hagler:

"The Racial Wealth Gap as a Barrier to Middle-Class Security," published by Center for American Progress (available here: https:// cdn.americanprogress.org/wp-content/uploads/2016/09/07090906 /RWRW-RaceAndEthnicity.pdf).

I grew up hearing "pretty is as pretty does," but I didn't realize until I read Monica Carol Miller's *Being Ugly: Southern Women Writers and Social Rebellion* (Louisiana State University Press, 2017) that the phrase was connected to the ideological apparatus of being a nice white lady.

The sadistic cruelty of white women is on vivid, excruciating display in Stephanie Jones-Rogers's book *They Were Her Property: White Women as Slave Owners in the American South* (Yale University Press, 2019). She gathered the evidence for this book by going through the accounts of formerly enslaved people and, in an interview, spoke about how emotionally damaging that process was for her as a researcher. This book was important for me in understanding the sadism that so frequently exists beneath the veneer of nice white ladyhood, so I am especially grateful to her for doing this work.

The quote by Kirstjen Nielsen using the term "animals" to refer to immigrants was widely reported and, specifically, was used in reference to members of the M13. Nielsen excoriated those who criticized her use of this term as "defending gang members" (https:// dailycaller.com/2018/05/18/nielsen-scorches-dems-defending -gang-members). Her boss frequently referred to immigrants as "animals" (https://www.newsweek.com/trump-immigrants-animals -people-undocumented-930029).

Reporter Nikole Hannah-Jones has documented white parents' efforts to fight the desegregation of public schools. The public radio program *This American Life*, July 31, 2015, "The Problem We All Live With," Episode 562, is a two-part episode that includes reporting on white women pushing back against efforts in present-day Normandy, Missouri. Hannah-Jones also wrote about her own struggle with racial segregation in New York City schools for the *New York Times*

*Magazine*, June 12, 2016. I first learned about the white mom on the affluent Upper West Side intent on maintaining racial segregation from NY1, my local news station, in 2018. In 2020, radio producer Chana Joffe-Walt mentioned this story in her excellent podcast series for the *New York Times*, "Nice White Parents."

### Chapter 1: "Karens": Weaponizing White Womanhood

In the 1980s, I read Paula Giddings, *When and Where I Enter: The Impact of Black Women on Race and Sex in America* (W. Morrow, 1984), and that shaped some of my thinking about the issues discussed in this chapter. I also read Jacqueline Jones's *Labor of Love, Labor of Sorrow: Black Women, Work, and the Family, from Slavery to the Present*, which taught me so much that I had not learned in my Texas public school education. I read all I could about Ida B. Wells-Barnett, and it is Paula Giddings's book that is now the definitive resource on her life: *Ida: A Sword Among Lions: Ida B. Wells and the Campaign Against Lynching* (HarperCollins, 2009). The story about her encounter with Lady Somerset and Frances Willard is drawn from here.

Again, Stephanie E. Jones-Rogers's phenomenal *They Were Her Property: White Women as Slave Owners in the American South* (Yale University Press, 2019) was invaluable. Reading it alongside Craig Steven Wilder's *Ebony and Ivy: Race, Slavery, and the Troubled History of American Universities* gives a fuller picture of the brutal system of chattel slavery and the mechanisms used to justify it. For the continuing effects of it on descendants of enslaved people, I read Joy DeGruy's *Post Traumatic Slave Syndrome: America's Legacy of Enduring Injury* (Caban Productions, 1994). Adam Goodheart's *1861: The Civil War Awakening* (Vintage, 2012) taught me about the distinction between "masters" and "owners."

I developed my thinking for much of this chapter through a series of columns at *Huffington Post* in 2018, including a piece on Carolyn Bryant, after news of her recanted testimony became public: "The Word of a White Woman Can Still Get Black People Killed"; a piece on white women in family separation: "Why the Face of Family Separation Is a White Woman"; and articles on white women mainstreaming white supremacy, in the GOP, and in power: "Laura Ingraham Is Mainstreaming White Supremacy, but She's Not Alone," "White Women Who Vote GOP Aren't 'Voting Against Their Own Interests,'" and "White Women in the Trump Administration Do Not Deserve the Benefit of the Doubt." I am grateful to Chloe Angyal for that opportunity and for her keen editing, which always made my writing clearer, sharper, and less jargon filled.

The quotes I used for the discussion of Karen memes from André Brock and Apryl Williams are in a story for *Time* magazine, July 6, 2020 (available online here: https://time.com/5857023/karen-meme-history-meaning/). And I learned much from Apryl Williams's analysis in "Black Memes Matter: #LivingWhileBlack with Becky and Karen," *Social Media+ Society* 6, no. 4 (2020).

On the United Daughters of the Confederacy (UDC), I consulted Karen L. Cox's *Dixie's Daughters: The United Daughters of the Confederacy and the Preservation of Confederate Culture* (University Press of Florida, 2003) and Elizabeth Gillespie McRae's *Mothers of Massive Resistance: White Women and the Politics of White Supremacy* (Oxford University Press, 2018).

I first wrote about the early white feminist movement on Racism Review, http://www.racismreview.com/blog/2014/02/18/trouble-with-white-feminism/, and in it, I reference these books: Barbara Andolsen, *Daughters of Jefferson, Daughters of Bootblack: Racism and American Feminism* (Mercer University Press, 1986); Nancy F. Cott, *The Grounding of Modern Feminism* (Yale University Press, 1987); Lori Ginzberg, *Biography of Elizabeth Cady Stanton* (Hill and Wang, 2009); Beverly Guy-Sheftall, *Words of Fire: An Anthology of African-American Feminist Thought* (W. W. Norton, 1995); and Louise Newman, *White Women's Rights: The Racial Origins of Feminism in the U.S.* (Oxford University Press, 1999).

Subsequently, I consulted Lisa Tetrault's *The Myth of Seneca Falls: Memory and the Women's Suffrage Movement, 1848–1898* (UNC Press Books, 2014). And I read this article, "White Suffragist Dis/Entitlement: The Revolution and the Rhetoric of Racism," in *Legacy* 30, no. 2 (2013): 243–264, by Jen McDaneld. It gives a much more thorough and nuanced account of the racism in Stanton and Anthony's publication, *The Revolution*, than I was able to include here.

On the great migration north, Isabel Wilkerson's *The Warmth of Other Suns: The Epic Story of America's Great Migration* (Vintage, 2011) is essential, beautiful reading.

This excellent reporting by Sarah Posner, "'Radically Mainstream': Why the Alt-Right Is Celebrating Trump's Win," for *Rolling Stone*, November 28, 2016, includes the story about "Emily," her white guilt and her relief in finding white supremacists on 4chan. Seyward Darby's writing both in *Harper's Magazine* and in her book *Sisters in Hate* was useful in fleshing out the everyday life of women on the far right. I first wrote about the Far Right in *White Lies* (Routledge, 1997) about the gendered rhetoric of extremist rhetoric, as well as the way it maps onto more mainstream versions of white supremacy. I followed that with *Cyber Racism* (Rowman & Littlefield, 2009), about how those same groups moved online, the threat from a globally networked white supremacy, and how white women made extremist ideology their own in ways that fit seamlessly with feminism. More recently, I have written about the rise of the Far Right for *DAME* and *Contexts*: "Rebekah Mercer Is Leading an Army of Alt-Right Women," *DAME*, September 26, 2017; "Twitter and White Supremacy, a Love Story," *DAME*, October 19, 2017; and "The Algorithmic Rise of the 'Alt-Right,'" *Contexts* 17, no. 1 (2018): 60–65.

The story about the mob of white women beating Black women is based on reporting by Carlos F. Hurd, for the *East St. Louis Post-Dispatch* newspaper in 1919. It is included in an excellent 2020 article for *National Geographic* by Deneen L. Brown, "Remembering 'Red Summer,' When White Mobs Massacred Blacks from Tulsa to D.C.," (https://www.nationalgeographic.com/history/2020/06 /remembering-red-summer-white-mobs-massacred-blacks-tulsa-dc/).

I first read the quote from Carolyn Bryant ("That part's not true") in a 2017 article by Sheila Weller, "How Author Timothy Tyson Found the Woman at the Center of the Emmett Till Case," in *Vanity Fair* (https://www.vanityfair.com/news/2017/01/how-author-timothy-tyson-found-the-woman-at-the-center-of-the-emmett-till-case). The full account is in *The Blood of Emmett Till*, by Timothy B. Tyson (Simon & Schuster, 2017).

There is an extensive history of racist fears among white people behind the push to establish the infrastructure of the 911 emergency call system. Prior to this, to summon the police people had to dial a ten-digit number to a local law enforcement office. The 911 call system was established in the United States in 1968 as a response to the street uprisings in twenty-three cities during the summer of 1967 demanding an end to racial oppression. See "The Little Known, Racist History of the 911 Call System," by Katrina Feldkamp and S. Rebecca Neusteter, *In These Times*, January 26, 2021 (https:// inthesetimes.com/article/911-emergency-service-racist-history-civil -rights). This history is unremarked upon in the 2015 documentary *The Witness*, directed by James D. Solomon, about the Kitty Genovese murder.

### Chapter 2: The Trouble with White Feminism

I read Hazel Carby's "'On the Threshold of Woman's Era': Lynching, Empire, and Sexuality in Black Feminist Theory," *Critical Inquiry* 12, no. 1 (1985): 262–277, and her piece, "White Woman Listen! Black Feminism and the Boundaries of Sisterhood," in *The Empire Strikes Back: Race and Racism in 70's Britain* (Routledge, 1982), 212–235. Both had a big impact on me as I was discovering intersectionality in the late 1980s at the University of Texas at Austin. Following that, Patricia Hill Collins's writing, especially "Learning from the Outsider Within: The Sociological Significance of Black Feminist Thought," *Social Problems* 33, no. 6 (1986): 14–32, and her book *Black Feminist Thought: Knowledge, Consciousness, and the Politics of Empowerment* (Routledge, 1990), has shaped my thinking since I first read her.

In the 1990s, I read *Words That Wound: Critical Race Theory, Assaultive Speech, and the First Amendment*, by legal scholars Mari J. Matsuda, Charles Lawrence III, Richard Delgado, and Kimberlé Williams Crenshaw, and it profoundly changed my thinking about intersectionality. I read it and it made me reassess the radical, mostly white, Marxist feminist scholars I'd read before that, such as Catharine MacKinnon's *Feminism Unmodified* (Harvard University Press, 1987) and Andrea Dworkin's *Intercourse* (Basic Books, 1987). It was during this time that I read Elizabeth Spelman's *Inessential Woman: Problems of Exclusion in Feminist Thought* (Beacon Press, 1988), and that further developed my thinking about the way feminism gets distorted when viewed through a gender-only lens.

In her now-famous article "Mapping the Margins," legal scholar Kimberlé Crenshaw situated intersectionality through a critique of white feminist initiatives around violence against women. Danielle McGuire's book *At the Dark End of the Street: Black Women, Rape, and Resistance* (Penguin/Random House, 2011) is an important work that helped me understand more fully both the freedom struggle and the fight against sexual assault. Similarly, Aishah Shahidah Simmons's documentary *NO! The Rape Documentary* is invaluable for understanding the intersections of race and sexual violence.

A good deal has been written about the Women's March 2017, but none better than Lauren Michele Jackson's take in her book *White Negroes* (Beacon Press, 2019). And the art created by the collaboration between Angela Peeples and Kevin Banatte in the photo from that day is priceless for all that it captures.

Mikki Kendall has been a teacher of mine, and so many others, since she started the #SolidarityisforWhiteWomen hashtag on Twitter. Her book *Hood Feminism: Notes from the Women a Movement*

*Forgot* (Penguin/Random House, 2020) was a crucial and clarifying reminder for me that issues like food insecurity, clean water, the living wage, and access to education are feminist issues.

Statistics broken out by race and gender are difficult to find in any arena, and perhaps especially so when it comes to incarceration. Therefore, I am grateful for the 2015 report on incarceration rates by Jamal Hagler published by American Progress, which does this (https://www.americanprogress.org/issues/race/news/2015/05/28 /113436/8-facts-you-should-know-about-the-criminal-justice-system -and-people-of-color/).

The quote from Andi Zeisler is from "The Pussyhat Is an Imperfect, Powerful Feminist Symbol That Thousands Will Be Wearing This Weekend in DC," by Mattie Kahn, *Elle*, January 17, 2017 (https://www.elle.com/culture/career-politics/news/a42152 /pussyhat-project-knit-protest/).

I continually learn from Mariame Kaba about transformative justice, accountability, mutual aid, and abolition in the age of the prison-industrial complex, and much of the writing here about carceral feminism is inspired by her. I am so grateful that her wisdom and visionary insights are available to a wider world in her book *We Do This Til We Free Us: Abolitionist Organizing and Transforming Justice*, edited by Tamara Knopper (Haymarket Books, 2021). The works of three scholars are foundational for thinking about prisons: Angela Davis's *Are Prisons Obsolete?* (Seven Stories Press, 2011), Ruth Wilson Gilmore's *Golden Gulag: Prisons, Surplus, Crisis, and Opposition in Globalizing California* (University of California Press, 2007), and Michelle Alexander's *The New Jim Crow: Mass Incarceration in the Age of Colorblindness* (The New Press, 2010). All of these have shaped my thinking here, and the damage of carceral feminism seems clearer under the powerful light from these books. I first encountered the phrase "carceral feminism" in 2010 (about the time I was reading *The New Jim Crow*) in an article by Elizabeth Bernstein, "Militarized Humanitarianism Meets Carceral Feminism: The Politics of

Sex, Rights, and Freedom in Contemporary Anti-Trafficking Campaigns," published in *Signs* 36, no. 1 (2010): 45–71. I am indebted to all those who are working to end policing and the prison-industrial complex, and I look forward to the day when these issues are understood as feminist issues. For white evangelicals' advocacy for harsh criminal justice policies, I consulted Aaron Griffith's *God's Law and Order: The Politics of Punishment in Evangelical America* (Harvard University Press, 2020).

The discussion of The Wing and other corporate feminist enterprises was drawn largely from reporting in the *New York Times, Fortune*, and the *Los Angeles Times*. The accounts about the white women forced to resign are from reporting by Heather Grossman in "The Workplace Reckoning for White Feminism: A Roundup of Who's Out," published June 18, 2020, on Boss Betty (https://bossbetty.com/culture/the-workplace-reckoning-for-white-feminism-a-roundup-of-whos-been-shown-the-door/). Allegations were also reported here: "Jen Gotch Resigns from Role at L.A. Brand Ban.do After Racism Accusations," Khanh T. L. Tran, *Los Angeles Times*, June 10, 2020 (https://www.latimes.com/lifestyle/story/2020-06-10/jen-gotch-resigns-los-angeles-brand-bando-racism-accusations).

Alison Phipps's book *Me, Not You* arrived right on time for me. As I was struggling to articulate what it was about the #MeToo movement that seemed so white, other than the obvious press attention showered on white celebrities, Phipps showed me how this was connected to the global dominance of white bourgeois women in a variety of domains. Her writing was also invaluable in helping me understand the Trans-Exclusionary Radical Feminists (TERFs) and how their misbegotten idea of feminism is linked to whiteness and white supremacy.

Lauren Chief Elk is an Indigenous woman and among the first people to critique the work of V (formerly Eve Ensler), and I learned a great deal from her writing online, especially her open letter (https://chiefelk.tumblr.com/post/49527456060/an-open

-letter-to-eve-ensler). I first wrote about Eve Ensler and what I call "vagina feminism" at Racism Review in February 2015 (http://www .racismreview.com/blog/2015/02/10/white-feminism-v-day/). Since then, I've discovered lots more writing about the V-Day enterprise: Sealing Cheng's insightful work, "Questioning Global Vaginahood," *Feminist Review* 92, no. 1 (2009): 19–35, and Kim Q. Hall's "Queerness, Disability, and The Vagina Monologues," in *Hypatia* 20, no. 1 (2005): 99–119, about how *The Vagina Monologues* reinforces systems of patriarchy, compulsory heterosexuality, and ableism. From writer and activist Harriet Lerner, I learned about the way "vagina" is a misnaming of women's bodies. The quotes from the Mount Holyoke student group are taken from "Vagina Monologues Playwright: 'It Never Said a Woman Is Someone with a Vagina,'" by Oliver Laughland, *The Guardian*, January 16, 2015.

The "Open Letter from Black Women to the SlutWalk" was republished with permission by the Black Women's Blueprint in *Gender & Society*, October 2015.

The quote from Gloria Steinem's statement following the verdict in the Weinstein case is mentioned in *Variety*, February 24, 2020 (https://variety.com/2020/film/news/weinstein-verdict-gloria -steinem-1203513693/). For a thorough discussion of Harriet Jacobs's perceptive analysis of the law as creator of white women's virtue (and conversely Black women's supposed lack of it), see Christina Accomando's "'The Laws Were Laid Down to Me Anew': Harriet Jacobs and the Reframing of Legal Fictions," *African American Review* 32, no. 2 (1998): 229–245.

### Chapter 3: The Shallow Promise of the Wellness Industry

There is a good deal of scholarship on bodies and health that undergirds this chapter but that is not directly cited or quoted. Susan Bordo's *Unbearable Weight: Feminism, Western Culture, and the Body* (University of California Press, 1993) and Judith Butler's *Bodies That Matter: On the Discursive Limits of Sex* (Routledge, 1993) shaped some of my thinking about this chapter. I read Michel Foucault's classic *The History of Sexuality* when I was at the University of Cincinnati studying with Patricia Hill Collins. Her work on *Black Sexual Politics* (Routledge, 2004) has also shaped my thinking here. Since then, the rise of "fat studies" as a field of critical inquiry has been very generative for me especially as it intersects with queer studies and critical race theory, particularly the work by Bianca D. M. Wilson, Zoe Meleo-Erwin, Kathleen LeBesco, and Natalie Boero. Sondra Solovay and Esther Rothblum gathered much of this work together in their edited volume *The Fat Studies: Reader* (New York University Press, 2009).

I first encountered the scholarship in critical public health while I was employed in the field of public health, and it was like oxygen to me. Deborah Lupton's *The Imperative of Health: Public Health and the Regulated Body* (Sage, 1995) was paradigm shifting for me. Similarly, the edited volume by Jonathan Metzl and Anna Kirkland *Against Health: How Health Became the New Morality* (New York University Press, 2010) challenged all my assumptions about health and bodies in the very best way.

I read Mary Douglas's *Purity and Danger* (Routledge, 1966) at the suggestion of Lester Kurtz, when he was my dissertation cochair, in the early 1990s. Eager to finish the dissertation, defend it, and get on to the next thing, I wasn't able to incorporate Douglas's work at the time, so I am glad to be able to include this note here at long last.

In preparation for this chapter, I read all that I could find on the subject of self-care, and the one article that did the most to help me understand this cultural turn inward is Koritha Mitchell's 2018 "Identifying White Mediocrity and Know-Your-Place Aggression: A Form of Self-Care," published in *African American Review* 51, no. 4 (Winter): 253–262.

In thinking about contemporary food cultures, I discovered the work of Leah Penniman and her 2018 *Farming While Black* (Chelsea Green Publishing), which helped me put food into a broader, racial context. For me, this book was very much in conversation with Julie Guthman's 2011 book *Weighing In: Obesity, Food Justice, and the Limits of Capitalism* (University of California Press). Around the same time, I read Rachel Slocum's article from 2007, "Whiteness, Space and Alternative Food Practice," *Geoforum* 38, no. 3 (2007): 520–533. Together, these works helped me to understand how it is that white bodies come to dominate farmer's markets and why these will not make us healthier (however we define that and should that be something we want). As I was reading these two works, I discovered Danya Glabau's 2019 article "Food Allergies and the Hygienic Sublime" in *Catalyst: Feminism, Theory, Technoscience* 5, no. 2, pages 1–26. In it, she writes, "Gender, family, and race in the idealized home: The ads and features in *Allergic Living* often reinforce an idealized mother–child relationship as the seat of safety and purity in the allergic home." I am still thinking about this and how it captures something true about my own mother's drive to keep our house "hospital clean" as a form of love.

To sharpen my thinking about the clean eating trend, I found Laurie Penny's "Life Hacks of the Poor and Aimless" in *The Baffler* very helpful (https://thebaffler.com/war-of-nerves/laurie-penny-self -care). Shayla Love's "The Dark Truths Behind Our Obsession with Self-Care," in *VICE* (https://www.vice.com/en/article/zmdwm4/the -young-and-the-uncared-for-v25n4), helped me see the connections between the paucity of self-care related to the broader failure to provide adequate mental health care for those who need it. I would never have thought about the connection between soap and "clean eating" if I hadn't read Dana Berthold's "Tidy Whiteness: A Genealogy of Race, Purity, and Hygiene" in *Ethics and the Environment* 15, no. 1 (2010): 1–26. Donica Belisle's article "Eating Clean: Anti-Chinese Sugar Advertising and the Making of White Racial Purity in the Canadian Pacific," *Global Food History* 6, no. 1 (2020): 41–59, was gratifying to read because it connected clean eating to the protection of white women.

I did not know much about yoga when I began writing this chapter, so I am grateful to several scholars for writing about this, especially Shefali Chandra, whose article "'India Will Change You Forever': Hinduism, Islam, and Whiteness in the American Empire," published in *Signs* 40, no. 2 (2015), clarified so much for me about white women seeking enlightenment in and through yoga and in and through India. Chandra writes:

> The current global war and its concerted racialization appears (when it does at all) [as] a fantastical backdrop to the white woman's healing. Herein emerges the longer connection to transnational whiteness: the concerted disregard of history and context. The ability to transcend history and social conflict, the power to universalize one's desires through contact with the other, remains a hallmark of the kind of white racial power crafted through colonial encounters. . . . the idea of India that guides the global passage of whiteness, that coheres the recovery of the white woman and thus absolves the United States of its imperialist reality. Pain and alleviation, the women's desire for regulation, and India's palliative role—all these accelerate the conjoining of whiteness with Hindu culture. The new, racialized terrain of the post-9/11 world directs white women toward India as they stage distinctions from British colonialism, seemingly ignoring the existence of the current war even as they echo its discourses.

Rumya Putcha's powerful writing, "Necropower and the Cult of White Woman Wellness" (available online here: http://rumyaputcha .com/insta-influencers-and-the-cult-of-white-woman-wellness/), was crucial for me in understanding how the pursuit of yoga and other Indian-influenced practices was connected to white womanhood. Putcha writes:

> To be sure, claims to "New Age culture" as something that can be bought or sold, taken on or off at will exposes the nefarious logics of

American imperialism and its deathly, necropolitical impulses. And when aligned with so-called women's issues, like access to healthcare, claims to feminism tend to excuse impact and instead center intentions. This mechanism, by which white women are taught to see themselves as perfect victims in turn feeds the self-centered rhetoric of "my best interest at any cost." This is what many postcolonial feminists refer to as imperial feminism—a recognition that white women's liberation has always come at the expense of black, indigenous, and women of color. Put another way, the mechanisms by which "white women wellness" operates in 2019 is just the latest iteration of imperialist thought by which white women capitalize on their racial privilege to get their own needs met and in the process uphold the very white supremacist patriarchy that plagues our society at large.

I am also grateful to Ayu L. Saraswati for unlocking the mystery of white women's tanning practices for me. Her article "Cosmopolitan Whiteness: The Effects and Affects of Skin-Whitening Advertisements in a Transnational Women's Magazine in Indonesia," *Meridians* 10, no. 2 (2010): 15–41, includes a brilliant methodological design and is the first I've ever read that puts the critique of skin-whitening practices next to an analysis of skin tanning. She writes: "None of the whitening ads hint at one's ability to take control of how white one's skin can be, these tanning ads explicitly employ the language of choice and control, an apparatus of white supremacy. Aveeno, for example, sells 'moisturizer that lets you customize your color.' Olay puts it even more strongly by advertising 'the color you control.' Hence here, the anxiety of getting too dark is eliminated because Caucasian women can control how 'bronze' their skin can be."

As I was writing this chapter, I was lucky enough to read an early draft of a chapter from Chloe Angyal's 2021 book *Turning Pointe: How a New Generation of Dancers Is Saving Ballet from Itself* (Bold Type Books). Her writing helped me see the way (some) white women are encoded in Western culture and high art. She writes: "A body that is rigid, obedient, and disciplined, remade from something natural and unruly into something refined and well-behaved. Proper."

I knew very little about mindfulness when I started writing this chapter and am fortunate that I discovered Ronald Purser's *McMindfulness: How Mindfulness Became the New Capitalist Spirituality* (Penguin/Random House, 2019). Purser's book helped me understand why and how what used to be called Transcendental Meditation has become so popular with Google executives and other corporate managers. Through his work, I discovered another scholar's writing, Melissa Fisher, who helped me see this through a gendered lens. Her 2017 article "White Corporate Feminine Spirituality: The Rise of Global Professional Women's Conferences in the New Millennium," in *Ethnographies of Conferences and Trade Fairs* (Palgrave Macmillan), gave me the wonderful anecdote of the drummers who opened the women's corporate leadership conference. Her writing helped me place white women's embrace of mindfulness within the rise of a new transnational white corporate spiritual feminism.

### Chapter 4: Love and Theft

I did not plan to write a chapter on white women's cultural appropriation, identity tourism, or outright theft of racial identity. In fact, I had sent what I believed was a complete draft of the book to my editor and agent, when a brave few Latinx scholars called Jessica Krug on her charade, and I knew I needed to write this chapter. So, I am grateful to those Latinx scholars (unknown to me) for speaking up. Part of the reason I didn't plan to write about this is that I feel like it's just outside the reach of my expertise, and I felt like all that needed to be said had been said better, already. I am grateful that I got to read up on all this, and in a hurry, as it was the distraction I needed in the fall of 2020.

I started, as I had with previous chapters, with books I'd read in graduate school. I reread bell hooks, *Black Looks: Race and*

*Representation* (South End Press, 1992), which reminded me of her crucial take on how the commodification of race works and why it is so alluring for white people. I was glad, too, to be reminded that she was reading and citing James Cone's Black liberation theology, which has only become more meaningful for me since I first read it.

I also reread Eric Lott's *Love and Theft: Blackface Minstrelsy and the American Working Class* (Oxford University Press, 1993). I reached out to Eric, another wonderful CUNY colleague, to ask him if I could use his book title for this chapter and he graciously agreed. (I only learned afterward that I was in good company since Bob Dylan had used "Love & Theft," with quotations marks, as an album title.) Eric also alerted me to a newer work of his, *Black Mirror* (Harvard University Press, 2017), which proved to be invaluable, not only for what he had to say about Rachel Doležal but also for his chapter about Joni Mitchell's affinity for blackface throughout her career. (I had no idea; my ignorance of pop music is vast.) He also situated her flirtation with Blackness in the context of what usually gets called the riots in Watts, which were happening at the same time that musicians like Mitchell were hanging out just a few miles away, seemingly unaware. As he writes, "In the wake of Watts, in other words, Laurel Canyon scarcely batted an eye." The quotes from Joni Mitchell I included in this chapter are from "Joni Mitchell, Unyielding," by Carl Swanson, published on The Cut, February 2015.

In writing this chapter, I discovered the writing of Lauren Michele Jackson and I have learned so much from her that I had to go back and revise an earlier chapter to include some of her brilliance. Her 2019 book *White Negroes: When Cornrows Were in Vogue and Other Thoughts on Cultural Appropriation* (Beacon Press) taught me and it elevated me. Her writing is like sitting down to coffee with a very smart friend. I am grateful to her for learning about Dora Charles, who I am ashamed to say I didn't know about until now, but that's how whiteness works and I have to unlearn it all the time. Since I started this chapter thinking about the example of Krug's theft, I was so fortunate to read Lauren Michele Jackson's words about that case in *The New Yorker* (September 12, 2020).

I will again and without parentheses confess that my ignorance of pop music is vast, so I was grateful to Tressie McMillan Cottom for explaining Miley Cyrus to me (and the rest of the world). And, of course, she did it with her characteristically sharp, and award-winning, writing. Her 2013 article about Miley Cyrus, "Brown Body, White Wonderland," appeared in *Slate* and is fantastic (https:// slate.com/human-interest/2013/08/miley-cyrus-vma-performance -white-appropriation-of-black-bodies.html). In it, she writes, "I suspect it isn't the white male audience for whom Cyrus performs her faux bisexual performance. That is choreographed for the white male gaze against a backdrop of dark, fat black female bodies and slightly more normative *café au lait* slim bodies because the juxtaposition of her sexuality with theirs is meant to highlight Cyrus' supremacy, not challenge it. Consider it the racialized pop culture version of a bride insisting that all of her bridesmaids be hideously clothed on her wedding day." Originally, I had a long passage about it, with block quotes of Cottom's writing. Unfortunately, that paragraph had to be jettisoned in a subsequent draft, but I am glad to include it here. Her book of essays, *Thick*, was a finalist for a National Book Award, and in 2020, she received a MacArthur Genius Award.

I first wrote about the Rachel Doležal story when it erupted in 2015 on the Racism Review blog (June 12, 2015). Since then, I've read just about every news report or article or interview with her. Among this vast trove, three pieces stick with me. First, there is journalist Goldie Taylor's take that was filled with so much empathy ("I would eagerly link arms with you, lead you to my table to break bread and share my culture with you") and accountability ("but you lied") that I'm still thinking about it (*Blue Nation Review Archive*, June 12, 2015). Ijeoma Oluo's "The Heart of Whiteness," from the *Portland Mercury* (April 19, 2017), is one of the most uncomfortable accounts of an interview I've ever read and one of the best character studies. Doreen St. Felix's review of the documentary about her, "The Rachel Divide" (*The New Yorker*, April 26, 2018), left me with a haunting unease about her as a white mother of Black sons, as did the film.

As I worked on this chapter, blackfishing kept coming up and I wasn't sure what to think about it. Fortunately, I found a news story that quoted Alisha Gaines, who seemed to understand what was happening in this Instagram-based practice. Then I found her book *Black for a Day: White Fantasies of Race and Empathy* (UNC Press, 2017), and read it with gusto. As a child growing up in Texas, I had read John Griffin's *Black Like Me* and was deeply affected by it, but I did not know about Grace Halsell's *Soul Sister* or her other adventures with racial identity until I read about her in Gaines's book. I am also grateful to Mark Anthony Neal, professor at Duke University and host of *New Black Man in Exile*, for an interview he conducted with Gaines that taught me even as it entertained me ("White Fantasies of Race and Empathy," season 8, episode 21, May 9, 2018).

Thinking about white people's cultural appropriation of Black culture made me think about the blues, and that led me to Joel Rudinow's essay "Can White People Sing the Blues?" (*Aesthetics*, pp. 250–255, 2017), which I found useful for placing the behavior of white women into a larger cultural context of the plunder white people do.

As I wrote this chapter, even more scandals about white people's identity theft of racialized others began to emerge: a graduate student studying in Krug's former department, a chemistry professor in New England. Scholar Dorothy Kim reminded me of the connection between these instances and the 2011 scandal surrounding the online persona known as "Gay Girl in Damascus," and the work of Lisa Nakamura and her brilliant piece for *Hyphen* magazine called, "Syrian Lesbian Bloggers, Fake Geishas, and the Attractions of Identity Tourism" (July 15, 2011). I know Nakamura's work in my bones, it feels like, but for me it existed in a different epistemological bucket labeled "the internet" and not "white women's cultural appropriation," so I hadn't been thinking about her work in this context. Once I did, the connection was obvious. Her piece "Syrian Lesbian Bloggers" follows her much earlier, and field-establishing, article, "Race in/for Cyberspace: Identity Tourism and Racial Passing on the Internet" (*Works and Days* 13, nos. 1–2 (1995): 181–193). That piece went on to become part of her iconic first book, *Cybertypes: Race, Ethnicity, and Identity on the Internet* (Routledge, 2002). There's a thing that happens in New York City when you travel mostly underground, and you think of neighborhoods and sections of the city as distinct and separate. Then when you travel aboveground, by bus or cab or bike, and you suddenly see a heretofore invisible few blocks that are like a missing puzzle piece between two sections you didn't realize were so close together. That's exactly how this felt, rediscovering Nakamura's work here.

For a long time now, I've been interested in my father's insistence on his (fictive) Native American identity and the work that did for him, and all the other white people who also claim an Indigenous link without any evidence. Because of this, I have been compelled and delighted to read many Native American scholars and others who have plunged into this field of study. Among the key readings I consulted for this chapter are Shari M. Huhndorf's *Going Native: Indians in the American Cultural Imagination* (Cornell University Press, 2001), which I appreciate for her discussion of *The Education of Little Tree*. Circe Sturm's book *Becoming Indian: The Struggle over Cherokee Identity in the Twenty-First Century* (School for Advanced Research Press, 2011) has been so helpful for me in understanding "race shifters" (like my father) and why the pull of Cherokee identity is so seductive. I am especially indebted to Kim TallBear both for her work in this area, her superb book *Native American DNA: Tribal Belonging and the False Promise of Genetic Science* (University of Minnesota Press, 2013), and for her public scholarship. Her podcast *Media*

*Indigena* is excellent. And I am especially grateful for the way she spoke up for me on that podcast when I was attacked by the Far Right in October 2017 after I made some of the arguments in this book on Twitter.

The story about William Wages, brother-in-law of Rep. Kevin McCarthy (R-Calif.), who claimed to be "1/8 Cherokee" in order to benefit from a Small Business Administration loan program designed to assist Native Americans, was widely reported (for instance: https://www.latimes.com/local/california/la-na-pol-mccarthy-contracts-20181014-story.html). No charges were filed, and those in authority were reported to have "shrugged" at the case (https://www.govexec.com/management/2018/10/sba-shrugs-report-house-majority-leaders-law-may-have-misused-small-business-contracts/152042).

I began this chapter by talking about my own identity tourism (and racism) in my childhood "Cherokee princess" costumes at Halloween. Much of my thinking about the racism of our American Halloween tradition comes to me from a peer-reviewed article by Jennifer C. Mueller, Danielle Dirks, and Leslie Houts Picca, called "Unmasking Racism: Halloween Costuming and Engagement of the Racial Other," in the journal *Qualitative Sociology* 30, no. 3 (2007): 315–335. The American holiday at the end of October each year is the occasion for the display of much racism and sexism from white people, such as the couple who in 2015 dressed in blackface as Ray and Janay Rice (he had been caught on camera physically assaulting her). An article at Gothamist featured a picture of the white couple and the headline RAY RICE HALLOWEEN COSTUMES COMBINE BLACKFACE AND DOMESTIC VIOLENCE JOKES. As I began to think about Halloween, news of the Karen masks broke and I noticed how white women were becoming "monsters" in the collective imagination. This led me to cultural studies and Monster theory, developed by Jeffrey Jerome Cohen. I am grateful to Rebecca Tiger for introducing me to this theory and for talking with me at length about how it applies to white women.

## Chapter 5: Protecting White Families

I read Michèle Barrett and Mary McIntosh's *The Anti-Social Family* (Verso, 1982) and Adrienne Rich's *Of Woman Born: Motherhood as Experience and Institution* (Norton, 1976) when I was becoming a lesbian and a feminist, and both of these radically critical books shaped my experience of those emerging identities. In graduate school, Christine Williams introduced me to the work of Freud and the writing by psychoanalytic sociologists and feminists, such as Nancy Chodorow's *The Reproduction of Mothering: Psychoanalysis and the Sociology of Gender* (University of California Press, 1978) and Lynn Chancer's *Sadomasochism in Everyday Life* (Routledge, 1992). Williams also introduced me to Stephanie Coontz's *The Way We Never Were: American Families and the Nostalgia Trap* (Penguin/Random House, 1992). It would be hard to measure how important Joe Feagin's work has been on my own, but for this chapter his book with Kathryn McKinney, *The Many Costs of Racism* (Rowman & Littlefield, 2005) and *The White Racial Frame* (Routledge, 2009), were particularly useful. All of these books shaped my early thinking for this chapter.

In 2012, I devoured more than read Sharon Patricia Holland's *The Erotic Life of Racism* (Duke University Press, 2012). Her retelling of an encounter with a nice white lady was so clear and resonant that I regret that I could not figure out a way to work that into the main text of this book. However, I am glad to be able to include it here. She writes:

A few days after Tupac Shakur's death in 1996, I pulled into a Safeway parking lot in Palo Alto, California, with my friend's fifteen-year-old daughter, Danielle. We were listening to one of Shakur's songs on the radio: because he was a hometown boy, the stations were playing his music around the clock—a kind of electromagnetic vigil, if you will. An older (but not elderly) woman with a grocery cart came to the driver's side of my car and asked me to move my vehicle so that she could unload her groceries. The tone of her voice assumed fruition—it was not only a request but a demand that would surely be met. The Southerner in me would have been happy to help; the critic in me didn't understand why she simply couldn't put her groceries in on the other side where there were no other cars or potential impediments. I told the woman I would gladly wait in my car until she unloaded her groceries—that way, there would be plenty of room for her to maneuver.

While she did this, I continued to listen to Shakur's music and talk with Danielle. We were "bonding," and I was glad that she was talking to me about how Shakur's death was affecting her and her classmates. When I noticed that the woman had completed her unloading, I got out and we walked behind her car toward the Safeway. What happened next stayed with me as one of the defining moments of my life in Northern California. As we passed the right rear bumper of her car, she said with mustered indignation, "And to think I marched for you!" I was stunned at first—when something like this happens to you, you see the whole event in slow motion. I recovered and decided that I had two options: to walk away without a word or to confront the accusation—to model for Danielle how to handle with a modicum of grace what would surely be part of the fabric of her life as a Black woman in the United States. I turned to the woman and said, "You didn't march for me, you marched for yourself—and if you don't know that, I can't help you."

More recently, I read Elisabeth Gillespie McRae's *Mothers of Massive Resistance: White Women and the Politics of White Supremacy* (Oxford University Press, 2018). I read this in conversation with the release of the second edition of Vron Ware's *Beyond the Pale: White Women, Racism and History* (Verso, 2015), which led me to look for more ways to situate my thinking about white women within both colonialism and postcolonialism. I read Margaret D. Jacobs's extensive comparative historical account *White Mother to a Dark Race: Settler Colonialism, Maternalism, and the Removal of Indigenous Children in the American West and Australia, 1880–1940* (University of Nebraska Press, 2011). I also discovered Raka Shome, *Diana and Beyond: White*

*Femininity, National Identity, and Contemporary Media Culture* (University of Illinois Press, 2014), and that book offered me a number of key insights about the way ideas of white womanhood circulate globally. The quotes from Ann Watt and Jason Hillard are from Raka Shome's article "'Global Motherhood': The Transnational Intimacies of White Femininity," *Critical Studies in Media Communication* 28, no. 5 (2011): 388–406.

I am indebted to film scholar Leo Cortana, who helped me understand how the melodrama in *The Blind Side* works. An article by Erin Ash, "Racial Discourse in 'The Blind Side': The Economics and Ideology Behind the White Savior Format," *Studies in Popular Culture* 38, no. 1 (Fall 2015): 85–103, was also very helpful. The quotes from Michael Oher about scenes in the film are taken from this article.

As I was writing this chapter and struggling with how to talk about the whiteness of heterosexuality, Jane Ward's wonderful book *The Tragedy of Heterosexuality* (New York University Press, 2020) arrived right on time, like the gift that it is.

In another project, I am writing a memoir and for many years I've been researching Oklahoma, the Homestead Act (1862), and how those mostly white men who "made the run," as my great-grandfather did in 1889, were viewed at the time. Archives of newspapers around the end of the nineteenth century have been very useful in that research. The fuller quote I included from the *Kansas City Times*, February 26, 1885, reads:

> The difficulty now is not to get men to go west and occupy wilds [*sic*] lands and redeem them to profitable uses, but to furnish the lands for those who are anxious to go, and whose only hope of bettering their condition lies in that direction. There is something due to these homeless white men. They are at least entitled to lands which are lying idle under conditions of a superficial and indefensible character. If the Indians had reduced these lands to farms or otherwise utilized and improved them, there might be some force in the clamor about protecting the poor red

man against white cupidity and robbery; but they have not cultivated one acre in a thousand—and the government has kept them in food and clothing like so many helpless and dependent children. The experience of thirty years has shown, in short, that the solution of the Indian problem does not depend upon sustaining and prolonging the policy of devoting large bodies of the public domain to alleged Indian use and advantage. If the dream of making the Indian race agricultural and self-supporting is ever to be realized it must not come through great possessions of real estate, but through a better conception of what land was made for and how a living is to be obtained from it.

There is a vast literature on the facts and figures that get poured into the bucket called "the racial wealth gap," and I have read much of it, but many years ago. No one has done a better job synthesizing this literature and giving it a powerful moral clarity than MacArthur Award Winner Nikole Hannah-Jones, who wrote "What Is Owed," for *New York Times Magazine*, in June 2020. She writes:

Wealth, not income, is the means to security in America. Wealth—assets and investments minus debt—is what enables you to buy homes in safer neighborhoods with better amenities and better-funded schools. It is what enables you to send your children to college without saddling them with tens of thousands of dollars of debt and what provides you money to put a down payment on a house. It is what prevents family emergencies or unexpected job losses from turning into catastrophes that leave you homeless and destitute. It is what ensures what every parent wants—that your children will have fewer struggles than you did. Wealth is security and peace of mind. It's not incidental that wealthier people are healthier and live longer. [There is a] . . . perhaps intentional forgetting, that the racism we are fighting today was originally conjured to justify working unfree black people, often until death, to generate extravagant riches for European colonial powers, the white planter class and all the ancillary white people from Midwestern farmers to bankers to sailors to textile workers, who earned their living and built their wealth from free black labor and the products that labor produced. The prosperity of this country is inextricably linked with the forced labor of the ancestors of 40 million black Americans for whom these marches are now occurring, just as it is linked to the stolen land of the country's indigenous people. Though our high school history books seldom make this plain: Slavery and the 100-year period of racial apartheid and racial terrorism known as Jim Crow were, above all else, systems of economic exploitation.

As I was working on this chapter, I emailed my wonderful colleague and friend Michelle Fine to see if she could remind me of some of her work I'd heard her discuss in person before, and within seconds she sent me this reference: "The Breast and the State: An Analysis of Good and Bad Nipples by Gender, Race, and Class," *Studies in Gender and Sexuality* 11, no. 1 (2010): 24–32, which unlocked so much for me about the psychology behind goodness and badness and race and motherhood and the state, all with her characteristic good humor. Her edited volume, with Lois Weis, *Off White*, has been crucial in shaping my thinking about whiteness.

Another wonderful colleague and friend, from a different institution, Koritha Mitchell, helped me identify the postcard with the image of Jesse Washington's body and reminded me of her insightful take on it in her essay "Love in Action: Noting Similarities Between Lynching Then and Anti-LGBT Violence Now" (*Callaloo* 36, no. 3 [2013]: 688–717). She also reminded me of Shawn Michelle Smith's excellent discussion of lynching postcards in *Photography on the Color Line: WEB Du Bois, Race, and Visual Culture* (Duke University Press, 2004). Mitchell's 2011 book *Living with Lynching: African American Lynching Plays, Performance, and Citizenship, 1890–1930* (University of Illinois Press) has become one of the standards in the field, and I regret that I wasn't able to include it more fully here.

The argument at the heart of this chapter, that white families are key to reproducing white supremacy, had been germinating for a long time. When I read Thandeka's compelling *Learning to Be White: Money, Race, and God in America* (Continuum Publishing, 2007), I understood more clearly how I could make that argument, and for that I am grateful to her for this work.

### Chapter 6: The Lie That Is Killing All of Us

W. E. B. Du Bois's essay "The Souls of White Folks," in *Darkwater: Voices from Within the Veil* (1920), is essential reading for anyone interested in whiteness, and it informed my thinking for this chapter. I first read Du Bois in graduate school, thanks to Joe Feagin. It was only much later that I discovered my training was anomalous and that Du Bois was not included in sociology curricula across the United States. Thus, I am grateful to Aldon Morris's work, *The Scholar Denied: W.E.B. DuBois and the Birth of Modern Sociology* (University of California Press, 2015), for correcting this error in the field and revitalizing Du Bois for a new generation. For this chapter, I also consulted Marilyn Lake's "'The Discovery of Personal Whiteness Is a Very Modern Thing': WEB Du Bois on the Global and the Personal," in *Historicising Whiteness: Transnational Perspectives on the Construction of an Identity* (University of Melbourne, 2007).

Along with Du Bois, Jonathan Metzl's *Dying of Whiteness: How the Politics of Racial Resentment Is Killing America's Heartland* (Basic Books, 2019) profoundly shaped my thinking for this chapter. Metzl has created a powerful empirical indictment of the way whiteness is destroying all of us, and the truth of it seems to lead the evening news on a daily basis. It was at around the same time I read Natasha Stovall's "Whiteness on the Couch" (Longreads, August, 2019), and it both confirmed many of the things I had been thinking about whiteness and fundamentally shifted how I understood it. And, as if that was not enough, it was also beautifully written, and for all that I am grateful.

As I was reading Metzl and Stovall, I stumbled across the work of Cheryl Matias and Ricky Lee Allen, "Loving Whiteness to Death:

Sadomasochism, Emotionality, and the Possibility of Humanizing Love" (*Berkeley Review of Education* 4, no. 2 [2013]), and this helped me to connect my argument about sadomasochism in white families and the intergenerational trauma of being raised white. Part of what I appreciate so much about their account is that they delve into love, not a subject that sociologists regularly venture into. Matias and Allen write,

> Essentially, we contend that the emotional aspects of whites' commitment to whiteness, specifically their understanding of loving whiteness and, ultimately, the white race, plays a major motivational role in perpetuating a system of white domination. . . . what does love, or its distortion, have to do with how whites refuse to undo their unhealthy racial coalition and unjust structural power? Are white commitments to the white race born out of love or some other psychic condition? Or said differently, is the white race a loving community, one that grows love for both whites and people of color? For if the ontological opposite of love, hope, and humanity is apathy, despair, and monstrosity, then nowhere is the study of love more crucial than in theoretical postulations about whites' loveless membership in the white race and phobia of the painful possibility of finding love beyond whiteness.

Liz Garbus's 2011 documentary film *There Is Something Wrong with Aunt Diane*, about the Schuler family and the Taconic crash, was important for my thinking about white women's deaths in this chapter.

For the section on deaths of despair, I read Anne Case and Angus Deaton's *Deaths of Despair and the Future of Capitalism* (Princeton University Press, 2020), along with most of the reported pieces on the trend in rising rates of certain kinds of death among white people. Case and Deaton are rigorous in their quantitative analysis, and it was their research that first began to spark my thinking about how whiteness might be killing us. I appreciate, too, their critique of

American capitalism but, somewhat surprisingly, did not find much in their analysis that is useful for understanding whiteness.

I also consulted Diane Miller Sommerville's historical account, *An Aberration of Mind: Suicide and Suffering in the Civil War Era South* (UNC Press Books, 2018), which helped me locate suicide within the landscape of whiteness in America. Sommerville also reminded me of the suicide(s) in Thomas Dixon's novel *The Clansman*. Dixon's novel, of course, inspired D. W. Griffith's 1915 film *Birth of a Nation*, which was screened by President Woodrow Wilson at the White House and who heaped praise on it.

I am no literary scholar, but I appreciate those who are for all they help me understand. Martin Dine's article about *The Virgin Suicides* ("Suburban Gothic and the Ethnic Uncanny in Jeffrey Eugenides's *The Virgin Suicides*," *Journal of American Studies* 46, no. 4 [2012]: 959–975) helped me enormously. I am also grateful to Diana Rickard for reminding me about this novel and about the trope of the depressed white housewife in popular culture.

Hua Hsu's excellent reporting in "The End of White America," for *The Atlantic* (January/February 2009), was very helpful for me in writing this chapter, and the quotes I included in this chapter from Matt Wray are from his interview for that article. Matt Wray is, as the article describes him, one of the founders of what has been called "white-trash studies," a field conceived as a response to the perceived elite-liberal marginalization of the white working class. I regret that I wasn't able to include more of his excellent work in this chapter.

For this chapter, I read Sara Ahmed's *The Promise of Happiness,* in which the central concept is the "affect alien." Ahmed writes, "The struggle against happiness as a necessity is also a struggle for happiness as a possibility." Ahmed's scholarship, and the example of her life, is a guiding light for all of us queer affect aliens.

Barbara Ehrenreich's work has been a model of publicly engaged scholarship for me for a couple of decades, so I was glad to be able to incorporate her book *Bright-Sided: How Positive Thinking Is*

*Undermining America* (Picador/MacMillan, 2010). Her critique of positivity and how pernicious it is in American culture was very useful for my thinking in this chapter, particularly about breast cancer. For thinking about the tyranny of the pink ribbons branding that has encircled breast cancer, I learned from Samantha King's book *Pink Ribbons, Inc.* (University of Minnesota Press, 2006) and the documentary of the same name from 2011 directed by Léa Pool and produced by Ravida Din. The dual-format *Pink Ribbons, Inc.* of book and documentary is a model of publicly engaged scholarship that I hope to be able to do one day with my own work.

### Conclusion

Nell Irvin Painter's *The History of White People* (W. W. Norton, 2010) has shaped much of my thinking for this book. And, despite having turned her attention to painting and memoir writing, Painter spoke out through several interviews and op-eds during the spring and summer of 2020, and for that I am grateful.

Neal Caren is quoted in the *New York Times* in an article titled "Black Lives Matter May Be the Largest Movement in U.S. History," from July 3, 2020.

In the weeks just before the 2020 election, there were dozens of news articles about white women changing their minds about voting. The quotes here are from an article by Bess Levin called "White Women Apologize for Saddling the World with Donald Trump," published in *Vanity Fair*, October 20, 2020.

In thinking about the small percentage of white women who have fought back against white supremacy, *Deep in Our Hearts: Nine White Women in the Freedom Movement* (University of Georgia Press, 2000) was a useful reminder.

In addition to Gerda Lerner's classic text *The Grimké Sisters from South Carolina* (UNC, 1967), I also drew on Mark Perry's *Lift Up Thy Voice* (Penguin Random House, 2001) for information on the Grimké sisters. There were other white women abolitionists, such as Lucretia Mott. Mott, like the Grimké sisters, was inspired to denounce slavery because of her religious beliefs. However, Mott, like Susan B. Anthony and Elizabeth Cady Stanton, jettisoned her commitment to abolition when it came to the Fourteenth and Fifteenth Amendments to the Constitution. In this political battle, they saw these amendments as granting the vote to Black men "ahead of" white women, and therefore did not support them.

The stories about Anne Braden and Carla Wallace are drawn from the documentary film *Anne Braden: Southern Patriot* (2012) by Anne Lewis and Mimi Pickering. It is available online at https://www .annebradenfilm.org/.

The quote from Stephanie Kimou is taken from an interview by Catherine Cheney in "INGOs Can Help Dismantle Development's 'White Gaze,' PopWorks Africa Founder Says," an article in DEVEX, a development industry publication (available online here: https://www.devex.com/news/ingos-can-help-dismantle -development-s-white-gaze-popworks-africa-founder-says-96237). Susan Sandler's $200 million gift was widely reported, including in the *New York Times*, September 14, 2020 (https://www.nytimes .com/2020/09/14/us/politics/Susan-Sandler-donation-racial-justice .html).

The information about the "It's Ok to Be White" meme came from a research report produced by the Media Manipulation Project, written by Brian Friedberg and Joan Donovan. It is available online here: https://mediamanipulation.org/case-studies/viral-slogan-its -ok-be-white. I did not have space here to thoroughly document the important work that Angela King, Gwen Snyder, Emily Gorsenski, Talia Lavin, Joan Donovan, and Brian Friedberg and many others are doing in beating back the Far Right, but I have a deep respect for what they face on a daily basis. In the future, I hope we can work together on some kind of reparative care for those who spend eight hours a day (and more) staring down into the abyss of hard-core white-supremacist ideology. It is truly soul destroying.

Claudia Rankine's book *Citizen* (Graywolf Press, 2014) is a powerful work of prose/poetry and I have been grateful to be able to teach with it. I have been following her emerging work on whiteness since then, including the launch of the Racial Imaginary Institute in Lower Manhattan. The quotes I used here from her speech at ArtsEmerson are from a recording I found online (https://youtu.be/uCEfUMesedE). In March 2020, I had tickets to her play *Help*, a show based on her interviews with white men about their privilege. Then The Shed, where the play was to be staged, shut down because of the pandemic. The quotes I use throughout this chapter are from the filmed rendition of the play *November*, by Phillip Youmans. I transcribed parts of the film myself through multiple viewings. I am so grateful for the filmed version of the play, which helped me enormously in thinking through how to end this book.

In thinking about whiteness studies, I am indebted to my friend and colleague Jennifer Gaboury, who has invited me to speak on "whiteness" in her class at Hunter College and who has spent many afternoons with me tucked away in some off-campus watering hole talking about the field. I'm also lucky to be in conversation with several other CUNY colleagues, all experts on whiteness in their own domains: Linda Martín Alcoff, Sarah Chinn, Michelle Fine, and Eric Lott. Each of them has helped me think through this section on whiteness studies in ways that have honed my thinking. In this section, I reference scholars who think we should say we are "not white," and here I was thinking of (the late) Noel Ignatiev, whose *How the Irish Became White* (Routledge, 1995) influenced a generation of whiteness scholars. Ignatiev and John Garvey's journal *Race Traitor* were important venues for arguing that "treason to whiteness is loyalty to humanity." More recently, Ta-Nehisi Coates has taken up the mantle of James Baldwin (albeit without the queerness) to make a similar argument. In *Between the World and Me*, one of Coates's refrains is "those who believe themselves to be white." Like Baldwin, Coates's prose is elegant, but it's unclear what those of us raised white should do. In her 2015 *The Future of Whiteness*, Linda Martín Alcoff addresses the "race traitor" position, which she refers to as "eliminativism," and offers a rigorous critique of this stance as untenable. Instead, Alcoff suggests that we could reclaim whiteness by developing a "double-consciousness," a concept coined by W. E. B. Du Bois. Certainly, whiteness studies in general owes its origin to W. E. B. Du Bois, whose essay "The Souls of White Folks" was published in 1920. Several other pieces shaped my thinking for this discussion, including Richard Dyer's *White* (Routledge, 1997), Toni Morrison's *Playing in the Dark* (Harvard University Press, 1992), Alfred J. Lopez's *Postcolonial Whiteness: A Critical Reader on Race and Empire* (SUNY Press, 2005), David Roediger's "Is There a Healthy White Personality?" in *Counseling Psychologist* 27, no. 2 (1999), all of Joe Feagin's work, especially *The White Racial Frame* (Routledge, 2009), and Jonathan Metzl's recent *Dying of Whiteness* (Basic Books, 2019), mentioned in the previous chapter. The breadth of this field is well beyond the scope of this brief discussion and, indeed, the book itself. I apologize to all those I left out.

I am grateful to Patricia Hill Collins for the opportunity to spend time with her at the University of Cincinnati as Charles Phelps Taft postdoctoral fellow. Her book *Black Feminist Thought* (Routledge, 1990) changed my life in profound ways and has shaped my scholarship since I first read it.

I am indebted to Alondra Nelson for her brilliant scholarship, her warm heart, and her generous friendship. And I'm grateful to her for letting me use the story of our conversation over breakfast in Michigan. I am especially grateful to all the women of FemTechNet for the invitation, to Lisa Nakamura for hosting us, and especially to Sharon Irish for writing a blog post about the event that helped refresh my memory of the polar vortex from a distance of several years later.

The suggestion to take an inventory is based on a technique used by ethnographers, life coaches, and professors. The exercise Jennifer Mueller designed is "Tracing Family, Teaching Race: Critical Race

Pedagogy in the Millennial Sociology Classroom," *Teaching Sociology* 41, no. 2 (2013): 172–187.

My first involvement in political activism happened at UT–Austin during the protests against apartheid in South Africa. It was during that time when I read George Fredrickson's classic text *White Supremacy: A Comparative Study of American and South African History* (Oxford University Press, 1981). The push to "divest" from South Africa as a way to erode support for apartheid proved to be an effective rhetorical and political strategy. It's my hope that we could learn from that example as we reflect on the ways we invest in our own version of apartheid, and how we might begin to reverse that process. My thinking for this point was also shaped by the writing of Elijah Cummings on "white spaces."

The call to reimagine kinship comes from thoughtful writing by several key scholars, including Ruha Benjamin's 2018 piece "Black AfterLives Matter: Cultivating Kinfulness as Reproductive Justice," in *Boston Review*; Christina Sharpe's 2016 essay "Lose Your Kin," in *New Inquiry*; Kim TallBear's chapter "Making Love and Relations Beyond Settler Sexualities," in the 2018 volume *Making Kin Not Population*; and Jane Ward's 2020 *The Tragedy of Heterosexuality*. My questions about having a safety plan are based on personal experience and on recent reporting about an anonymous woman from rural Missouri whose brother has joined a right-wing militia. Talking to a reporter, she said: "Unless you have a brother who has guns in every room of his house, and who is in a hate group, and who is ruining his family and his children's lives, then don't tell me about having empathy for people" (Anna Silman, *New York Magazine*, December 3, 2020). The story about Helena Duke was widely reported, including in this article, "Lesbian Teen Outs Mom as Capitol Rioter After Being Kicked Out for BLM Support," *Them*, January 12, 2021 (https://www.them.us /story/lesbian-teen-outs-mom-capitol-rioter-after-kicked-out-blm -support).

As a research assistant for Joe Feagin, I first learned of internment camps for Japanese Americans during WWII and that the US government paid a small amount in reparations forty years later. Since then, I have thought that reparations are the very least the US government can pay for enslaving a whole group of people and profiting from that stolen labor. My thinking for this point has, in more recent years, been shaped by the writing of Ta-Nehisi Coates, Nikole Hannah-Jones, and Sandy Darity on reparations and the debt that raised-white people owe. For information about the work white women did in establishing Confederate monuments, I'm thankful for Karen Cox's book *Dixie's Daughters: The United Daughters of the Confederacy and the Preservation of Confederate Culture* (University Press of Florida, 2003).

I am grateful to the people working to make Standing Up for Racial Justice (SURJ) a reality, and it was through their website I first encountered the document by Tema Okun, "White Supremacist Culture," which has been very helpful for me and many others in seeing the everyday manifestations of white dominance.

I am thankful to Tony Amato for pointing me in the direction of Ann Russo's article "Brokenheartedness and Accountability," *Journal of Lesbian Studies* 21, no. 3 (2017).

I am indebted to Keeanga Yamatta-Taylor's *How We Get Free* for enlivening the Combahee River Collective Statement for me once again, and to Barbara Ransby for her meditation in that volume.

The title of the last section is a reference to an oft-quoted line from a commencement address that Toni Morrison gave to the graduating class of Barnard College in 1979. The complete sentence the phrase comes from is, "You are moving toward freedom and the function of freedom is to free somebody else." The full context of the speech is often lost when the partial quote is shared, but it is worth noting here because it is directed to an audience of mostly white women. In it, Morrison deploys Grimm's fairy tale of Cinderella and her stepsisters who were "not ugly" in the original version but "fair and lovely," a code for whiteness. She uses the fairytale to remark on the way women treat each other: "I am alarmed by the violence that women do to each other: professional violence, competitive violence, emotional violence. I am alarmed by the willingness of women to enslave other women." She never says "white" or "whiteness," but it is clear to whom she is speaking based on her book from more than a decade later *Playing in the Dark: Whiteness in the Literary Imagination* (Harvard University Press, 1992). The quotes from her about our "very, very serious problem" are from a taping of *The Charlie Rose* show, May 7, 1993.

**Jessie Daniels** is a writer and a professor. She is a professor of sociology at Hunter College and of sociology, critical social psychology, and Africana studies at the CUNY Graduate Center. She also serves as faculty affiliate at the Harvard Berkman Klein Center and research associate at the Oxford Internet Institute, University of Oxford. She is the author of several books, including *White Lies*, and her writing on race has appeared in the *New York Times*, in *Huffington Post*, and on NPR. She lives in New York City. She tweets @JessieNYC.